CRITICAL ACCLAIM FOR
ROGUES & PATRIOTS

"Nick Crane is the kind of guy you can count on. He's smart, tough, and persistent, a throwback to the classic American PI, in the mold of Marlowe and Spade, the kind of guy who runs into the burning building rather than hit the fire alarm. So, be prepared to buckle up for this wild ride."
—Charles Salzberg, Three-Time Shamus Award nominee, author of *Man on the Run,* and winner of the Beverly Hills Book Award

"In *Rogues & Patriots*, LA PI Nick Crane's courage and cunning are put to the test as he battles sinister super patriots. A heart-pounding tale of espionage, friendship, and one man's unwavering resolve against dark forces."
—Michael D. Sellers, award winning-writer and director of *Eye of the Dolphin*

"Patrick H. Moore has written a book to savor—vivid characters and crackling, high-voltage dialogue… Moore is a master of poetic detail that captures the era's howling rage while creating a dark and menacing mood."
—John Nardizzi, PI of the Year and Shamus award finalist for *The Burden of Innocence*

"*Rogues and Patriots* by Patrick H. Moore is fast-paced, taut, and lean. Moore has evolved into a seasoned and uncompromising author who crafts stories that so ingrain themselves into your psyche that it's darn near impossible to put his books down."

—Max Myers, award-winning author, screenwriter and film director

"Moore has produced a thought-provoking and suspenseful thriller as PI Nick Crane squares off against a creepy cabal of paramilitarists intent on taking power. Set against the intensifying political divides of our time, *Rogues and Patriots* builds the action and plot twists with masterful, page-turning precision while offering an insider's portrayal of the investigator's world and the desperate, colorful characters who inhabit it."

—John Brown, Los Angeles private investigator

"LA PI Nick Crane is in serious trouble. A gang of alt-right aristocrats are trying to destroy him. Thank God he has friends; he will need every one of them. Luckily, Crane is the king of stealth. He will dig deep to draw on every ounce of strength, courage, and cunning that he possesses. All this in order to survive and beat back the evil that threatens our country."

—Ellen Sanders, reader of great fiction

"Patrick H. Moore enthralls us once again, taking us on another mesmerizing tour of America's underbelly with our favorite private eye, Nick Crane. This story cooks from beginning to end as Nick Crane thrills us with his inimitable panache."

—Kirk Sanders, Silicon Valley technologist

ROGUES & PATRIOTS

BOOKS BY PATRICK H. MOORE

The Nick Crane Thrillers
Cicero's Dead
27 Days
Rogues & Patriots

A Grifter's Song
Setting the Record Straight

PATRICK H. MOORE

ROGUES & PATRIOTS
A NICK CRANE THRILLER

Copyright © 2024 by Patrick H. Moore

All rights reserved. No part of the book may be reproduced in any form or by any electronic or mechanical means, including information storage and retrieval systems, without permission in writing from the publisher, except by a reviewer who may quote brief passages in a review. Without in any way limiting the author's [and publisher's] exclusive rights under copyright, any use of this publication to "train" generative artificial intelligence (AI) technologies to generate text is expressly prohibited. The author reserves all rights to license uses of this work for generative AI training and development of machine learning language models.

Down & Out Books
3959 Van Dyke Road, Suite 265
Lutz, FL 33558
DownAndOutBooks.com

The characters and events in this book are fictitious. Any similarity to real persons, living or dead, is coincidental and not intended by the author.

Cover design by Margo Nauert

ISBN: 1-64396-364-3
ISBN-13: 978-1-64396-364-8

*To Warren Larry Foster, Vietnam veteran,
American hero, and friend unto death.
May he find the peace that
every Vietnam veteran longs for.*

*And to Ellie Eich, my good friend and
unflinching literary advisor,
without whom this book
may have never seen the light of day.*

PART ONE

CHAPTER ONE

The frowning corpse of Roberto Diaz was found by a jogger on Friday morning at six a.m. on a windswept hillside in East Los Angeles. Cause of death still unknown. Time of death according to the ME, around two a.m. Not an accident, not according to my LAPD friend, narcotics detective Tony Bott. Roberto had been Tony's best informant, and my friend was beside himself with anguish and rage.

Twelve hours before the body was discovered, Tony had charged into my office on the third floor of the Poseidon Building, near Third and Alameda. All wound up. First, he told me he'd been called down to the old Spring Street Courthouse by a federal prosecutor named Sam Blaylock, who'd told him that henceforth his best informant, Roberto Diaz, would be off-limits. Starting today, Diaz would report to one of Blaylock's DEA agents. He would work for a new DEA-ICE task force dedicated to combating drug trafficking, sex trafficking, and human smuggling. Not to mention narco-terrorism and murder-for-hire. The whole nine yards.

"It was strange," said Tony. "Blaylock was all casual and

dismissive. Like jumping a man's informant was no big deal. He never even apologized. But I controlled myself. Got out of there fast. I figured I had to talk to Roberto, see how he felt about this, but when I called him, his voicemail was full. So I paged him. That was three hours ago. He still hasn't gotten back to me. That's not like Roberto. I'm worried." Tony paused. Took a deep breath. "So listen, Nick, listen to what happened next. Either I'm crazy or something weird is going on."

Tony stopped, pulled a bandana out of the pocket of his Tommy Bahama walking shorts and mopped his forehead. He was wearing his casual designer clothes: Izod pullover and Polo deck shoes to go with the shorts. And the mirrored Ray-Bans pushed up on his forehead. Why this instead of his usual dirty white boy riding-in-the-Mexican-car undercover look—black jeans, colored tee-shirt, and blue bandana? Or his basic go-to-court look—Dockers, bland polo shirt, casual shoes?

Simple. He had a date right across the street from my office at the Third Street Korean Bar & Grill. At seven p.m. Or as Tony explained:

"This woman came up to me in the parking lot outside the courthouse. Right after my meeting with Blaylock. I was steaming. And plenty worried too. 'Cause Roberto is kind of a simple guy. Those sharks are the last people he needs to be working with. That's when I felt her breathing on the back of my neck. I turned around, and she gave me a big smile. She looked about forty. Stylish enough, I guess, but a bit wizened in that clubwoman kind of way. Wrinkles around her mouth and eyes. She says, 'Hey, Tony, got a sec? I need your help with your old informant Roberto Diaz. That prick Blaylock wants me to shadow him. He thinks Diaz won't suspect anything 'cause I'm a woman. Says he wants to know what Diaz is really doing. Yeah, right. How the hell should I know? I'm in over my head. Maybe we can catch a drink later, and you can give me some tips?' She acted like we were pals. It made no sense. And why in hell would Blaylock want his own informant followed? I deadpanned, and she said, 'Look, I'm Tami Wheat. I'm a new investigator with the U.S. Attorney's Office. And I need your help. C'mon, Tony, be a sport. I would so appreciate it.'"

He paused for breath while I mulled it over. Tony was right. It made no sense.

"Then," said Tony, "I was about to ask her why she thought I could help, but I stopped myself. 'Cause I figured if I helped her out, it might help me stay connected to Roberto, when and if he surfaces. So what I said was, 'Sure. I can meet you for an hour or so. Around seven. But I'll have to bring a friend 'cause we already have something planned for the evening.' She didn't like it, and I told her to take it or leave it. I guess she decided to take it."

I rubbed the back of my neck. Thinking. Spoke. "It does seem weird. Why in hell would she come up to you five minutes after Blaylock gave you the black spot? It makes no sense. I never told you this, but three years ago Blaylock was the AUSA on a twenty-pound federal meth case where my lawyer friend Jack Snow got the client a year and a day. A year and a day! With no cooperation. Outrageous! I remember thinking at the time that it seemed kind of sketchy."

"Something's up with that Blaylock fool. I can feel it." Tony nodded firmly. "And Roberto's been spooked for a while now. He was approached by some undercover guys about a week ago in a North Hollywood bar. He managed to shake them, but he was freaked out. Said he was going to disappear for a while. Which was fine up until today, when I learned what the Feds have planned for him. He's not here legally. They'll hold that over his head."

"Does Roberto have a local case?"

Tony grinned. A bit sheepishly.

"I know. He's working off a case that's never even been filed. Jack Snow says that's pretty much taboo among the Feds, but that you local boys do it all the time."

"He's right," said Tony. "Those federal bastards have no

mercy. They put you to work setting people up, and then they still send you to prison. Whereas we local boys have heart."

CHAPTER TWO

At seven o'clock we walked across the street to the Korean Bar & Grill. A smiling Tami Wheat greeted us halfway down the bar. "Gentlemen. How nice of you to be on time!"

"Always," said Tony. I stepped forward and introduced myself as Nick. Perfunctory handshake.

Tami was about what I expected—on the petite side, toned and tan with a determined look in her close-set blue eyes. She was wearing expensive jeans, a frilly white blouse, and a brown leather bomber jacket.

"It's too noisy in here for conversation," I said, nearly shouting. "Let's sit on the patio." Outside, we sat in swinging chairs suspended on chains under a bamboo awning. A moment of awkward silence, waiting for the drinks to arrive. I stepped into the breach. "Nice place, huh? Whenever I get the chance, I sit out here with a Pellegrino while I write up my case notes."

Our drinks arrived. More chit-chat. Then Tony got down to business. "So, what can I do for you, Ms. Wheat? You said something about needing pointers on how to shadow Roberto Diaz."

"That's right," said Tami. "But please call me Tami. I'm pretty new to this game, and although they trained me, I've never done surveillance on my own before. And because Diaz has disappeared, I've got to figure out how to find him."

Tony and I exchanged a quick glance. Was it possible Blaylock and his team had not yet located Roberto? This would help explain why Tami had appeared out of nowhere, asking Tony for help.

"Just so you know," said Tony slowly, "I can't find him either. The damned guy has disappeared. And this can be a slow game. I've had informants disappear for months at a time and then reappear with a new target." He paused and shook his head, his lips set in a hard line. "But more to the point, why on earth should I throw you a bone when your people have made it crystal clear you're stealing my prize informant?"

"Wow!" said Tami. "You're angry. I would be too, I suppose." A moment of silence. Then she plunged ahead. "But there's no need to be defensive. We're all on the same side here, aren't we? I mean, we all want to indict these drug trafficking bastards and lock 'em up. Protect our borders and all that good stuff."

"I wonder," said Tony, cracking a half-smile, which, given his mood, dripped more menace than mirth, "if we are on the same side? The way I see it, your people want to fuck me and use Roberto. Then when he runs out of information, you'll indict him for trafficking and lock him up. Then, when he's done his time, you'll deport him. A bad deal all around."

Tami was shocked by Tony's vitriol. At least she looked shocked. My friend's cell phone pinged, and he punched in his code. Stared at his screen, worry lines erupting across his forehead.

I stepped in. "Here's what you need to understand, Tami. Detective Bott has every reason to be angry. The standard procedure here in LA is for our federal colleagues to share informants with local law enforcement. It's been that way for decades. And here you and your team go and break the rules. Without any reasonable explanation."

Tami shrugged, a casual lifting and falling of her shoulders. Almost too casual. "I understand. And just so you know, like any good conservative, I have great respect for precedent. But this situation is different. We are a brand-new state-of-the-art task force, and we are taking all due precautions to keep everything in house. In order to avoid any possible slip-ups."

Tony looked up from his phone. Treated Tami to his best scowl. Went back to his readout.

"That's completely out of line," I said. "You're implying Detective Bott would screw things up unless he's cut out completely. That's downright insulting. Not to mention ironic, considering here you are trying to persuade my friend to help you out with Roberto when, according to your boss, Sam Blaylock, he's not even supposed to go near the damned guy."

Tami looked at Tony, who was ignoring her. Looked at me and smiled. Broad, friendly, and phony as hell. "Why should you be insulted? It's no skin off your back. You're not law enforcement. In fact, Mr. Crane, unless I'm mistaken, you're one of those rare PIs who never even was a cop."

Hit me like a gut punch. This woman, notwithstanding her green and helpless act, knew exactly who I was and what I did for a living. Which made no sense. Unless...I took a long pull from my Heineken.

At that moment, Tony's phone pinged again. This time, he swiped up, glanced at the number, frowned, and held the phone to his ear. "Holy shit." The blood drained from his face. "Gotta roll." He stood up, flung down some bills, and was gone within seconds. I had a bad feeling. Diaz.

And I had problems of my own. Here I was, alone with this peculiar woman, who seemed to know more about me than she had any business knowing. I decided to probe. "Sorry my friend had to leave. I didn't see that coming. But I'm curious. How did you know I'm Nick Crane? We've never met before."

She looked at me. No smile this time. Instead, a measured, thoughtful look, like a hunter surveying her prey. "Well, if you really want to know, we know all about you, Mr. Crane. We know you've almost lost your investigator's license countless times for breaking the rules. It's amazing you still have a license to carry. Suffice to say, you're not too popular in certain circles."

She was baiting me. Much as I wanted to, I decided not to bite. I stood up, nodded shortly, and walked away, leaving her there on the patio, one hand wrapped around the waist of her St. Pauli Girl, the other reaching for her phone.

CHAPTER THREE

Outside, I took a careful look around. Thursday night, and Third Street was jumping. People were queuing up in front of the Bar & Grill. Down on the corner of 3rd and Traction, the sushi and the exotic hot dog joints were mobbed. No one looked suspicious, which meant nothing. It was a big crowd. Anyone could be watching me. I crossed the street. Buzzed my way into the Poseidon Building and took the stairs up to the third floor, where Albert, the janitor, was mopping his way to the end of the hall.

I locked my office door behind me and spread out my guns on my desk. My Colt Commander 9mm looked as tough as ever, my Walther P22 compact and dangerous. Picked up the Colt and aimed it at my investigator's license on the wall next to the door. Hadn't fired it in a while.

Phoned Tony. No answer. Then Bobby Moore, my long-time partner at Nick Crane & Associates. "Fuck, Nick! Tony just called me. He's beside himself. He's talking about chickenshit federal double-crosses and how they jumped his informant Roberto, who's now vanished. What's that all about?"

"Long story. Where is he now?"

"He's out searching for Roberto. So am I. We're in separate vehicles. I've got a bad feeling, Nick."

"Yeah. Something is seriously rotten. And what Tony didn't tell you, because I just found out myself, is I might also be in their crosshairs. The Feds, that is. For some unknown reason. I'm gonna phone Jack."

Jack Snow has been my personal lawyer for close to twenty years. I have the bad habit of getting collared now and then and keep Jack on retainer to deal with it. I also work occasional cases with him. Jack doesn't spring for a pricey downtown office or posh Century City digs. Instead, he's content with his modest second story quarters in Monterey Park on the edge of the San Gabriel Valley. He works alone except for his legal secretary Sylvia. Jack started out in the Federal Public Defender's Office. He knows who's who and who's doing what. If he has a fault, it's that he's too busy and often doesn't answer his phone. I left a message.

Then I sat down with a fresh thirty-six-inch square of whiteboard and a black magic marker. On the top left, I wrote U.S. Attorney's Office and on the far right, LAPD. Then, in parentheses under the headings, I added (AUSA) and (Detective). I started to write their names and stopped.

In my mind's eye, under AUSA, I filled in Human Smuggling, Sex Trafficking, Murder-for-Hire, Drug Trafficking, and Narco-Terrorism. Under Detective, I filled in CI. Tony might be right. The AUSA Sam Blaylock might be dirty. I wasn't sure how or why. But if Tony was right, it meant Blaylock was probably hooked up with a host of other miscreants. Rogue agents. Crooked lawyers. Hired guns. Bad actors of every stripe and color.

This was new terrain. I'm used to dealing with psychopaths in my major cases, which, in a sense, has made it easy. They're predictable creatures, weighed down by their massive egos and rigid self-absorption. Half the time, they come looking for you, but it seemed unlikely Blaylock would follow their example. If he was dirty, it was probably simply for money and power, two muscular and persuasive motivators. And he, or someone connected to him, had dispatched Tami Wheat to approach Tony. Which had led to our aborted meeting at the Bar & Grill.

And how in hell did Ms. Wheat know who I was? It made no sense, yet it made all too much sense. They were conspirators and I was their mark. But why, and for whom? That was the question. I had just poured a cup of coffee when the phone rang. Jack.

No matter how bad things might really be, Jack Snow always sounds like he's just won the California lottery. I let him ramble on for a long minute before telling him we had to meet ASAP.

"You're in luck. I'm dictating a memo."

"At your office?"

"Where else?"

"Don't go anywhere. I'll be there in thirty minutes."

I holstered both guns and was about to lock up when the phone rang.

"Hello, is Nick Crane available?" A cultured accent. I couldn't quite place it.

"This is he."

"Oh, excellent. I was hoping to catch you. I'm Amina. Amina Hosseini. I know this is rather sudden, but I need to talk to you. Within the hour, if possible. I have an emergency matter and I need your help."

"Within the hour? I'm on my way out."

A long sigh. "Look, I think you'll be interested. And I'm prepared to pay a substantial retainer. But it has to be tonight; I can't get away very often." Plaintive now. Then with more confidence. "I'll explain everything when we meet."

When we meet? Or if we meet? Something about the wistful quality in her voice, or maybe I liked her accent. I agreed to meet her at eleven at Abel's All-Night Kitchen on Soto Street in East Los Angeles. She was pleased. Thanked me.

Surveillance would likely focus on the front of my building. I left by the side door, which led directly into our parking lot, then drove my Chrysler 300 out the back gate onto Rose Street. East on Traction through the Arts District and across the tragic, old Fourth Street Bridge, where the homeless melt into the alcoves. Diverted south on I-5, Garfield exit. Precautionary. Got gas at a Valero station. North on Garfield, across Highway 60, and north into Monterey Park. Slowed down to make the left onto Jack's street, which pissed off the driver behind me. He got up on my ass, honked, and accelerated past me. Caught a glimpse of a dark-colored van. Jack's building was down the block on the right. I parked in back.

Jack buzzed me in and handed me a cup of coffee.

As part of his unflagging optimism, Jack rarely says anything bad about anyone. You could be a rank-to-the-bone killer, the dirtiest defense lawyer in LA, hell, even a child molester, and Jack will soliloquize about what a *bon homme* guy you are. Everybody loves Jack, but no one really understands him.

"Remember that federal meth case we did about three years ago?" I paused, tested my coffee, piping hot, the way Jack likes it. "Our client got a year and a day, despite twenty pounds of crystal meth and bullshit cooperation. Sam Blaylock was the AUSA. I can't remember the client's name."

"Can't forget that one. His name was José Diminuendo." Jack grinned and ran his slender fingers through his spiky brown hair. "Sometimes, you get lucky."

"Nah. You're just good...Have you done any other cases where Blaylock was the prosecutor?"

Jack thought it over. "I think I have. He's a piece of work. Known for handing out sweetheart deals. Unless he's in a bad mood. Then he'll fuck you." Jack laughed. "Gotta love it, Nick. We meet some corkers. We really do."

Jack brought up a file on his computer screen, scrolled down a bit, and snapped his fingers. "Bingo. Sylvia is damned good. She's got the file cross-referenced and alphabetized by AUSAs, judges, and clients." He spent a few minutes clicking around, nodded a few times, coughed, cleared his throat, and straightened up. "How do you like that? I gotta draw this guy more often. Four cases over the last three years. All great results. And one of them even drew the Honorable Charles Doggett. You know how tough he is." Jack grinned and knuckled his forehead. "Judge Doggett gave Blaylock hell right there in open court and then gave him the sweetheart deal he wanted. Which made my client very happy. I didn't have to do anything."

"Hmm...Were they cooperation cases?"

"That's the funny part. None of them were. Instead, Blaylock trotted out all the mitigating personal stuff—health problems, family problems, sick children, infirm grandparents. It was crazy. Like he was the defense attorney."

Jack's phone buzzed. He let it go to voicemail.

"Don't you think that's a little strange, Jack? A year-round fire sale?"

"It's strange, but good strange. Don't look a gift horse in the mouth. Why? What's on your mind? You seem amped up."

I didn't answer. In the grip of memory. Quietly, shielding my anticipation, I asked, "Wasn't there another AUSA not unlike Sam? Six or seven years ago? Who also handed out *bon homme* deals? It was mostly coke but also some meth and money laundering. I think he might've left the department, maybe under a black cloud..."

"As far as I'm concerned, they all leave the U.S. Attorney's Office under a black cloud. Ruin a bunch of lives and then slide into a cushy berth with a white shoe law firm..."

That's about as cynical as Jack ever gets. "No, this was different. As I recall, it had something to do with blatant prosecutorial misconduct at a high-profile trial. Kind of thing that will ruin your chances of ever getting a white-collar job."

Jack mulled it over. Then he snapped his fingers. "Oh yeah, I know who you mean. Stan Timberlake. He withheld the fact at trial that he'd arranged for his key witness, a bank manager at one of the big downtown banks who'd been working with a Colombian money launderer, to keep her job in exchange for her testimony. That did not sit well with Judge Eggers. Stan left the department under a very black cloud. The white shoe boys wouldn't touch him, so he became a private criminal defense lawyer. Makes a wonderful addition to the ranks."

"I don't suppose you know whether Timberlake and Blaylock were friends?" My offhand tone belied my curiosity.

Jack grinned, showing strong yellow teeth. "*Were* friends? They *are* friends. About a week ago, Ben Boxer told me he ran into them having drinks at Musso and Frank in West Hollywood. He said they looked depressed and intoxicated, in no particular order. But I wouldn't read too much into it, unless, of course, you insist."

"Bad habit of mine." I laughed, finished my coffee, stood up, and gave him a hearty handshake. Jack will cheer you up in the worst of times.

CHAPTER FOUR

I walked into Abel's All-Night Kitchen a little after eleven p.m. Business was decent. Three couples and several small groups. And a bedraggled-looking man at the counter. No sign of Amina Hosseini. Took a seat at a table for two with a good view of the front door. At ten after eleven, a tall woman wearing black jeans, earbuds, a purple shirt, and a black leather jacket walked in. Surveyed the joint, spotted me, waved, and walked over. Took off her earbuds and smiled. White teeth and elegant cheekbones. A nose ring dangling from one of her nostrils. And long rose brown hair. Middle Eastern?

I stood up to greet her. "I'm Nick Crane and I assume you are Amina."

"Yes, I'm Amina. Amina Hosseini."

An attractive woman, a hint of wariness in her caramel-colored eyes.

We sat down across from each other. Asked her if she was hungry. She was. So was I. We ordered coffee and blueberry pancakes. Waited for the food. Small talk about the neighborhood. Amina said she'd heard even East Los Angeles was in the process of gentrification, but that she didn't see much visual evidence.

"Give it time." I chuckled. "Another ten years and all of LA County will be luxury condos, like what you see on Wilshire Boulevard."

"Maybe. I hope not." She paused. Gave me a keen look. "So just to make sure, you're Nick Crane, right? The private investigator with your office on Third Street?" Her voice casual, perhaps too casual.

"That about covers it. You wanna see my license?"

She shook her head. "That won't be necessary."

The pancakes arrived and we dug in. No matter what the situation, food always seems to generate harmony. After a few minutes, I pushed back from my plate and smiled. "So, what's this all about?"

"Where do I start?" She shrugged and smiled. More white teeth. Elegant in black. She put down her fork and sipped her coffee. "I guess I should start at the beginning. I'm Iraqi American. We came here when I was ten, my father Mohammad and me. My mother is dead. I went to boarding school all the way through high school."

"Figures. You wear it like a subtle fragrance."

Her lips curved into a smile. "Thanks. I attended the Westover School for Girls in Middlebury, Connecticut. Old World grace in New England."

I nodded. "And after that?"

"Hawthorne College in New Hampshire. I majored in Theater Arts and minored in English Lit."

Hmm. Took a moment to phrase it. "Were you on the production side, or were you an actor?"

"I was an actor. I started from the bottom and worked my way up. It took me a while to develop my acting chops."

"You persevered. That's the important thing."

"It was a good challenge. My father, who donated generously to the theater department, came to all my plays. In my senior year, I played Desdemona in *Othello* and Maggie in *Cat on a Hot Tin Roof*. But then, when I graduated, it was on to Georgetown Law School."

"So then, you're a lawyer?"

She shook her head. "I wish. I'm not a U.S. citizen yet. I was hoping I would be by now, but it hasn't worked out that way."

"It's tough. I know quite a few people in your position. What do you do instead? Some kind of legal work, I imagine?"

She smiled. Mournfully. "It's nothing I'm proud of. I do admin work at ICE."

ICE? Hmm...Seemed odd given her immigration status.

She read my mind. "It's the last place I want to work. My father and I escaped from Saddam Hussein's dictatorship when I was a little girl. And here I am working at an agency that rounds up immigrants and sends them back to some of the worst places imaginable. But I don't have a choice." She hit the table with her left fist. Firmly. Rattled our coffee cups and silverware. Angry now, her features sharpened. She controlled herself and took a sip of her coffee. Put her cup down. Looked at me. Somewhere in her earth-toned, gold-flecked eyes, I saw fear or vulnerability or both. Then she nodded her head as if making a decision.

"Here. This will explain a lot." She took a deep breath. Reached into her purse and took out a small spiral notebook. Opened it and handed it to me. "I wrote this ahead of time to give you a general sense of why I contacted you. I thought it might be easier than trying to explain everything."

> My father and I are in danger. I'm forced to work at ICE by my husband Miles Amsterdam. He keeps me under house arrest except when I'm at work. Once every week or two, I get to go out with my girlfriend Jennifer. Miles thinks I'm with her tonight.
>
> It's even worse for my father. His name is Mohammad Ghaffari. I want to hire you to go to Boston to talk to him. He'll explain everything when you see him, but basically, I need you to devise a plan to rescue both of us. Get us both to somewhere safe where we can regroup

and decide what to do next. But you can't phone him because all of his calls are monitored, and you can't go to his house because my husband keeps armed guards there around the clock.

    You come highly recommended, and I believe you can find Mohammad on your own. Once you contact him, arrange to meet him at a safe location. He'll do anything to save me and to help himself. I'll pay you a $10,000 retainer to get you started. My girlfriend Jennifer will drop it off at your office on Saturday morning at eleven o'clock. That's all I can raise at such short notice, but my father is a very generous man and will pay you handsomely if you can help us.

CHAPTER FIVE

I read her note twice from beginning to end. She waited, impassive now. I probed. "So then, your husband Miles Amsterdam forces you to work at ICE."

She nodded.

"How did you get referred to me?"

She hesitated. Averted her eyes and nibbled at a clear-coated finger nail. I waited. Finally, she nodded her head and met my gaze. "Okay, Mr. Crane, I'm going to be very straight with you. What I'm asking you to do will not be easy, and I want you to know who you're dealing with. I heard about you from Miles's friend Desmond Cole. Like my husband, Desmond is a powerful man. He's too much of a chameleon to be entirely trustworthy, but he's not as bad as my husband."

Hmm...I asked the obvious question. "Does this Desmond fellow know why you want to talk to an investigator?"

She looked past me. Thinking. Squared her shoulders. Turned toward me. "I think he probably does. And please realize, Mr. Crane, I'm speaking candidly."

"I do realize that. Thank you."

Her gaze, steady now. "Okay. Here's the situation. Desmond Cole has known my husband for almost thirty years. They're long-time friends and colleagues. I think Desmond does feel some sympathy for me and my father, because he knows how unfair our situation is, but because of his friendship with Miles, he doesn't try to intervene directly."

"I see. Did you ask him to recommend a PI?"

She pondered, toying with a lock of her rose-brown hair. "It was nothing like that. It happened out of the blue. Desmond is often at our house. It was a Sunday, a few weeks ago. We had just had brunch on the patio. Miles went to take a call, and Desmond said in a calm, matter-of-fact way, 'There's a PI in town you might want to talk to. His name is Crane, Nick Crane. He has an office on the edge of the Arts District. He knows how to get things done.' Then Miles returned and sat down with us. Desmond winked at me and that was it. It made sense when I thought about it afterwards. Though he won't come right out and say it, Desmond knows my husband is delusional."

"Delusional or not, I imagine Desmond and your husband are both uncompromising conservatives, right?"

"Miles is. Definitely. He wasn't always, but he is now. It's hard to say with Desmond because of his fickle nature. He's good at telling people what they want to hear."

I nodded slowly. "Not exactly a glowing recommendation. So, tell me this. Why would this Cole fellow even know about me?" Right then, it hit me. Like with Tami Wheat. Neither of them should even know my name.

Amina. Calm now and resolute. I was the agitated one. "He and Miles both know about you," she said. "I'm going to tell you why."

I sighed. Tried not to look totally grim. Gave her a weary nod instead. This was shaping up to be one of those godforsaken nights when everything goes sideways.

"It all goes back to the death of Frank Constantine."

"Oh, shit!"

She paused, very solemn now. Waited. Spoke. "You've been on Miles' shit list ever since then. Pardon my French. Miles and Frank were best friends going all the way back to their childhood. Miles is bent on revenge."

Stunned. No other way to put it. Frank Constantine. Military psychiatrist. Serial killer of women and advocate of "gentler, kinder" torture techniques. My team and I had taken him out seven long years ago. And now here he was, back from the grave.

I shook my head and sipped the dregs of my coffee. Picked up my fork. Put it back down. "I'm speechless. Which virtually never happens."

She reached out across the table. Warm, slender fingers gripping my left wrist. "I'm sorry, Mr. Crane. May I call you Nick?"

An automatic nod. She took her hand away.

"Don't think I like being the harbinger of doom, but you need to know the truth." She paused again. Thinking. "I think you, me, and my father are all in jeopardy. In my case, it's not like he beats me or starves me, but there's always that possibility. Miles is a violent man with crazy ideas about loyalty. The sword of Damocles he holds over our heads is the the threat of deportation, which would be disastrous. Because my father and I came here under unusual circumstances, we were not granted normal refugee visas, which, of course, could eventually lead to citizenship. And we've been strongly discouraged from applying for green cards. Were it not for this, I would have left Miles some time ago. Unfortunately, my husband is an influential man with important friends." She paused. Looked at me, her brown eyes flooded with hope and the desire to trust. Someone.

"Okay," I said. "Thank you for explaining that. And just out of curiosity, do you happen
to know a woman named Tami Wheat?"

She nodded slowly and ran a hand slowly through her long lustrous hair. "I'm acquainted with her. I don't know her well. I met her a few years ago. She was working for the Roach Consortium, making speeches and doing general PR. It was obvious she and I were on different wavelengths. I made a mental note to avoid her. Then, about six months ago, I discovered she was back in my husband's orbit. Then, last week, I ran into her again at a joint DEA-ICE task force meeting."

Interesting. Very. I waited. She wrinkled her forehead. "At the meeting, I learned DEA and ICE had formed a task force to combat drug trafficking and other related crimes. And there was talk about a high-level LAPD informant being taken over by the DEA to work for them exclusively."

She paused and I nodded slowly. "So that's how this began. That's why the U.S. Attorney's Office stole a good cop's best informant, a good cop who happens to be my friend."

Amina's turn to nod. She picked up her fork and stabbed at what was left of her pancakes.

"Hang on," I said. "I need to think this over." I stood up and wandered over to the jukebox. Light rock and norteños. And a little leftover grunge. I stood there, staring at the song titles. *Tony and Bobby Moore have often claimed that most of the weird stuff is initiated off-the-books. ICE doesn't make the decisions. Neither does the DEA. Nor does the U.S. Attorney's Office. Rather, the truly extreme stuff is initiated by rogue actors with no official allegiance to any reputable agency.* I turned around and walked back to our table. Sat down facing her.

"Okay, then. Help me out. Who exactly was at the meeting? Your husband Miles, right, and Tami Wheat?"

She nodded. "Yes. They were there. Along with three or four ICE and DEA agents. And an Assistant United States Attorney who everyone called Sam. Plus, there was a big, scary-looking guy named Oliver Tragg who seemed to know my husband quite well."

"How would you describe your husband's relationship with Tami Wheat?"

She snorted. "They're close. Too close. Miles is a sneaky bastard, and I have the feeling he and Tami are cooking something up."

I nodded. "And who is this Tragg fellow?"

"That I don't know. He looks paramilitary. I don't think he's with ICE or the DEA. Here's something, though, I think you'll find interesting. After an hour or so, everybody left except for the key figures."

"And who were they?" I looked at her. She was counting on her fingers.

"It was just the four of them. Miles, Tami, Sam the AUSA, and Oliver Tragg." She nodded slowly. "I was off to the side and couldn't hear much."

"Who does Miles work for?"

"No one. He contracts with ICE. His job is to interdict illegal border crossers."

"What about Tami?"

"She told me she's moved on from the Roach consortium. She's currently working as a publicist for the private prison industry."

"Ugh. My kind of woman." I frowned. "And what about this Tragg fellow? The scary looking guy?"

"All I know is he looks paramilitary."

"So then, out of the four, only the AUSA, Sam, has an actual position with a normal agency."

She thought for a moment. "I think that sums it up."

I needed to think this through. Which was not going to be easy. I took out my wallet and extracted some bills. "Well, Ms. Hosseini," dropping thirty dollars on the table, "this has certainly been illuminating. And I'm definitely interested in your proposal, but I want to think it over for a day or two before I commit to anything."

"What?" She sat bolt upright, her eyes dark with sudden anger, her lips curled into a look of disdain. "I don't believe it. You're going to walk away from a most lucrative and interesting case? I expected more of you." Again, her lips twisted into a look of scorn.

I shrugged. "I didn't say I don't want the job. I want to think it over. You need to look at it from my point of view. Here you are, trying to hire me to execute a plot against your husband, a powerful man who you live with and who you say is imprisoning you and your father. Isn't that a little weird?" I sat back and waited.

A long pause. Then she brightened. Spoke. "Okay. I don't disagree. It is a little weird. But the truth is, given how much Miles hates you, I think it's in your best interest to help me and my father. My father has considerable resources, and it will pay off in the long run. I can virtually guarantee that. On the other hand, you can refuse my offer and wait for Miles to cut your legs out from under you, which would be stupid, and I don't think you're a stupid man. But if you help us, and if you succeed, you'll be the beneficiary of my father's largesse. Which could be life-changing. I truly don't think you have much choice." Her turn to sit back. A look of triumph in her earth brown eyes.

"So you really believe your husband and his gang of cowboys are going to come after me? Over what happened to Frank Constantine, who, by the way, we tried our damnedest to keep alive."

"Nick," she said, so softly I had to lean forward to hear, "I have heard the story far too many times—from numerous sources. I am fully aware you and your team did everything in your power to keep Frank alive. I'm also aware Miles is going to try and bury you."

There is depression, something most of us have experienced. But there is also something deeper, a sense of grim finality that can destroy all hope in a man. Also known as endgame.

And there is counterpunching. Something I'm pretty good at. I decided to take the job.

CHAPTER SIX

I met Tony Bott at a back-to-school night in 2008, when my daughter Maleah was eleven. He'd walked up and introduced himself. Had the feeling he knew who I was. With his thick black hair and even thicker eyebrows, and his warm brown eyes and strong jawline, Tony had a face you don't easily forget. He told me he was LAPD, narcotics, and I told him I was a PI with my own company, Nick Crane & Associates. He raised an eyebrow. Grinned and stuck out a hand. "Indeed. You're that Crane asshole people talk about." We shook hands gravely.

We had interests in common. Hoops, beer (foreign and domestic), weapons, history, politics. And an addiction to danger. Throw in abusive childhoods and the mutual realization that our so-called justice system leaves one helluva lot to be desired. Tony may be a cop, but he knows the system is rigged. Which is why you'll never catch him arresting some poor jerk over any petty shit. And he'll go out of his way to help out people in need. We became good friends and even better drinking partners.

When I worked the Frank Constantine serial killer case in 2011, Tony plunged right in with me. Was there when the deranged aristocrat willed his own death rather than surrendering. Neither Tony nor I pulled the trigger. For which I am glad. Frank's personal assistant, tall, gangly Henry Taylor, shot and killed Frank with a Ruger semi-automatic. Truth is, I'd done my best to forget about Frank Constantine, his sins and excesses. Not easy. A military psychiatrist engaged in "gentler, kinder" torture research, he was highly regarded in intelligence circles. Frank's "problem" was his uncontrollable need to strangle women.

On a night I'll never forget, somewhere on the edge of Benedict Canyon, Tony and Bobby and I found Frank's torture records in neatly labeled file folders in one of his safe houses. We snatched them and cached them in Bobby Moore's safe house. Two weeks later, representatives of an unidentified agency, dressed in black, carrying sidearms and driving brown panel trucks, showed up and retrieved Frank's torture records. End of story, or so I had hoped…Seven years had passed. No black helicopters in the sky. No inopportune surveillance. Until now.

Saturday afternoon, September 30th. Thirty-two hours since Roberto's corpse had been discovered on the East LA hillside. Tony and I were flying to Guadalajara, on our way to Culiacán in the Mexican state of Sinaloa, where Tony would offer his condolences to Roberto Diaz's wife, Señora Iglesias, and give her a chunk of Roberto's "fuck you" money. Even in the grave, he would still be supporting the spokes and layers of his large Mexican family. While we were in the air, Tony told me what he knew about Roberto's murder. In fits and starts, like it hurt him to talk about it. "Roberto's face was…all contorted when they found him…The ME said his heart stopped…At maybe two a.m. Friday morning…They don't know why…Think it might have been a heroin overdose. Bullshit. Roberto never touched the stuff…"

Normally, a hard-bitten, narcotics detective like Tony adopts an attitude of genial contempt toward his informants. Not with Roberto. Something about Roberto's obsession with supporting his Mexican family and one day bringing them to America had rung a bell with Tony, who was only third generation himself and had had his own gaggle of rambunctious kids to argue with, yell at, and care for. His paternal grandfather, Abraham Botwinick, had read the tea leaves and brought his family to New York in 1933.

The smoking gun, according to Tony, was three-fold. First, Blaylock jumps his informant. Second, ten minutes later, Tami Wheat accosts him and asks for his help shadowing that same informant. Twelve hours later, Roberto dies in agony. "It's just too damned strange," said Tony. "As you know, normally, DEA, ICE, and the U.S. Attorney's Office love sharing snitches with local law enforcement. So why not this time? What the hell is going on?" As our plane began its descent into Guadalajara, Tony grabbed my arm and muttered, "This is what fries my ass! Roberto was almost out. He had one last target, a big coke dealer named Javier Fincus. Shit. Shit. Shit." Like most CI's, Diaz mainly ratted out his competition and protected his connections. He had planned to "graduate" to that great American dream, real estate. Condos. Wilshire Boulevard condos. As suggested by his friend Raymundo Ochoa, an ex-Federales captain, also on the dance card for this expedition. Tony had met Raymundo fifteen years ago, when the Federales had sent him up to LA as part of an LAPD training exchange program.

I said nothing about my own grave concern—Frank Constantine had clawed his way out of the crypt, at least in the mind of an ICE contractor named Miles Amsterdam, and revenge against beleaguered old Crane was now on the table. And nothing about Amina Hosseini and her father, either. That could wait.

In Guadalajara, we transferred to an Aerolittoral Embraer E-190 for the hop to Culiacán. Over the Sierra Madre, then a smooth descent to the Aeropuerto Internacional, a strikingly modern delta fueled by drug money. Out into the warm subtropical evening, slashes of scarlet cutting the fog at dusk.

Five minutes later, an Escalade pulled up alongside us. A granite-faced *sicario* got out of the passenger seat. Walked over and handed Tony Raymundo's business card. Said his name was Arnulfo and that Don Raymundo was waiting for us. A Mercedes pulled in behind the Escalade. We picked up our bags and climbed into the back seat of the SUV. Arnulfo got back in, and we pulled out into traffic, the Mercedes on our tail. Backup can be a good thing. In *any* dark and bloody land.

Fifteen minutes later, we reached Raymundo's fortress, a multi-story, tile-roofed mansion surrounded by manicured lawns and a circular driveway filled with Harley-Davidson classic "hogs," a Buick Enclave, and a Ford F-150. We walked up to a huge door with a gold jaguar knocker, surrounded by faux Corinthian pillars and luxurious potted palms. Not my style. But not too shabby for an ex-cop.

CHAPTER SEVEN

Raymundo Ochoa was the whole package. Wavy black hair streaked with gray. Powerful shoulders, a Zapata mustache, and a livid three-inch scar running diagonally across his right cheek. His .40 caliber S&W, M&P semi-auto pistol in an old-fashioned side holster. He smiled. "Don Antonio! So long, no see. Safe trip?"

"Always safe with you on my side, Don Raymundo," said Tony.

He ushered us into the anteroom. Shifted his head a little to one side and squinted at me through his right eye. "And you are? Wait. I know you. We met deep-sea fishing in July. I was up in Newport Beach on business. Small world, as you Americanos like to say." It was true. Vague memory of a cheerfully drunk Raymundo bragging about closing high-end real estate deals for his international clientele.

"I believe we were too far gone that afternoon to introduce ourselves properly. I'm Nick Crane." I met the man's firm grip.

"Raymundo Ochoa, at your service. You are LAPD?"

"Detective *privado*."

"*Habla español?*"

I shook my head.

"Then it's *muy afortunado mi madre* insisted I learn English when I was a little boy. It's been *muy útil* in my career...Did you know, Don Antonio, I'm retired now?"

"Ernesto Cardenas told me you'd been thinking about it."

"*Sí*. I am retired El Capitán now. What a great relief. What *gloriosa libertad*! And how is our friend Ernesto? I believe he is also El Capitán?"

"*Exactamente*. He plans to retire in a year or two."

"Progress," said Raymundo, his brown eyes amused as he led us across a broad expanse of light marble tile into a high-ceilinged parlor, where he directed us to make ourselves at home. "I believe in progress."

Tony handed him a bottle of Buchanan's Red Seal 21 blended scotch. Ochoa chuckled. "In case I was in short supply, *mis amigos?*"

"Not likely, but just in case," said Tony.

Raymundo rang a bell and a maid appeared. He spoke to her in rapid-fire Spanish and handed her the Buchanan's. Five minutes later, she returned with three glasses on a tray, an ice bucket, the Scotch, and a collection of expensive cigars arranged in a silver display case.

"A little voice told me not to drink with dinner tonight. Now I know why. So I can start fresh with *mis compadres*."

The maid poured us each three fingers of the light amber beverage. Raymundo and Tony took theirs neat, I opted for ice. "*Gracias*, Maria." Raymundo waved her away, and she left the room, silent as time.

"*Salud!* To our health and continued prosperity. And many young and beautiful women." The scotch was smoky yet smooth, welcome after a long day. "Not bad, *mis amigos*." Raymundo ran his hand across his mouth. "The drink of *policia* and narcotraffickers everywhere."

Tony smiled. "*Mis informantes* swear by it."

Raymundo and Tony drank rapidly while I nursed my scotch, a fact that did not elude our host's experienced gaze. They never discussed Ochoa's fingers in the drug trade. Never discussed his relationship with Roberto. Or whether the three of them had ever even met? What ten-moves-ahead chess game was being played? For the moment, though, just a couple of cops and an LA PI sharing good scotch. Raymundo said the best thing about being a retired *El Capitán* was the steady stream of business propositions that came his way.

He explained that while he rarely said no to an intriguing real estate venture, he drew the line when it came to human smuggling, and of course we had to end the cancer permeating Mexico and the U.S., the drug trade. Having gotten that off his chest, he lamented the current state of narco-trafficking, in which the cartels were at each other's throats and torture and beheadings and mass murder were the order of the day.

"And to think many *Jefes* live here in *mi propio barrio*. They're probably drinking Buchanan's and smoking fine Cubano cigars like we are." He drew on his cigar thoughtfully and exhaled a plume of blue smoke. "Of course, you know all that. I'm sure things are *muy diferente* in Los Angeles. Such a lovely city." He smiled. Sarcastic devil.

Tony took a thoughtful sip of Buchanan's. Deliberating on how best to deflect Raymundo's challenge. Then he answered. "*Mi amigo*, I am very glad to see you. You look well, and it appears you are doing well now that you're enjoying your retirement. My *compadre* and I greatly appreciate your hospitality. We are here, though, because of an unfortunate matter."

"I know," said Raymundo. He did not seem surprised. "Although you are observing *el decoro*, I see sadness in your eyes."

"Yes, Don Raymundo. We are here because I must pay my respects and deliver my condolences to the widow of our dear friend Roberto Diaz."

"Roberto? *Ay Dios mío.*" Ochoa grimaced. Bit his lip and reached for the scotch. "Poor Roberto. I'm so sorry to hear that. How was he killed?"

Again, Tony deliberated. Again, he drank before responding. "We're not sure yet, Don Raymundo. It's still early in the investigation. All we know is something is wrong, and the facts don't add up."

For a moment, Ochoa's eyes were distant, as if remembering things better left unsaid. Then he spoke. "I can see you are *muy triste*, Don Antonio. It is a strange thing with you Americanos. Here in Mexico, where no one escapes corruption, we are not upset by it. Yet in America, which is just as corrupt and much more powerful, and therefore much more *peligroso* than my little Mexico, there are still idealists like you who are upset by what we see as everyday occurrences. But I can't help wondering, and because I respect you, Don Antonio, I must ask. Are you purer than the corrupt ones?"

"I wish I could say I am. But I can't." This time, Tony didn't hesitate. Nor did he drink before answering. "All I can do is try to be a man of my word."

"*Hombre de palabra*. That's all any of us can do. So, what can I do for you, Don Antonio?"

"What I'm hoping is you would be willing to drive us out to Don Roberto's widow's house in El Tamarindo in the morning, so I can offer her my condolences." Tony knew Ochoa knew this was expected. The sign of the cross, as it were, for Diaz's service to both Tony and Ochoa.

Raymundo pondered. He rubbed his tired brown eyes and scraped at the scar on his cheek. Then he drank. Finally, he spoke. "I will do that for you, Don Antonio. I will do it willingly. But I ask one thing in return. I have a nephew, Pedro Salazar, who I am very close to. He went to the university in Mexico City, where he got his law degree. He came home, and like *los hombres jóvenes* sometimes do, he got caught up with the wrong people. He is currently in the prison in Guadalajara. He will be extradited to Los Angeles soon. It will be *un desastre*. As long as he is here, *el está bien*. We take care of him, and we have compadres at the prison. But if he is taken to an American prison, he will be lost…" Raymundo paused, his eyes glistening.

Tony did not answer at first. He looked at me and I nodded. Then Tony refilled his glass with Buchanan's, and then he toasted the company. "*Salud.* I can't promise anything, but we will do what we can to make sure he's protected."

"*Gracias,*" said Raymundo. "That's all I can ask."

After that, Tony and Raymundo got down to some serious drinking. The retired captain regaled us with colorful narco stories. What he had "heard" or "discovered," all the while wearing the grimace of all-too-human reality. Tony responded with lively tales of stakeouts, arrests, confiscations, and the occasional shootout. I wasn't in the mood to get drunk. Instead, I drank slowly, listened with one ear, and puffed cautiously on a fine Cuban cigar. While mulling over Amina's predicament. And my own. Raymundo's phone rang frequently, and he mostly let it go to voicemail. On two occasions, though, he answered, excused himself, and strode to a corner of the room, where, standing under a bust of Benito Juarez, he spoke quietly into the speaker.

After the second call, he returned beaming, sat down, lit up a fresh cigar, and leaned back, puffing luxuriously. "Ah, *mis compadres*, life is good if you are lucky and keep your eyes and ears open. Over the last few years, I've been introduced to several wealthy foreigners, Saudis and East Indians, who are buying high-end properties in our lovely resort communities, especially around Puerto Vallarta. It looks like my biggest deal ever is about to go through. I will make…no, it would be obscene to tell you how much I will make. Let me just say it will be a sum fit for a king. This calls for a celebration. Señor Nicolas, why are you drinking so slowly? I remember you did not hold back on the fishing boat."

"He's like that," said Tony. "Some of the time."

"I like a cautious man," said Raymundo, fixing me with the steady yet unsteady look of an experienced drinker. "Just so he's not too cautious. From the look of you, I don't believe that is the case."

I shrugged.

"Actually," said Tony, "*mi compadre is muy loco.*"

We wound it down sometime after two a.m. Raymundo led us to a lavishly appointed guest room, where I collapsed onto one of the king-sized beds. The room was spinning, but only a little. I slept.

CHAPTER EIGHT

Sunday morning. Raymundo Ochoa's guestroom. The black dog attacking like a sledgehammer. Tony felt even worse. We gulped down black coffee the maid served in white china mugs. Just before we left the house, Tony handed Raymundo the envelope containing the Señora's money. "Down payment," he said. "I'll arrange to have the rest of it delivered, a chunk at a time."

We were on the road by eight a.m. in Raymundo's F-150. The highway from Culiacán to El Tamarindo was in good repair, and we rode three abreast in the cab. Raymundo appeared none the worse for wear and, between phone calls, described the lush farmlands with great enthusiasm. "Pumpkins, watermelons, cantaloupes. *Muy bien.* And the healthy vegetables. Broccoli, cabbage, lettuce, kale, even Brussel sprouts, we have it all." Tony responded in monosyllables, and I managed an occasional grunt.

"*Santa Madre de Dios.* I wouldn't have gotten drunk with you boys if I'd known you were such pussies. But don't worry. It's *muy* early and the narcotraffickers are all still asleep. No one is likely to shoot us. Besides, everyone knows I'm…What do you Americanos call it?" He fondled the butt-end of his handgun with considerable familiarity.

"You're strapped," said Tony.

Roberto's wife lived on a small goat farm a few miles outside of El Tamarindo. We pulled into her driveway, which was shaded with poplars and elephant trees. The chickens, which had been pecking in the dirt, scattered. Two dogs began to bark, and a young boy with dark hair and a friendly, open face came running up to the cab. When he saw Raymundo wearing khakis with two Americanos looking vaguely like DEA agents, the boy stiffened and drew back.

"*No te preocupes,*" called Raymundo. "*Por favor trae a tu madre. Asuntos oficiales.*"

Now the boy looked even more worried. He stared at us and plucked at his hair. Then he nodded and retreated toward the adobe farmhouse. "Let's get out," said Raymundo. "This will not be easy. I will not give Roberto's wife the money now, not in front of everyone. She would be insulted. I will take care of it after suitable time has elapsed."

Tony nodded grimly. We got out of the truck and stood there. It was still cool and there was little humidity. After five minutes, a thirty-something woman, dressed neatly in jeans and a brightly colored work shirt, walked toward us. Her body language betrayed acute anxiety, and as she drew closer, she faltered.

"Señora," said Raymundo gravely, "*no estamos aquí para hacerte daño.*" He walked slowly toward her with us in his wake. Raymundo stopped a few paces away, turned, and nodded to Tony, who stepped up next to him.

"*Mi compadre tiene un mensaje para ti.*"

Although it was a still morning, a series of dust devils appeared out of nowhere and spiraled haphazardly around the yard.

"Señora Iglesias," said Tony quietly, his face riveted with strain, "I wish to apologize on behalf of the *Estados Unidos.*" Raymundo reached out and took his arm. He translated and nodded to Tony.

"*Su marido*, Roberto Diaz, and I worked together. Roberto was my *muy bien compadre* and *un hombre valiente*. He was killed two days ago. We're not sure who is responsible, but we are investigating. I am so sorry."

His weathered face grave, Raymundo translated. Señora Iglesias broke in stages, her face cracking, her shoulders slumping, but she did not weep. Then she recovered, straightened up, and began shouting at us in Spanish, calling us *pendejos* and *maricónes* and other insults I didn't recognize.

Tony bowed his head and stepped back, folding his arms across his chest. Then he recovered and spoke with great clarity. "*Por favor,* Señora, I am investigating *su marido's* murder. I will not rest until I have solved it. I give you my word."

Raymundo translated carefully, emphasizing each word. Then Tony spoke again. "The American government will make arrangements to fly his body here as you wish."

"*El gobierno estadounidense hará los arreglos para volar su cuerpo aquí tal como lo desea.*"

"I am so sorry. Roberto was a good man and he was *mi compadre.*" Tony's voice broke. A dust devil passed between him and Señora Iglesias.

The widow stood there staring at us. Slowly, her rage fell away, step by step, into bitter resignation. Then she backed away, as if we were somehow lethal. I had the feeling we were. Once she had put enough space between us, Señora Iglesias turned and walked slowly toward her house. She stumbled once but did not fall.

Raymundo drove us back to Culiacán and dropped us off at the airport.

CHAPTER NINE

A somber flight home. You wouldn't have known it, though, at thirty thousand feet. The glorious twilight over the Pacific, the endless sky streaked pink and rose and turquoise. Such a beautiful fucking world. A bump and a skid and we were back down in it.

Sport bag in hand, his shoulders slumped, Tony started toward the escalator. Stopped halfway and turned around. Came back. When he reached me, he pulled me over against the wall. Spoke quietly. "Listen Nick, there's something else. I need you to listen to me. Roberto had a lover from El Salvador named Elene Eliade. She's a smart woman who speaks good English—"

"You sound like you know her..."

"Fuck you, Nick. I do know her. Anyway, this goes way back. Roberto met her in Guadalajara, where she was treated like an indentured servant. She already had a daughter named Abrecia. Elene and Roberto had a daughter together, who they named Gloria. Roberto paid to have all three of them smuggled into the U.S. He suggested she find a job somewhere in the heartland, thinking they would be safe there. For the past four years, she's been working on a farm in Morgan County in southern Ohio near a place called Liberty Center. Her kids were doing fine, and Roberto would visit every so often. He was really close to little Gloria and Abrecia just loved him. Sweet guy, you know. He liked kids."

A catch in his throat. I looked at him. Knew where this was going. Maybe.

"The fuckin' immigration people picked them up a week ago Saturday, five days before we met Tami Wheat at the Bar & Grill." He stopped. Looked at me. Tony never cries, but there was moisture in his dark brown eyes. "Listen, Nick, they separated the little girls from their mother. They're being held in a foster home on a farm outside of a town called Gallipolis, right there on the Ohio River. Pending removal. I don't know where their mother is. I'll find out." He stopped. Looked at me. "I gotta do something."

"I thought the new orders are to reunite the mothers and children."

"It's tricky," said Tony. "If they were reunited, they'd be held in some hellhole of a tent city down on the border, where they would apply for asylum. Elene might get it because she's originally from El Salvador and will arguably be killed if she's sent back, but the girls are Mexican citizens. They don't stand a chance. God knows what will happen to them if they're deported. They'll be dumped in Guadalajara, where they don't know a soul."

"How do you know they're Mexican citizens?"

"How do you think? They were born there."

I must have given Tony a questioning look. "Listen, Nick, I'm not an idiot. I've spoken to their lawyer. He seems like a sharp guy. His name is Lyndon Naismith, Esquire. These hicksville lawyers still call themselves Esquire." Barest flicker of a smile.

"What does he say about the girls getting deported?"

"He says it's most likely a slam dunk. His strategy is to keep them right where they are, where he thinks they're safe, for as long as possible. In case the tide turns and the immigration authorities relax the present standard."

I thought about it. Rubbed my forehead. "They're not going to relax the standard. You and I both know that. But you said the girls are on a farm. Is that good or bad?"

"That's the first thing I asked Lyndon. He said the conditions were basic, but the foster parents, the Munsons, are decent people, and the girls weren't being mistreated. They go to school every day just like American kids. The Munsons have been in the foster care business for a long time and have a good reputation. I agree with Naismith, Esquire." This time Tony did smile. "They're obviously better off there on the farm than they'd be in a tent city or in one of those private jails, where they pack 'em in like worker bees."

I said nothing. Tony leaned in closer. "Listen, Nick, I've met these girls. Roberto flew them out here. We all went to Disneyland together, his kids and mine. His girls are sweethearts. They speak really good English." He stopped. Sport bag in his left hand. Right fist clenched. Tony is a big, strong man. I've seen him hurt people.

"Maybe," I said casually, "I could look into it. Maybe come up with a plan to somehow shepherd them to safety."

He looked at me. Looked away. Back to me. People hide the hope they're feeling. Tony was no exception. "Maybe you should look into it. I would really appreciate that." He offered me his hand, which I shook. Then he turned and started to walk away. Stopped and turned around. "Thank you, Nick. I'll email you all the information."

Found an airport Starbucks and ordered a dark roast. Sat there letting it cool, musing over Amina and Mohammad and my own vexing situation. And now Elene's two daughters were added to the mix. My client list was expanding. Amina, her father Mohammad, Gloria, and Abrecia... A final sip of my coffee, then down the escalator to Arrivals to meet my Uber.

CHAPTER TEN

I stepped off the escalator and there she was. Tami Wheat holding an arrival sign with a skull and crossbones instead of a name. Big smile when she saw me. Gave her the middle finger salute and reached in my pocket for my phone. Texted "SOS" to my partner Bobby Moore. He could track the GPS locator in my boxers, as long as I had them on.

Took a hard left into the baggage crowd. No dice. Three burly Middle Eastern types wearing Arab robes and headgear sandwiched me out of nowhere. Stuck a gun in my ribs and hustled me out the door into an SUV. Muttering in English. Hmm. One fella pulled a hood over my head. The snap of plastic restraints and the sharp pinprick of a needle. Off to la la land. Until rudely awakened by a pail of cold water sloshed over my head. Naked, chained to a chair, under bright interrogation lights. Hoped they'd delegated disposal of my clothes to their weakest link.

Out of the brightness appeared three shadows, which slowly took form. Tami Wheat in her expensive jeans and leather bomber jacket. Grinning like the cat that swallowed the canary. Definitely enjoying herself more than at the Bar & Grill. A tall, aristocratic Yalie type flanked her. Those ole "ice blue" eyes, angular thin features Bryn Mawr girls would call handsome, a good tan, and a $500 haircut. A bespoke suit, starched white shirt, and one of those J. Press-type striped ties. Blue Eyes said his name was Miles Amsterdam, which somehow didn't surprise me. What did surprise me was how quickly he and his crew had struck. Cursed myself for being unprepared.

The third caballero was a whole different breed. Think Seal Team Six on speedballs. Biker vest over a Marshawn Lynch jersey. The Beast. How subtle. Looked like a knife blade had dug trenches in his forehead—ancient scars that looked like shrapnel wounds. His broken nose pointed to three o'clock. Truly, a new standard of ugly. The guy had a bad habit of gnashing his teeth while slip-slapping his rubber truncheon against his thigh. Growled out his Spook Land name, QB Tragg, as moronic a tradecraft as the goon himself. Clearly, this was the Oliver Tragg Amina had met at the DEA-ICE meeting.

Introductions out of the way, Tami spoke first. "The reason you are here, Crane, is you poisoned Roberto Diaz with potassium phosphate. Less than eight hours after we met at that shitty little bar on Thursday night. The poor man died in agony. You, my friend, are truly an asshole."

I'd anticipated some kind of stitch up, but this was a shocker. But too absurd to be truly worrisome. I said, "Ms. Wheat. What a pleasure! You're looking good as always. But I didn't realize you had such a big imagination. You really should put it to better use."

The gorilla whacked me in the ribs with his truncheon. Pain. The beast could also speak in a kind of guttural way, two parts gravel, one-part nasal drip. "Listen, shit bird. Here's how we're going to do this. I'm going to ask you questions. You will answer the questions promptly and truthfully. Or else I'll…" He gestured toward my man-parts. "Cut your boys off. So where were you at two a.m. on Saturday morning?"

Naked, chained to the chair, I sensed Tragg and I had a rendezvous with destiny, and I knew I would enjoy grinding a motorcycle boot into his ruined face. But from his question, I gathered there was some problem with their timeline. They were trying to find out what I could prove definitively before building their frame around it.

"Where do you think I was at two a.m.? I was asleep at my house in Avocado Hills."

"Exactly. You were asleep at your dump on Peter Maple Drive, where we found the potassium traces this morning. You weren't too careful, were you, you fucking traitor?"

"Hey, have a little respect. That's my house you're pissing on. Where I happen to have cameras in every room. Whatever you planted will be obvious, not that you'd have any way to tie your phony traces to Roberto Diaz's body. If you even were in my house."

This brought a couple more whacks in the ribs and more guttural spewing. "Crane, shut the fuck up! We disabled your security system before we went in." Beast in my face, saliva splattering. If he's this angry, they must have some problem. Or else he's just insane.

Miles Amsterdam pirouetted into the breach. His was a warm, soothing enema of a voice, fluid and almost sorrowful, as if it pained him to see me in this dire position. "We've been watching you for some time now, Mr. Crane. From your recent track record, it hasn't been easy for us to figure out whose side you're on. Maybe you're on no one's side except your own. Which is pure insanity in today's world of accelerating threats and clear and present danger to the American way of life. Sadly, your most recent actions represent, in the opinion of our principals, very bad and inexcusable choices."

"Principals?" I asked. "Or principles? Which you so clearly lack."

Amsterdam smiled. Ignored my conclusion. "Take last Thursday, for instance. You and an LAPD narcotics detective named Anthony Bott met with Ms. Wheat at seven p.m. at the Third Street Bar & Grill. It was not a successful meeting. You and Officer Bott purposely pissed off and antagonized my colleague." He reached out and put his right hand on Tami's leather-clad forearm. "After you walked out of the bar, you crossed the street and entered the Poseidon Building, where you keep an office for your failing detective agency. Then you did nothing of interest until Saturday, when you and Mr. Bott flew to Culiacán.

"Based on your outrageous professional misconduct at the Bar & Grill, we had placed you under surveillance. Which is how we know you spent Saturday night and Sunday morning with one Raymundo Ochoa, one of the most corrupt men in Mexico, discussing how best to obstruct an ongoing federal investigation into human trafficking." Amsterdam smirked. "Ah, Mr. Crane, you really should know better than to interfere in a federal investigation. But some people have a death wish, I guess."

My gaze flickered from Amsterdam to Tragg to Wheat and back to Amsterdam. No sympathy from this crowd. I felt like I'd been slapped or spun around. How did Amsterdam know about Ochoa? I was almost certain no one had followed us in Culiacán, and yet...

I spoke. "My turn to ask a question. Why on earth, knowing the law as I do, would I ever interfere in a federal investigation into human trafficking or any other crime, for that matter?"

"That's what we keep asking ourselves," said Tami Wheat. "But given your bad track record combined with the fact you were not only rude but also made singularly unpatriotic remarks when we met on Thursday night, it's clear you are toxic to our free society..."

"Gee, thanks for the vote of confidence. Next question." I had not been Mirandized, which meant this interrogation was not official.

As if he'd read my mind, Amsterdam purred, "I'm sure you're familiar with the term 'extraordinary rendition.' Not my favorite method of executing justice, but the option is definitely on the table."

Madness. I was an American-born citizen living in the U.S. This meant extraordinary rendition was not technically available or necessary to arrest and question me. Rendition means private arrest outside the U.S. What these miscreants were actually doing was illegally detaining an American citizen, which is a serious federal offense. Also known as false imprisonment.

Amsterdam smiled, his lips curling up in a sickly, irregular curve. "I'll tell you what, Mr. Crane. Let me spell it out for you. Lay our cards on the table, so to speak. First, we could bind you over on a charge of obstruction of justice for interfering in a federal investigation into human trafficking. Second, there's the Diaz murder, which, based on the truly malevolent nature of the crime, carries the death penalty. Third is your theft of classified documents from Frank Constantine, which has a ten-year cap. And even such a lengthy sentence would not begin to pay for the fact you killed a most valiant American who also happened to be our friend. You, Mr. Crane, are a sick sonofabitch and the walking, talking definition of a threat to national security."

"I didn't kill Frank Constantine. His handyman, Henry Taylor, shot him."

Amsterdam ignored me. He turned to Tami, who handed him a manila folder. He leafed through some papers, nodding and pursing his lips. "And now, as a kind of bonus, if you will, we have evidence that in addition to obstructing justice, you are also conspiring to commit terrorist acts against the United States. Among other things, you and Officer Bott spent Saturday evening and Sunday morning conspiring with your friend Ochoa, who, we have probable cause to believe, is smuggling Saudi and Yemeni nationals into this country who, in turn, are planning terrorist acts even as we speak."

Made no sense. Why would Raymundo Ochoa be involved in human trafficking? Or terrorism of any kind. Unless... Suppose that in return for Saudi financing of his real estate deals, Ochoa had lined up coyotes to transport a few trusted Saudi retainers (the kind with no visas) stateside, perhaps to check out their own American properties...But why would Ochoa, a wise and experienced hand, not cover himself with his old Federale connections? In order to avoid any slip-ups that might expose him.

"Officer Bott and I were there hoping Captain Ochoa would help us offer our condolences to Roberto Diaz's widow."

Amsterdam nodded. Ran a hand through his immaculate hair. Another ghoulish smile. "It's a good cover story and even believable...except for the fact we have solid evidence you and your pal Bott were there with the ulterior motive of planning terrorist acts against the United States."

"Which is why I want to break you into little pieces," growled Tragg.

Amsterdam stared at me. Pale flat eyes. No smile this time, ghoulish or otherwise. Thin mouth set like a knife cut. "Let's not get off track. Six or seven hours after you and Officer Bott insulted my colleague here," gesturing toward Tami, "Roberto Diaz died in agony in a field just a few miles away. Thirty-six hours later, you're in Culiacán discussing with Ochoa how best to smuggle terrorists and sex slaves across the border."

I yawned. Deliberately. "That's crazy. I never engaged in any such conversation. And I know nothing about smuggling anyone, sex slaves or terrorists, across the border."

"Right, and I used to play bongos in the Clifton Chenier Orchestra." Tragg and Tami snickered like they got the joke. Truth is, there were no bongos in the Clifton Chenier Orchestra, God rest his Cajun soul.

"You're lying, Crane," said Amsterdam. "The problem is you're no good at it..." He paused. Smirked and nodded emphatically. "Here's how I see it. On the one hand, you're working with that Ochoa bastard to smuggle sex slaves and terrorists into the country, and on the other hand, you're obstructing our investigation into those very acts. And you have absolutely no idea who we really are." *You got that right.* "You think we're ICE or DEA and my colleague here," gesturing toward Tami, "is DOJ or works for the U.S Attorney's Office. But you would be wrong thinking such naïve thoughts, Mr. Crane. You have no idea who you are dealing with." Okay, time for the gut punch. Every nightmare has a climax.

Tragg's turn. "Listen, motherfucker, I play fair. I give a man the benefit of the doubt, and I will go to the fucking wall for any decent, loyal American. But after looking at the evidence, there is one fact and one fact only. You, Crane, are a fuckin' traitor, and that's why I'd like to beat you to death with my bare hands. And I will. But not yet. Not until we get to know each other better." That ugly grimace. I'm going to enjoy killing this species of vermin. Reminded me of an old Thelma Ritter noir film where she tells her son, "I've stepped on better things than these guys."

So many times, with Bobby Moore and Tony at the safe house, I'd listened to them discuss the New Game. Not the old Great Game that pitted the Russians against the Brits in India and Afghanistan or any other traditional Old World rivalry. The New Game was different. Americans fighting and scheming against every shadow on the sidewalk. Bobby and Tony were obsessed with the machinations of all manner of free-lance actors. Rogues of every stripe and pedigree. And the infinite layers of deceit all covered up as "state secret privileges." Bobby would say, "*At its simplest, the game is double and triple and most likely quadrupling on from there. But the question is always the same. Cui bono? Who benefits?*"

Decided I'd heard enough. "Time's up, my friends. I've been patient. I've listened to each of you spew your happy horseshit. But now, I want a lawyer. And I want my Miranda rights read. Until that happens, I will answer no further questions."

Tragg guffawed. "Another liberal pussy who wants to read terrorists their rights." Amsterdam added, "You know better than that, Crane. Rights are reserved for loyal Americans, not national security risks."

I said, "I demand the right to habeas corpus guaranteed to all American citizens by the Constitution."

Ms. Wheat's turn. She smirks, "Wow. An armchair lawyer as well. But amateur. Decidedly amateur. Habeas rights don't apply to you, Crane. You are going nowhere until we are satisfied you are not a threat to national security. You stole Frank Constantine's classified research records seven years ago, and now you are conspiring to smuggle sex slaves and terrorists across our borders. Will you never learn? And just in case you weren't aware, there is no statute of limitation for the destruction of federal property. And our sources tell us that at least one-tenth of Frank Constantine's classified research material was missing when the agency retrieved the rest of it."

"Which means you're facing up to ten years in prison on that alone," said Amsterdam, a little too casually, "under 18 U.S.C., Section 1361." He paused. Another sickly smile. Continued. "Of course, there may be other options." Oh boy, here we go.

On cue, Tragg snarled, "Not my preference, you sick fuck. I want your pussy ass in the ring, where I can legally kill you with these." Raised his hands in a passable pugilist's stance. "In fact, ever since I heard about you, I've been wanting to beat some red, white, and blue sense into your leftie skull." He must know about my boxing? But how could he? Not a soul in Los Angeles knows I was a pretty fair Silver Gloves boxer in northern Minnesota when I was a kid. These creeps had resources. As I was to learn. Again and again. "Yeah, you little prick," said Tragg. "We know all about you. Little boy up there in the cold country with his little boy boxing gloves. Think you can last one round with me? Your patty cake style won't even pass the giggle test." So Tragg's ego was out of control. Good to remember.

"Tragg, what I've heard about you is that when you're in the ring, you flap your hands like a two-year-old announcing a bowel movement. You're a fucking disgrace to the Marquess of Queensberry. Did Miss Manners teach you how to box?" Tragg came at me with his fists, but Amsterdam suppressed a smirk and held him off. Whispered to him *sotto voce*, and then Tragg laughed, a harsh metallic sound like the rasp of a broken screen door.

"As you can see," said Amsterdam, "my colleague is passionate about protecting the homeland."

I'd heard enough. Go time. "Whoever or whatever you and your principals are, this detention is illegal bullshit, and I can prove it. So, what the fuck do you want?"

Amsterdam smiled and held up his hands as if warding off my profanity. "It's not what we want that matters. It's what you want. Do you want to be whisked off to Poland or Egypt or even Syria, where torture is elevated to an art form? I don't think so. But because I am a patriot and believe in second chances, I'm willing to give you the option of walking through Door B, cooperating with us and saving yourself a lot of grief. We want information. On Ochoa, on Diaz, on Bott's investigations, and on his corrupt relationship with Ochoa. We want to know who's doing what with whom—when, what, where, and why. Once you've turned over all your intel, and if we believe you are being truthful and candid, not to mention effective, we can then decide how best to further utilize your talents.

"On the other hand, if we think you are not being truthful and candid, you will have an all-expenses paid vacation to a rather unscenic part of the world. There, our assets will complete your debriefing in a most painful manner. Real delicious...when viewed in a certain light. But we'd rather not go that route. We'd rather put you to work. We know you've got talent. We want you to go to Culiacán to get closer to Ochoa and his circle. According to our intel, you've gone fishing with him in American waters and visited him in Sinaloa. You guys are more than mere acquaintances. We want to build on this. Good help is always at a premium, and you can work off your crimes by serving your country. And be well paid in the process, which could rescue your failing detective agency. Quite frankly, it's a much better deal than you deserve, Mr. Crane."

Fishing in American waters? This could mean Raymundo's house was bugged. Unless the old captain was working for this batch of criminals? Which seemed unlikely, not his style. But did Amsterdam really think I would go for this sucker deal? Could this really be the endgame? And if I didn't cooperate, could they just kill me and bury the crime along with my body, even with Bobby and Tony still out there? Based on present circumstances, I was beginning to think maybe they could.

"Well, then," Amsterdam smirked, "you have something to chew on. Ms. Wheat and I have other plans for the evening, but we'll be back tomorrow to continue our debriefing. Fortunately, our friend Oliver here," a languid wave in Tragg's direction, "has kindly agreed to keep you company, so we'll leave you in his capable hands." Amsterdam produced an S&W .40 semi-automatic and shoved it against my left temple. Tragg unchained me from the chair and jerked me to my feet. Shoved me down the hall to a twelve-by-twelve cell. Pallet on the floor. Sink and toilet. All the comforts of home. The steel door clanged behind me, and I was plunged into darkness.

CHAPTER ELEVEN

Black and silent in the cell. The residue of recent light flooding the back of my eyes. And the unearthly buzz of silence. Lying on the pallet, I visualized my whiteboard. Up on the left Amsterdam/Spook Land with a line to, in the middle, Amina, where for the moment, I paused. Strange life she led, imprisoned by her deranged husband, she and her father Mohammad.

Amsterdam's outlandish description of my crimes, real and imagined, complete with job offer, was certainly peculiar, but what did it mean? And did he know about Amina hiring me to find and liberate her and her father? That seemed unlikely.

Solid line from Amsterdam to the Diaz murder and to the attempted stitch up of me as the perp with no discernible motive. His stitch up was flimsy, little more than an excuse to abduct me. Because the evening with first Tami and then Amina had been so unusual, I had taken precautions, printing out a date and time stamp from my surveillance camera when I got home. My neighbor Ted Avila was still up. I had him come over to take a picture of the stamp on his phone and then email it to both him and me. Methodical Crane.

I'd then called my daughter Maleah in Bucharest, where she and my ex-wife Cassady were touring with their dance troupe. Maleah is a talented dancer and we chatted about how her performances were going. They were performing that evening at the Royal National Dance Center. I asked her to email me a list of all their performances. She interrupted and said she was sick of dancing and wanted to come to work for me as soon as she graduated from SF State. I groaned, couldn't help it. Then she told me she was kidding. Sigh of relief. Then she said she wasn't kidding. Damn. We chatted a while longer and signed off. I then sent a couple of time-dated emails and got some sleep. And passed slowly in front of my surveillance camera in the a.m. on my way out to meet the grieving Tony.

The stitch up failed because the timeline didn't work. I have a tracking device behind the bumper on my car, which connects to my phone and dashboard readout. For some reason, maybe intuition, maybe just dumb luck, I'd turned it on when I left the Beach Street Law Office in Santa Monica at three o'clock that Thursday afternoon. Bad traffic on the 10. Parked in my office parking lot at 4:27. Tony arrived at my office at 6:32. We walked across Third Street to the Bar & Grill at 7:02. Our server would surely remember us. Tony stormed out at around 7:42. Made my low-key exit six minutes later. My office security system would show my arrival time as 7:50 and my departure time as 9:05 when I left to drive to Jack Snow's office in Monterey Park. My car system would show I arrived at Jack's office at 9:43, stopping for gas along the way. Spent forty-five minutes with Jack, then drove to Abel's All-Night Diner to meet Amina. Arrived at 10:58. Left at 12:25 and arrived at my house in Avocado Heights at 12:55. Both my route and my timeline were airtight. No opportunity to hustle over to City Terrace to murder poor Roberto. Amsterdam's crew knew nothing about my precautions. And all my data was backed up in a cloud-based, password-protected database. Any bogus timeline they constructed would fall apart on the witness stand.

Nor did rendition make sense because it would be illegal in all fifty states and raise troubling issues for bureaucrats. Even in these uncharted times, this was too big a stretch. Why take such risks without any obvious rewards? I wasn't important enough and neither was Diaz. Which meant I was expendable. Just like Diaz.

Most likely, Amsterdam simply needed a fall guy. On which to project his own criminal activities. Which, I was beginning to believe, were not unlike what he was accusing me of. And because of the skeleton in my closet, I was the perfect scapegoat. My team and I *had stolen* Frank Constantine's torture records. And though an unidentified agency had retrieved most of them, I'd always suspected Bobby Moore had stashed the juicier tidbits at some unknown location *before the retrieval mission*. There was a slim but real possibility I could be indicted on the theory I had stolen and conspired to destroy federal property.

Amsterdam hated me for leading the small group of heroes who had brought Frank Constantine to justice. And if the principals actually existed, they probably hated me too.

But how did all of this benefit Amsterdam? And his overlords, whoever they were? Intuition told me terrorism was key here. But terrorism for or against whom? No idea why or what for. And there was definitely a weird intersection between Amsterdam's criminal intent, national security, and our local U.S. Attorney's Office.

Could not unpack it. Not yet. Where was the thread that leads to the Minotaur? I needed sleep. And where the fuck was Bobby? I began to doze.

Startled awake by that deep, nauseating, phlegm-filled voice. And the harsh light of a high-power torch. Tragg standing just inside my cell, the hall lights on behind him. Closed my eyes to protect them from the harsh glare and turned away, dropping to the floor. "Get off the floor, shit weasel. We're moving you and I'm putting you in restraints. It can be easy or hard. It's up to you, motherfucker." I didn't move. Tragg kept talking. "You thought you were so clever using that recorder in the GPS chip in your dirty underwear. But the lab boys found it, and we are sending you to a stinking rat hole in TJ as a reward." Said nothing. Good policy to let fools rant. He moved closer. "You know, Crane, there are plenty of good patriotic men and women who treasure our nation and can be counted on to fight for Team America against the evil cocksuckers. And then there are lefty creeps like you, dog turds who respect nothing and stand for even less."

TJ would be curtains. Could not allow Tragg or anyone else to take me there. Play for time. Bobby couldn't be far. "Listen, you fuckin' numbskull, you don't know jack about me. I could have been the light-heavyweight champion of the world. And I'll prove it if I ever get in the ring with you. I'll beat you to a fuckin' pulp."

My father Adam was a violent alcoholic. Old guy voted independent, loved boxing. Taught me the manly sport and hit me himself more than a few times, love taps, to teach me the ropes. I caught on quickly. Had to. I thank him now for those lessons, even though I hated him at the time.

Tragg snickered. Nastily. "My colleague wanted you to know that we know your ex-wife and daughter are out of the country. We know when and where they are returning, their flight number, and all that good stuff. Your cooperation would be good insurance nothing bad happens to them. 'Cause we will be watching. Now get the fuck up before I break your knee-caps."

Right then, the hall lights went out. Had my eyes slitted, peripheral vision only, to prevent light blindness from Tragg's torch. Now the darkness was my friend. Two muffled explosions sounded down the hall. Tragg turned around, peering out into the corridor, but almost immediately his animal brain registered his mistake. He whipped back around to face me. Too late. I was airborne. He never saw my head, but he sure as hell felt it as I rammed into his solar plexus and drove him into the wall. Big man dropped like a stone. Put all my weight into a knee drop straight to his testicles. Satisfying crunch. His scream would wake Dracula. Even after Van Helsing took him out of the game. Left rabbit punch to the kidney. Right cross to the temple, and Tragg was out. The smell of tear gas slithering into the room. Bobby's team from the 2nd Marines doing their job.

I stripped off Tragg's pants, jersey, and shoes, staying low and trying not to breathe the gas. Footsteps. A masked shadow emerged from the gloom and a voice whispered, "State secrets." Bobby.

"Privileges," I answered. Put on the spare gas mask Bobby handed me. Pulled on Tragg's pants, jersey, and shoes, and scooped up his wallet and phone. No sign of my Walther. Bobby's gun light swept the room.

"Gorillas?"

I shook my head. "Just this fool." Terrible desire to kick Tragg hard in the head. Did not.

We double timed down the hall into a reception room. Four shadows in masks at one end. At the other end, Amsterdam's security people, a flailing tangled mass. Three looked Middle Eastern, maybe the same fools who abducted me. I said to Bobby, "Both the stunners and the gas?"

"Yeah, the stunners disoriented them, and then they fell all over themselves inhaling the gas." Good. The false imprisonment would be a workable defense to assault and battery. Better no death or permanent injury on our watch.

Bobby's crew were from the 2nd Marines, 6/2 combat team. Veterans of Desert Storm. Bobby met them at the VA. They became friends when Bobby realized they were as damaged and dangerous as he was. "How much?" I asked.

"Five stacks," said Bobby, his voice unnaturally loud. One of the Marines held out a gloved hand. Bobby shook his head. "I'll bring it by tomorrow. Meet me at the downtown VA on Temple at twelve noon."

Outside, we raced to Bobby's Dodge Charger, my feet slopping in Tragg's oversized shoes. Dashboard clock read two after two as we skidded off on National toward Venice. I'd been imprisoned for over eight hours.

"I guess the GPS chip did what it was supposed to do?"

"Yep. Easy as pie."

"Thank god you located me before they found my chip."

"Damned straight," said Bobby. "I checked your location again on the way over. Nothing. They must have disabled it."

"Probably smashed it with a hammer."

"Fuck them," said Bobby. "We've got plenty of replacements."

As Bobby drove expertly through the quiet streets, I searched Tragg's wallet. There he was, his nightmarish mug right on his driver's license. His name was Baron Woodley, born July 4, 1967. A member of the Conservative Coalition to Repeal the Affordable Care Act. Carried an NRA card, $200 in twenties, and smaller bills. I memorized his name and told Bobby to memorize his birthday. Then I ripped the bills in half and tossed them out the passenger-side window, followed by his wallet. Cached his cell phone in a patch of shrubbery behind an ampm store on National.

LA is a big place, 469 square miles. We checked into a fleabag hotel called The Mayflower on Wilshire, west of 110 and east of MacArthur Park. A rundown, out of the way place where low-budget conventioneers rent cheap rooms for downtown events. Our room had a big wet spot near the air conditioner. Burn marks on the furniture. Green mold in the bathroom. And a big square TV, ancient and forbidding. I didn't care. Paradise to me. After my night at the black site with Messrs. Tragg and Amsterdam, not to mention their vindictive pal, Ms. Tami Wheat.

PART TWO

CHAPTER TWELVE

In this business you develop contacts you never want to use. Except in extreme circumstances. Barry Camus is one of these contacts. A French hoodlum with a taste for dark-skinned women, Barry drew a seventeen-year bid in 1994 for two rapes he hadn't committed. Toughed it out in Pelican Bay and Ironwood. Now, five years after his release, finally off parole, gangster calm intact, women still come flocking. He rarely stays in one place for long and was currently living with his café-au-lait girlfriend in a pink stucco house in Mar Vista, east of Venice.

Like most ex-felons, Barry faces hiring resistance. But knows where to find the cracks between legitimate employment and indictable crime. Works as a male escort for older ladies. Unlocks cell phones and analyzes their contents. Sells fake IDs. Knows the latter might send him back to prison someday, but figures it'll be easy federal time.

At two p.m. that Monday afternoon, a yellow cab dropped me off in front of Barry's house. Bobby would arrive a bit later in a beige 2010 Accord with a clean title and up-to-date tags. Borrowed from our friend Leo Perez, who runs an auto body shop in East LA. Bobby would bring Amina's retainer, which her girlfriend Jennifer had dropped off on Saturday morning just before Tony and I caught our flight to Guadalajara.

Barry opened his door, shirtless. Eyed me warily. "The fuck you want?" A curt nod and he stomped down the hallway, a can of Coors Light in his left hand. He's like that. Permanently on edge. I followed him back to his den, a dimly lit cave with distressed wood paneling and cast-iron paperweights stretched across the mantelpiece. Barry grimaced, plucked a beer from a twelve-pack on the coffee table, and underhanded it to me. "Sit down, Nick."

I sank into the couch and gave him my best phony smile. Drank some of the watery beer. "Nice place you have here."

He softened. Barely. "Sorry 'bout the shitty beer, but I'm on a tight budget. Gotta move again. Need to dig up first and last month's rent. Haven't seen you for a while, Nick."

"'Cause I haven't been around, Barry. But I'm here now. Good timing, considering you need *dinero*."

"Talking to Bobby, I got the impression some bad kaka has come down."

"Yep."

"Murder?"

"None that I committed…Is Estelle here?"

He shook his head. "She and her girlfriends are off somewhere spending my money."

"Good. She doesn't need to hear about this." It cheered me up to know I didn't have a monopoly on the world's problems. I drank more beer.

"All right. What do you need?"

"Damn near everything." Counting on my fingers: "I need a phone unlocked. Need half a dozen false IDs including two sets of DHS Special Agent paperwork. Make me Bob Evans on one and Terry Fry on the other. And a dozen burners, some programmed for Eastern Europe. And a haircut, very short, and an ear piercing. And a suitcase."

Barry gave me a withering look. "I don't do DHS. DHS is a fuckin' cabinet position, whereas ICE is just another fuckin' agency."

Barry is smart *and* informed. I nodded respectfully. "Can you do ICE paperwork then?"

"It'll cost you extra." Wicked grin that man has. "And I think we should shave your head. That'll look better. More up to date. You do realize those foreign burners are expensive…"

I shrugged. "And I need clothes like a college English teacher might wear."

"*D'accord*. I'll phone Estelle. She'll take care of that. What size are you?"

I recited the magic numbers and sipped my beer. Barry rang up Estelle. Kidded with her a while, then passed on the information. Bobby showed up. He and Barry pounded each other on the back. The gangster embrace is alive and well in LA. Another sad beer materialized and Bobby joined me on the couch.

The men began to chit-chat, Barry on what never to do or say in prison, Bobby on how you should never feed cantaloupe or watermelon to goats. Then Barry wrote down a list of what I needed and told me it would cost $3,500, plus whatever Estelle charged me for the clothes. Bobby cleared his throat and looked at me. I nodded wearily. Bobby slapped Amina's retainer down on Barry's coffee table. I counted out his money and handed it to him. Pocketed the rest. Barry vanished into his bedroom and returned fully dressed, carrying an electric skull shaver. His touch was smooth and sure, Bobby crowding around giving advice. Afterwards, Barry took several snapshots on a digital camera. "Hang tight, *mes amis*. I'll be back in three or four hours. Don't go outside."

"Don't worry, Barry," said Bobby. "We'll just sit tight and drink your shitty beer." As he was leaving, I reminded Barry to pick up the cell phone from behind the ampm on National.

* * *

After Barry drove off in his Mustang, Bobby and I sketched out our plans. Bobby would sleep at the Mayflower. Until things got dialed back several notches. One of Leo's auto body men would feed his goats. Bobby would tail Blaylock and Timberlake and bring Tony up to speed. He would also surveil the Motor Avenue black site and check for messages at our office. Which he could do remotely. I would call Cassady and my daughter Maleah on a burner and warn them to stay in Europe until this had blown over. Hated the idea, but had no choice. I phoned my assistant Audrey and told her to steer clear of the office until further notice. Not the first time this has happened.

In contrast to Bobby, my job was simple. As long as I steered clear of Amsterdam and his criminal band. East to Boston and Hawthorne College in New Hampshire, Amina's alma mater. Ferret out one of her drama profs. Get him or her to talk. Then Mohammad. Pick his brain and devise a plan. On my way back to California, I would detour to southern Ohio to recce Gloria and Abrecia's living conditions…and figure out how to spring them.

I'd leave town in a 2014 Acura, which I'd pick up in Sun Valley before driving straight through to Salt Lake City, where I'd drop off the car and catch the Amtrak to Boston. Leo had given me a number to call when I arrived in SLC.

Barry got back around seven, Estelle right behind him. Could tell something was eating at the Frenchman. He handed over my burners and IDs without comment. The ICE IDs, encased in faux leather, looked highly professional. Barry watched grimly while Estelle outfitted me with my new wardrobe and expertly pierced my left ear before inserting a diamond-studded silver earring. Soon as she was done, Barry grabbed me by the elbow and pulled me into the den. Bobby followed, a bloodhound sniffing the air.

"What the fuck, Nick! When I opened up the iPhone, I damn near shit my pants. There was a tracking device built into the thumb-hold area where the battery goes."

Barry can get a little emotional. Maybe because he had to keep everything bottled up for so long in the joint. Or maybe he's naturally high-strung. I didn't think the phone was worth getting all steamed up over. And Barry had detected the tracking device. Which, after all, was his job. Tried to keep it light. "In that case, I guess you won't be analyzing the calls anytime soon."

"*C'est la vérité.*" Big sardonic grin. "I tossed it out on the 10. By now, it's been run over fifty or sixty times." Then he looked at me, his mouth a hard, straight line. "Good thing you didn't bring it to my crib."

I shook my head. "I'm glad I didn't." If I hadn't cached it, they would have tracked Bobby and me with ease. Probably before we even got to Barry's place. I'd just gotten out of one stitch up. Didn't need another. Barry took out his wallet and began counting out bills. Waved him off. "Keep it, *mon* fucking *frère*. You earned it."

His nostrils tightened and the bridge of his nose narrowed. "Look," I said, "sorry for the inconvenience, but I just paid you $3,500. I have the greatest respect for your talent and intelligence, but I'm not in the mood to be mindfucked over what could have happened."

Barry looked at Bobby. Bobby shook his large head and ran a blunt hand horizontally across his throat. Barry got the message. Shrugged. And kept the money. If Bobby hadn't been there? But he was. Like I said, there are certain contacts you never want to use.

Darkness fell. Calm now, Barry drank another Coors Light and started laughing at the thought of me impersonating an ICE agent. "You won't have any problem. Be your natural asshole self. *Tu es un mec.*" His way of apologizing. We loaded up the Accord. Bobby handed me a throwaway Beretta with a belt holster, something I wouldn't mind dumping in a pinch. I put it in the glove compartment. Had $6,500 in cash plus pocket change. I waited until Bobby's taxi arrived. Then I gave Barry a hearty phony handshake, kissed Estelle on the cheek, and embraced my friend. It was time, but before I slid in behind the wheel of the Accord, I stood there for a long minute, breathing in the cool damp air. Always wanted to live by the ocean. Never quite got there...

CHAPTER THIRTEEN

Drove all night, doubling back here and there to confuse any potential tail.

Dawn was breaking as I crossed into Utah. Pushed the Acura hard, traversing the stately red rock country. Reached St. George at around seven thirty and continued north to Cedar City. By now, Cassady and Maleah should be in the Bulgarian capital of Sofia.

After several failed attempts, I managed to get through to my ex.

"Nick?"

"Speaking."

"Thank God! It's been more than two days and Maleah is really worried. We've got a big show in less than four hours at the National Palace of Culture, and Maleah has to be on her game. So tell me, and this better be good, what the hell is going on?"

She's like that. Direct. I let her stew for a three-count. "Let's just say I'm facing a few complications. How many more performances do you have?"

"What do you mean, complications? You're in trouble again, aren't you?"

"Please answer my question. How many more performances?"

Cassady's long sigh said more than any accusation. "Five. Two here in Sofia, two in Athens, and the grand finale on the

Isle of Capri."

"Then you fly to London, right?"

"That's the plan. We're going to spend a day seeing the sights. London Bridge and Soho and Buckingham Palace. Then we fly back on British Airways…"

"I want you to listen closely. You and Maleah must not get on that flight. You need to extend your stay. Rent a car, drive up to the Lake Country, go to Stratford-on-Avon, maybe even Scotland. Hell, take the ferry across to Ireland. It's cheap. Go to all the places you've always talked about. But do not fly back home until I get this straightened out."

"Are you fucking kidding me?"

"No, I'm not. But don't let it ruin things for you and Maleah. I need a little more time, that's all. Oh yeah, I almost forgot. You and Maleah should both discard your phones and get new ones. Immediately."

Again, a long sigh, then silence.

I didn't try to reason with her. Instead, I asked her if I could talk to Maleah.

Cassady said nothing. Ten seconds later, my daughter came on the line.

"Dad?"

"Hi, sweetheart."

"I'm glad you called. I've been worried."

Her intuition is usually spot-on. "I'm sorry, sweetheart. I wish I had better news. Some stuff has come up, which I'm right in the middle of handling. So listen, I want you and your mom to stay in England for a while longer until I get this worked out. To be on the safe side. I'll let you know when things have calmed down. *Capiche?*"

"Dad, you promised you would help me move into my new apartment."

Maleah was about to begin her senior year at SF State, where she was majoring in Communication and minoring in Dance. Summers, she lives with Cassady north of Berkeley in a shabbily genteel Kensington Tudor.

"I'm sorry, sweetheart. I just need some time to sort this out. I'll make up for it. I promise. But like I said to your mom, you need to stay overseas a little bit longer. It's the only smart thing to do."

A long silence. Then Maleah spoke. "Is Bobby helping you?"

"Of course he is. Tony is too. But I want you to do something for me. For me and your mom. Be on your game tonight. You've worked for years to get to this point, and it's very important to both of us. Think about it. The National Palace of Culture. In a foreign capital. What an honor! I bet when you were a little girl singing Taylor Swift songs, you never thought you'd be touring the European capitals with your dance troupe."

Doing my best. Almost worked, but not quite.

"Listen, Dad, I know you're in trouble. And Mom knows it too. Don't try to change the subject."

I didn't. Instead, I was fighting the lump in my throat when the line went dead. When I called back, no one answered.

Reached Salt Lake City around noon. Phoned the number Leo Perez had given me. The swinging dick on the other end of the line said his name was Jared. Said he'd been expecting me and gave me directions to his house in a new upscale subdivision.

He met me out front. Tall and heavily muscled with coal black hair. Cold brown eyes. I handed him the keys to the Acura. His flash Lincoln Navigator, the recently constructed two-story house with pool, the hot girlfriend whom he virtually ignored when we walked in, and the preponderance of flat screens all screamed "trafficker." Although his eyes never smiled, he invited me in. Insisted I have a neighborly *cerveza* with him in his wood-paneled den. Said he had a trucking company in LA and had returned home to Salt Lake to decompress for a few days. He was aware of Roberto Diaz's death and kept shaking his head, saying how sorry he was. I wondered how he knew about Roberto, but I didn't ask.

Jared finished his beer. Said he'd drive me wherever I needed to go, but first he had to make a few phone calls. He left the room. I was sitting in a deep-cushioned black leather armchair. Put my beer down and closed my eyes. Drifting. But not too far from shore...

Jared dropped me off at the Gateway Mall, half a mile from the Salt Lake Amtrak station. We shook hands and he wished me well. I thanked him and promptly forgot about him. Until I saw the two guys watching me. Just as I was about to step into a Barnes & Noble to kill time. One was tall with a mullet. Wearing a long green peacoat in the 80-degree weather. The other was short. Lots of muscles and a Mohawk. And the familiar brown bomber jacket. Talk about a cold chill.

In the front door and out the side door. Pushed an old lady and her grandson out of the way. Not in the mood to be polite. Around the corner and down the block. Ducked into a bar. Gave a guy with missing front teeth thirty bucks to get me a cab. Knew it was risky, but I've done worse. Waited in the back room next to the pool table, where two guys about my age were playing eight-ball. They were scrubs, but it passed the time.

Toothless returned. Said the cab was outside. Restored my faith in humanity, and I gave him an extra Jackson. Had the cabbie take me to Sugar House, an upscale shopping area in South-Central Salt Lake. Walked into a Starbucks and eased back to the restroom. Came back outside wearing blue jeans, a dark blue, long-sleeved collared shirt, and a Seattle Mariners baseball cap.

Took a careful look around. Either I was in the clear or I was fooling myself. Went into the Barnes & Noble. Several hours to kill. Wandered back into the literature section. Selected a play called *Buried Alive* by Sam Shepard, which my paraplegic, part-time investigator and database expert, Greg Thurston, had recommended. Settled down to read in the bookstore café, keeping an eye on the street. *Buried Alive* was dark. About a Midwestern family that reminded me of my own.

Five o'clock. I packed up and walked outside. Two hours to kill. Refueled at the Olive Garden. Vermicelli and a glass of pinot noir. Then I took a cab to the train station, where I purchased a one-way ticket to Chicago from an elderly gentleman with a quivering jaw. No sign of Peacoat or Hardbody. I paid extra for a Viewliner Roomette and had no trouble smuggling my throwaway Beretta on board.

My sleeping compartment was good-sized, with a large, two-paneled window looking out over America. I sat down on the recliner seat and watched the countryside stream past. East of town, we climbed into the majestic Wasatch Range. My plan was to sleep and read from here to Boston. And figure out if and how Jared was connected to Peacoat and Hardbody. And whether they were all connected to Amsterdam and the despicable QB Tragg.

Weary, I fell asleep early. Time stopped, and then it started again. Dreamed I was standing in the door of a sunny bedroom. A young man, pale and drawn, lay on his bed. He was paralyzed from mid-thigh on down, his wheelchair at the foot of his bed. He asked me to tell him PI stories. Finally, he drifted off to sleep. I left the room and went outside. Heard him calling me, or maybe it was the wind, moaning and kicking up dust. Started back in, stopped, and listened. Silence…

Woke up at three a.m. Stumbled to my feet and walked to the window. Stared out into a dark and jumbled landscape. I couldn't tell whether the train was climbing or descending.

CHAPTER FOURTEEN

Greg Thurston had knocked on my door looking for work the week before Thanksgiving 2011. Told me later he'd been making the rounds—every PI office in town. Eager to break into the trade.

Frank Constantine was barely in the grave, and Cassady was in the process of leaving me, taking Maleah with her. I was making a half-hearted effort to shift into white collar work. A dark time. Too much Jack Daniels and a keen sense of my own mortality.

The morning I met Greg, I was struggling to set up a new database. Decided to test him. Gave him my chair and my username and password. An hour later, he had the database up and running. Paid him $100 cash right on the spot.

That was the beginning. For some reason, this Cal State, Northridge computer science major—a forelock of dark brown hair falling over his forehead—was convinced being a PI was right up there with dating Halle Berry or playing point guard in the NBA. He was a quick learner and was soon pocketing $400 weekly on a part-time basis.

My assistant Audrey and I taught Greg the ropes. Never saw a guy so happy serving a damned subpoena. And he loved going out on stakeouts with Audrey, who thought he was handsome, which I guess he was, if you like 'em young and eager. I felt fatherly toward Greg, and the stakeouts scared the piss out of me because of what could happen, even though they're rarely dangerous.

Then it did happen. The unthinkable. I had been retained by Grisholm & MacDonald, a white-shoe firm that was being paid by another firm that represented a Chinese-Cambodian businessman, Mr. Chee. Grisholm & MacDonald's job was to stall a class action case against Mr. Chee for allegedly violating the civil rights of his employees, including half-a-dozen litigious-minded Americans. They paid me well, not that I really gave a fuck about the money. It gave me something to think about besides my bleak personal life. I interviewed lots of witnesses and wrote lots of reports. Sometimes, I would interview the same witnesses a second time. Same questions, but I wouldn't always get the same answers. More reports. Stall, stall, stall. Bill, bill, bill. Mr. Chee was paying the bills for both firms. His firm had convinced him that this strategy was the best way to work out a settlement he could live with.

One evening, I sent Greg out to deliver a subpoena requiring Mr. Chee to appear for a deposition. When Greg arrived at the restaurant where Mr. Chee was dining, a civil rights demonstration was being held in the parking lot. No problem. The Long Beach constabulary was standing by. They told Greg to go right on into the restaurant and deliver the subpoena. Inside, he was swarmed by Mr. Chee's bodyguards, who beat him to a pulp. Then some thug picked him up and threw him across the room. He landed on his head and spine.

The fact that Greg, whom I'd tried to protect, was paralyzed from mid-thigh to the tip of his toes, all because of a fucking subpoena, was like a shot to the heart. The fact the thugs were eventually cleared of all criminal charges on a theory of diplomatic immunity made it that much worse.

I checked out for a while. No other way to put it. When I finally put down my shot glass and came back to work, my fledgling white-collar practice was in ruins. That was six years ago. Since then, I visit Greg regularly. Give him work that doesn't even need to be done to keep him occupied. He tears through it on his laptop. Asks for more. Refuses to blame me and still thinks being a PI is the most glamorous job in the world. On the days when his pain is bearable. On the bad days, he doesn't talk much. Just drifts with down-turned mouth in an oxycodone haze. I should have kept the kid chained to his databases, like a spirited dog on a very short leash. Of course, I should have. But I didn't.

Sat there for hours in the dark as the train bucked and fell, thinking about Greg and the fates sniping at us. Finally, I fell asleep. When I opened my eyes, we were at high altitude, dawn breaking over the Colorado Rockies. Spires of light. High alpine meadows. Forests of spruce and fir. Incredible.

Spent the day sleeping and reading. And thinking about my adversaries and my new client, Amina. Tami was pure evil, treachery seeping from her pores. Amsterdam was no better. No retreat and no surrender with this bastard. When handsome is ugly. Mouth like a knife cut. Cold eyes. Deep tan. And a $500 haircut. Intelligent flag waver. Hate the guy. He and Tami were the reason I was in this mess. And then there was Tragg. When ugly is ugly. Fat over muscle, a mesomorph gone to seed. Black ink tattoos like a common jailbird. Mucous boy, a sub-species flag waver with a broken nose pointing to three o'clock.

In contrast, Amina was an enigma. We had agreed—no contact until after I returned from Boston. Unless it was absolutely necessary. Operational security. I kept wondering if Amsterdam knew about our late-night tête-à-tête at Abel's. He hadn't mentioned it that godforsaken evening at the black site. Which meant very little.

Chicago is the end of the line for the California Zephyr. A four-hour layover before Boston bound passengers transfer onto the Amtrak Lakeshore Limited.

We rolled into Union Station, the big, broad-shouldered Chicago train terminal, at four thirty, fifteen minutes ahead of schedule. A case study in neo-classical overkill—says Tony, an architecture buff—the old pile is spooky at that hour. Tracks are way below street level. Hell, itself, can't be far off...The disembarking passengers stirred slowly and made their way, me among them, onto the concourse. No evidence I'd been made, but my nerves told me otherwise.

The station was huge. Several ways to get to street level, none of them good. Ambush would be elementary if I guessed wrong, and they guessed right. Decided to stall. Eased into the first available restroom and sat down in a cubicle. Pleasantly clean that time of morning. Opened up *Buried Alive*, but the words swam in front of my eyes. Put the book away and unholstered my Beretta. Waiting. Breathing slowly and easily. No rush. Let them tip their hand. Which they did thirty minutes later, as I was contemplating making my dash for freedom. First footsteps, then running water, and then a voice, high and whiny. "Why the fuck was the train early? Bastards are never early."

"Fuggedaboutit." The second voice deep and calm. "Asshole's around here somewhere. He's got to catch the Boston train at nine o'clock. God, I'm handsome. Kiss me, bitch."

"Kiss my ass."

"Dream on, baby. But listen, man, there's nothin' to worry about. We'll be on the train with him, and that's a beautiful thing. Let's go get something to eat."

Cold fury. They tromped out. I holstered the Beretta.

These guys were good trackers. Must have made me in Salt Lake, tipped off by Jared. Then flown to Chicago to greet me. I could not afford to make these kinds of mistakes.

Waited another thirty minutes. Then I sidled out of the restroom and made my way slowly up to ground level. A keen look in all directions. No sign of the trackers. Stepped out onto Canal Street. Danger zone. But I got lucky. An empty taxi came around the corner and I flagged it down. Got in and handed the bearded Middle Eastern cabbie two twenties. He put up no protest. Brief counter-surveillance before jumping out in front of the Chicago Loop Hotel. Paid extra for my own shower. The cost of doing business was spiraling out of control.

Cleaned up and lay on the bed. Empty the crowded mind. Impossible task, so I began planning Tragg's demise. And thinking about the little immigrant girls in Ohio. And wondering how Amina was doing...

When it was time, I went outside to catch a cab. A dogged sun was fighting through the haze, the smell of diesel in the air. I ducked down in the backseat of the first available taxi, shielding my face. More money. More counter-surveillance. When we pulled up in front of the square, low-slung Harrison Street Greyhound station, I convinced the elderly black cabbie to go in and buy me a ticket to Boston.

"Who are you, John Dillinger?" he smirked, handing me the precious ducat.

"Not hardly. I'm nobody. Nobody at all."

No cowboys staking out the Greyhound station. Not Peacoat and Hardbody or anybody else from their team. If they'd been there, I would've made them. But cowboys do not generally stake out Greyhound stations. Greyhound passengers are old people, poor people, people of color, people down on their luck, people who never had any luck at all. And the occasional college student on a shoestring budget. Still, I sussed every passenger before I relaxed in a seat near the back next to a heavyset white woman. Cindy. Bloodshot eyes. Work-roughened hands. We hit it off pretty good. Before long I was Youngster, and she was telling me her life story.

I listened politely until she ran out of gas. Then she took out a Christian end-of-the-world novel with ab guys and voluptuous women on the cover. Tired of *Buried Alive* and its relentless gloom, I dug into a John D. MacDonald novel called *The Deep Blue Good-by*.

CHAPTER FIFTEEN

Nine a.m. Thursday morning. Twenty-three hours out of Chicago. I got out at the Massachusetts Turnpike exit and caught a Yellow Cab into downtown Boston. On a whim, I had the cabbie drive by South Station. There they were, slouched against a brick wall twenty feet from the taxi stand. Hardbody's Mohawk was bright red. Peacoat had a stocking cap pulled down over his hair. I could've shot them both from the back seat of the taxi with my throwaway Beretta, but shooting folks in cold blood has never been my style. Instead, I had the cabbie step on it and take me to Seven Beacon Street, just north of the Commons, where Boston PI par excellence, Anthony Agresti, has his office.

I met Agresti at a death penalty conference at Asilomar near Monterey, California around the same time I met Tony Bott. Back then, Agresti struck me as young, eager, idealistic, and one of those guys who loses his hair way too soon. He was also a helluva drinker and could put me under the table with ease. Agresti has relatives in Northridge in the San Fernando Valley, and—quite a few years ago now—we'd spent several memorable nights together drinking and eating Chinese food on Ventura Boulevard.

Agresti may be the best PI on the whole Eastern Seaboard. He's comfortable giving the third degree to hoodlums in low places. At ease tracking sophisticated financial crimes with the help of state-of-the-art software. And when it comes to testifying in federal court? Trying to break Agresti on cross is tougher than penetrating Fort Knox.

When I walked into his office, I told his admin Valerie my name was Nick Crane and I needed to see her boss. She buzzed him. Sixty seconds later, razor sharp in a bold black-and-white checked blazer, Agresti came striding up the hallway, belting out the opening lines of "Stormy Monday."

He stopped, gave me a keen look, and broke into his trademark boyish smile. "Nick Crane. My man. Damn, it's been a long time. To what do I owe this pleasure?"

I shook my head and drew a knife hand across my throat.

"That bad?"

Huddled over coffee and croissants in Agresti's office, I filled him in. Watched his normally smooth forehead crease with concern. "Nick, I gotta tell you, you have a tremendous talent for wading into deep shit." I waved off the compliment. Agresti swallowed the butt-end of his croissant and washed it down with coffee. "You showed amazing restraint in not killing that Tragg sonofabitch when you had the chance."

"I struggle when it comes to killing a man in cold blood. Some kind of character flaw." A wry smile.

"Which I respect you for," said Agresti. He extracted a small notebook and a ball-point pen from inside his blazer and handed them to me. "Sketch it out for me."

I couldn't properly sketch it out on such tiny pages, so I wrote it out instead, dividing the factions and players into various categories. Enemies. Friends. Neutral parties. Agencies. Suspected crimes. Actual crimes. And question marks. Lots of question marks. I added the name Agresti under *Friends* and handed it to him.

While he studied it, I got up and walked around his office. Law books neatly arranged in built-in bookshelves. Soccer awards for his kids and reproductions of Boston sports figures and Revolutionary War scenes. Agresti took a long time.

Finally, he beckoned me over.

"I'm not sure what to tell you, Nick. This is pretty damned opaque. Suffice it to say you've pissed off some powerful people. I can speculate on what might be happening. Emphasis on might. This might have something to do with the alt-right's desire to manipulate the war on terror by instigating terror. They'll stop at nothing as I'm sure you're aware. Even false flag operations here at home. Anything to frighten the civilian population into complete submission. And it's only going to get worse. It will get harder and harder to tell real terror from fake terror. Like trying to tell real news from fake news.

"I hate to say it, but it looks to me like the genie has been let out of the bottle, and there's no way to coax it back inside. Amsterdam and his people see a terrorist under every woodpile. If they can't find one, they'll invent one. Our national dialogue is taking on all the tawdry aspects of a reality TV show, with Russia as co-star. What's key is the systematic assault on the free press and the expanding powers of the police state. Mass deportations are already underway. It's god, country, and torture, baby, god, country, and torture. While the real terrorists, both foreign and domestic, are hard at work. The fact Amsterdam mentioned "the principals" suggests they could be operating within at least quasi-official channels. Or," he paused and thought it over. "Or, they could be some kind of secret society."

"Pretty soon they'll be bombing the lunch crowd in Pershing Square. And we won't know if the perpetrators are real or fake."

"Sooner than you think, the way things are going," said Agresti. "What I can tell you for sure is you made a big mistake when you and your people walked off with Frank Constantine's torture research records. That automatically makes you an enemy of the state, which, as you know, cuts both ways. You could be liquidated or imprisoned and made a public spectacle. Or," he leaned toward me and spoke in a stage whisper, "you could be blackmailed to do their dirty work, which accounts for their bizarre job offer."

"Frank Constantine was a kidnapper and a serial killer of innocent women."

Agresti shrugged. "It doesn't matter. Frank Constantine was allegedly breaking barriers in the area of gentler, kinder torture research. He was respected. A talented man doing important research someone was underwriting. Those folks aren't ready to write it off."

Nodded my head slowly. Frowning. Agresti was right. "And, of course, I get no credit for doing my damnedest to keep the bastard alive. Not to mention, I was exonerated completely at the inquest."

Agresti stood up, adjusted his shirttail under his jacket. He looked at me, shook his head, and sat back down. "You were exonerated for Constantine's death. That is a fact. But if I'm not mistaken, and correct me if I'm wrong, Constantine's torture records were never even mentioned, right?"

I shrugged. He had me there. That was the 13,000-pound elephant tusking its way deeper into my skull.

"You're in deep, Nick, you're in deep. Amsterdam is clearly not a rational man. Neither is this Tragg idiot. You throw in Ms. Tami Wheat, and it just gets worse. My guess is whoever these folks are, they don't bear much resemblance to regular Company men who plan everything down to the gnat's ass, run it through headquarters, plan and reconnoiter, pick their nose, scratch their ass, and plan some more. These guys are more like Ollie North. Set the ball rolling and riff like jazz musicians. Improvise. Modulate. Change keys. But never punt. These guys are dangerous motherfuckers. When you and Tony met with Raymundo, everything fell into place. It gave them the semblance of a reason to pick you up. After all, we can hardly let a guy who steals classified government documents and conspires with suspected terrorists run around scot free, can we?"

I shook my head. Agresti was smart. "Say no more. I get it. I should never have stolen the torture data bank. Bad form. Period."

Agresti looked at me. Started to speak. Stopped. Did a drumroll with his fingers on his mahogany desktop. Then he reached out and put his hand on my forearm. "Sorry, buddy. I hate to say it, but I think you have very few options other than counterpunching, which according to rumor, you're pretty damned good at..."

I managed a weak grin. "Hell, even rats fight back when they're cornered. At least I think they do." I paused. Wasn't sure of the next step, but Agresti made it easy...

"So, what do you want me to do? Track down Mohammad, right?"

"Right, while I go up to the college in Nashua in New Hampshire—"

"—to collect information on Amina and her father."

"Something like that." *No, exactly like that.*

We talked for another fifteen minutes. Agresti would run the search engines to locate Mohammad. If necessary, he knew people in the Boston Arab community he could turn to. And he would run background on all three of my nemeses—Miles Amsterdam, Oliver "QB" Tragg, and Tami Wheat. "This should be fun. There's nothing I like better than rooting out pond scum."

That's where we left it.

CHAPTER SIXTEEN

Agresti went above and beyond. Outfitted me with a laptop, a pocket-sized notebook, and a classy Kensington briefcase. Even loaned me his old Honda Civic. On my way out of town, I picked up a Buck 110 Lockback Folding Hunter knife that I holstered on my right hip. I was wearing my pedagogue's tweed jacket, sweater, and khakis. My backup clothes and cheap gun were secure in Agresti's briefcase, along with my crime novels and *Buried Alive*.

Took Route 3 to Nashua and drove through town to the college. Parked in the visitors' lot behind the Phineas Morgan Center for the Performing Arts. Locked up the laptop and Agresti's briefcase in the trunk of the Civic. No clear danger, but with so many students milling about, it was impossible to be sure. Amina's alma mater was an obvious destination…for yours truly. Never underestimate the enemy. Sun Tzu dispensing wisdom. It would be hard for Hardbody and Peacoat to blend in with the student body, though, if they were on campus, which would make them easier to spot.

Hawthorne College was built right after the Civil War. Gothic Revival architecture. Old wood-framed buildings painted pink, rose, and coral. Steeply pitched roofs and a profusion of turrets, gables, and ornamental chimney pots gave the impression that Mad King Ludwig had relocated from Bavaria to staid old New England. I did my best to blend in. Just another academic type thinking about poetry and unrequited love. The well-heeled, young students barely gave me a glance. The Theater Arts building—a lovely, dusky rose color—stood adjacent to the Performing Arts center.

Cool and dim inside. Padded slowly down the hallway. Blind dead reckoning brought me to the departmental office. The admin, chunky with wild Goth hair and heavy eye shadow, looked up from his book. "Hello, there. Can I help you?"

"I'm pretty sure you can. I need to talk to one of your drama professors. Someone who's been here a while, say ten years. I need information on a student."

"Is this a legal matter?"

Smart kid. "No, it's personal."

"Ah, one of those." He rolled his heavily lidded eyes.

"You got it, brother. One of those. Personal and highly confidential."

The Goth plucked a lemon drop from a candy dish on his desk and guided it into his mouth. He looked at me. "Bad habit, I know. But it's better than the hard stuff."

"I couldn't agree more. So, who do you think I should talk to?"

The Goth kneaded his knuckles into his temples and grimaced. Looked longingly at the candy bowl. Spoke. "You really only have one good choice. Dr. Connie. Dr. Connie Reardon. She's the only one of the old guard who survived the recent departmental coup."

"The coup?"

"The regents wanted fresh blood, I guess. Younger professors with new ideas. Personally, I think it was a mistake. But don't quote me. As for Dr. Connie, maybe she'll talk to you, maybe she won't. She's temperamental."

"Where can I find her?"

"Right at the moment, everybody except yours truly is over at the theater auditioning for *Antigone*. Dr. Connie is there. You could walk over and wait until they're finished."

"What does she look like?"

"Hmm?" He pondered. Spoke. "She's neither short nor tall, in the middle, I suppose…Here's what you should do. Look for the woman who resembles a dock worker or a stonemason or maybe a house painter. She has thick black hair, cut short, combed back like James Dean or Elvis. She looks about fifty. She might be wearing white painter's overalls. Or maybe jeans and a blue work shirt."

My usual getup. "Does she have an office in this building?"

He checked his list. "She's in Room 204 on the second floor."

I thanked him.

Up to the second floor, where I found her office. Recced the hallway in both directions—windows sighting out across the campus and staircases to the first floor. I left the building and hustled over to the theater. No sign of Peacoat and Hardbody. Stood in back while my eyes adjusted to the dim light. The curious were scattered around the horseshoe-shaped auditorium, with the professors sitting together directly in front of the stage. I took a seat a few rows behind them. Could hear them talking quietly between auditions.

Antigone takes place in ancient Greece. That much I was able to discern. But as for the plot, I was lost. Except for one key fact. The heroine hangs herself because the king won't let her dead brother have a proper burial. That is sisterly love.

Grim, indeed, but that hardly dissuaded the parade of eager young thespians. I watched with interest. At first. Then the need for sleep took over, and I dozed off. Woke up with a start several times before going back under. The auditions ground on.

Finally, I was jogged awake by a strong female voice. A stocky woman in a purple sweatshirt with her black hair combed back was striding around the stage. She had the habit of placing her palms to her temples before speaking. She thanked the fledgling actors for their efforts. Reassured them their auditions would be thoroughly reviewed, and this was just the first of many monthly auditions. Then, she told everybody to "break a leg" and stepped off the stage. She conferred briefly with the other professors and strode up the aisle toward the front entrance. I followed discreetly. Outside it was Indian summer dusk. She headed toward the Theater Arts building and went inside. I was startled by the ominous sight of Hardbody and Peacoat, less than a hundred feet away, walking toward the center of campus. One tall, wearing his long green coat, the other short and broad. I eased into the shadows. It was them all right. Then, as if they could feel me watching, they turned around and started toward me. Changed their minds again and headed off in a third direction toward the commons. I ducked into the Theater Arts building and gave the professor five minutes to get settled. Then I went upstairs, walked down the hallway, and knocked on the door of Room 204.

CHAPTER SEVENTEEN

At first no answer, then footsteps. The door opened and Professor Reardon stood facing me. Broad of cheek, jaw, and forehead. An earnest, rugged face. Deep-set hazel eyes. Her sleeves rolled up, her forearms heavily muscled like a peasant woman tending her potato fields. She gave me a dubious look.

"I'm sorry to bother you, Professor. My name is Nick Crane. I'm a licensed private investigator. From Los Angeles." Handed her my license, which she perused briefly and handed back. "I've come all this way to try and help one of your former students."

"Sorry, Mr. Crane, I'd like to help but I've had a really long day. And I've got quite the splitting headache. I have office hours at eleven a.m. tomorrow. You're welcome to come back then." She took a step back, as if I would get the hint. Instead, I stepped quickly across the threshold. Black and white photos of Garbo and Marlene Dietrich on her walls. An old walnut desk, uncluttered.

"You're not listening, sir. I asked you to come back tomorrow." She held up both palms as if to push me away.

"Please, my client, Ms. Hosseini, is in serious trouble. So is her father Mohammad, who, if I'm not mistaken, donated generously to your department. My job is to help them, and I need you to help me. I just need some basic background information on Ms. Hosseini, who, I believe, had some good roles in some of your theatrical productions."

She hoisted herself up and sat on the edge of her desk, her thick, denim-clad legs dangling above the floor. She wore Doc Martens steel-toed men's work boots. I took the liberty of seating myself across from her in a straight-backed wooden chair.

"The admin downstairs said I should talk to you. He said you're the only one on staff who might be able to help. This shouldn't take more than five or ten minutes. I wouldn't have traveled three thousand miles to get here if it wasn't critically important."

She considered, frowning. It was a wonderful frown. A full-body frown. Good old thespian knowhow...I sat there patiently. Finally, she shook her head slowly. "I'm sorry, but like I said, I can't talk to you now. My head is pounding..." She slid off her desk and pointed at the door.

Ain't too proud to beg. "Please, Professor Reardon, I need your help. This young woman is in real danger."

Maybe it was the "young woman" or the "real danger." Or perhaps she had a conscience despite her frosty manner. She licked her lower lip and began chewing it pensively. Finally, she nodded. "All right. You win. What did you say her name is?"

"Amina Hosseini."

The professor nodded. "That sounds familiar. Give me a moment and I'll look her up."

She sat down behind her desk, logged into her computer, and began clicking. After a few minutes, she said, "Based on my records, and I've gone over this twice now, we have never had a student here named Amina Hosseini. So it appears we're at a dead end."

She sat back and folded her hands.

I let my face fall into a mask of despair. Acting. Probably none too well. But I did my best. "The woman I'm talking about majored in Theater Arts and minored in English Literature. She went to Georgetown Law School after she graduated from here. These are facts, not hypotheses."

This caught her attention. She ran her left hand slowly across her forehead. Looked at her fingers. Frowned and shook her head. Went back to her computer. More clicking. After what seemed like a long time, she spoke. "Help me out here, Mr. Crane. A woman named Adara Ghaffari did major in Theater Arts. And minored in English Lit. But she's clearly not the same person you're talking about. How do you explain this?"

Interesting. At some point, Adara must have changed her name to Amina. Perhaps it was Amsterdam's doing. Made a mental note to ask her about it next time we spoke. "I think there's a simple explanation. Amina and Adara are the same person. This poor woman is being harassed by some very bad actors. Her life may be in danger. Therefore, she's been living under a false identity for some time now. So please, let me describe her." I did in some detail, emphasizing her height and her rose brown hair, her striking cheekbones and gold-flecked brown eyes, her upper-class affect, and her cultured accent. When I was finished, I nodded firmly. "I'm sure they're the same person. What can you tell me about her?"

Professor Reardon deliberated, pursing her lips, nodding, rubbing her temples. Finally, she pushed her chair back and stood up. Came around to the front of her desk and hoisted herself up on it. Again. Then she stared at me—a hard, stony, hazel gaze. I gazed back. Calmly. After what seemed a long time, she softened. "All right, Mr. Crane. You've been patient. I'll give you that. Not to mention persistent. Here's what I can tell you."

I listened carefully, taking notes in Agresti's pocket-sized notebook. Adara had attended Nashua College from 2006 to 2010. She had played Cherie in *Bus Stop*, Marilyn Monroe's breakthrough role; Maggie in *Cat on a Hot Tin Roof*; Desdemona in *Othello*; and Blanche Dubois in *A Streetcar Named Desire*. And a few supporting roles in other plays.

I was impressed. "Wow! I guess she was a good actor."

The professor curled her lips upward in a semblance of a smile. I felt like cheering. "Not at first. At first, she was a screechy kid who kept drifting in and out of character. But she improved. My focus is on the upper division students, and I worked closely with her during her last two years." The prof nodded slowly, in the grip of memory. "What I liked about Adara was her zeal. She worked hard. I think she knew she was pretty awful at first. But she took criticism with a smile. And there was plenty of it. I don't sugarcoat things. As you may have noticed. She kept working hard and never complained about having to repeat a scene. In fact, she would often ask to repeat them when she felt her performance wasn't up to par. She was mature for her age."

"Did you ever meet her father, Mohammad?"

"A few times. He came to all her plays and attended our post-performance parties. He seemed the perfect gentleman. And you're right, as I recall, he was a generous donor to our department."

She paused. "Give me just a moment. I'm trying to remember something. I don't want to confuse Adara with another student." She began clicking her tongue against the roof of her mouth, like an old-fashioned clock ticking off the seconds. After a while, she stopped clicking and spoke. "Here's what I remember, and I think it's accurate. Shortly before Adara graduated, I pitched the possibility of her attending the Actor's Studio Drama School in New York or the Tisch School of the Arts at NYU. She was no Lillian Gish, but with more training and based on her solid work ethic, she could probably have ended up on Broadway." Professor Reardon smiled, a bit sadly. "Unfortunately, many of our talented young actors end up going into other fields."

I nodded sympathetically. "That's got to be rough. After all the hard work you and your colleagues put in. But I can't thank you enough for all your help, Professor Reardon. I have one final question. Did you ever meet Adara's husband, a tall, aristocratic blond fellow with a lean face? He would've been in his late forties, I believe."

"Hmm, he does sound familiar. Tall, you say?"

"Yes, I'd say he's about six foot one."

"That must be him, although, to my knowledge, they weren't married yet." She nodded her head firmly and slid off her desk. Faced me. "Adara's boyfriend stood out among the parents. He was ex-military, I believe, a patriot and a very cultured gentleman. He was also a generous donor to our department. He had studied poetry at Yale and liked to quote Eliot and Yeats. I believe he had some connection to the State Department. In fact, he recruited several of our graduating seniors for government positions. As I recall, he was simply mad about Adara and the feeling was mutual. It was sweet to see. I got to know him pretty well. Strange, I can't remember his name. It might have been Miles or Milton or something like that."

I thanked her, put Agresti's notebook in my shirt pocket, and stood up. Wanted to get out. Fast. Disturbing to discover this peculiar drama prof approved of Miles Amsterdam and his "patriotism." And his relationship with Amina/Adara. Even more disturbing to learn he would recruit students for "government positions." Although I knew the CIA and other agencies recruited heavily at elite colleges and universities, I had never encountered it personally before.

I thanked her again for all her help, said goodnight, and walked out into the hallway.

CHAPTER EIGHTEEN

If I'd been CIA working out of Moscow Station, I would've rappelled to the ground from one of the second-story windows...Instead, I stepped out onto the porch. Crisp and cold, moon waxing orange in the eastern sky. I walked rapidly toward the center of campus. To pull them in the wrong direction before flanking them. If they were watching me. And I was pretty sure they were. When I neared the student union, I took a long look around. No one. Took a long circuitous route, wandering past faculty homes and a commons area, which brought me back to the Performing Arts building. Skirted it on the right, moving rapidly along a paving stone walkway. Passed a series of blind indentations built into the wall. No sound apart from my own footsteps. But then, like Orpheus, I looked back. A tall figure in a knee-length coat was moving steadily toward me.

I broke into a run and rounded the rear corner of the building, stopping short when Hardbody stepped in front of me, his muscles rippling under a plain white tee-shirt. A muzzled nine in his right hand, the business end pointed at my chest. I was sandwiched. Peacoat coming up from behind.

"All right, Crane. Let's go." He jerked his head toward a Dodge cargo van in the parking lot.

The cold started in my bowels and rose to my throat. It happened fast. Spat in his face and he flinched. All the edge I needed. Caught him with an upthrust forearm, knocking the gun out of his hand. Drove my four-inch blade into his solar plexus. Bull-rushed him, twisting the blade deeper into his gut. Yanked it out. A second thrust. Not quick enough. Oxstrong, he shoved me back with both hands. Grabbed his gut, snarled, and launched himself. I side-stepped. Too slow. His right shoulder drove me to the ground. Then he was on top of me, powerful hands gripping my throat. Extreme pain, the cold splitting the top of my skull. I went limp. He relaxed for a millisecond. Big mistake. I drove the blade into the side of his neck. The sibilant crush of tissue and tendon tearing merged with his screams. Twisting the blade deeper was dark ecstasy. Motherfucker was gone. Rolled out from under him and kicked him hard in the side of the head. Crouched down over him and wiped my blade clean on a dry section of his tee-shirt. Big sadness 'cause he wasn't Tragg.

Spattered with blood, chest on fire where he'd shouldered me, I started toward Agresti's Honda, which was about twenty yards away. Ducked behind a car and surveyed the crime scene. There was Peacoat, frozen in place at the sight of his partner sprawled across the asphalt. I began back-pedaling toward the Honda. Not sure if he even saw me. Peacoat came out of his trance, grabbed Hardbody by the ankles, and began dragging him toward their cargo van, which was parked nearby. Cleaners. The surest sign of a "professional" organization. Peacoat was gonna package up his piece of dying meat.

I staggered to the Honda. Got in and pulled out of the parking lot. Made it back to Route 3, where I held it at seventy, shuddering, white knuckling the steering wheel. Damaged throat hurt like hell. I'd be whispering for a week.

Passed Lowell, where Jack Kerouac grew up. Turned off the highway and checked Google Maps. Found the old highway, 3A, a two-lane blacktop, which wound through the upscale suburbs, meandering toward Boston. Swallowed some ibuprofen. I'd taken a hard shot to the sternum. Nothing broken, but it hurt like hell. Throat swollen from Hardbody's beefy mitts, my voice gone. But alive. Had to get rid of my bloody clothes.

The Massachusetts countryside is full of freshwater lakes. Drove slowly till I came to a sign for Upper Mystic Lake. Parked when I got there and got out of the car carrying Agresti's bag. Cut through a patch of wooded parkland leading down to the lake. Stripped off my shirt and tweed jacket and khakis. Took off my shoes and socks. Filled the jacket pockets with sand and the largest pebbles I could find. Folded up the pants and jacket and tied the shirt around it. Made a tidy little package. Took a deep breath and waded into the water. At first, the cold was overpowering. Had to clench my teeth when the water reached my bruised chest. A few more breaths, and then I scissored out into deeper water. My father Adam taught me two useful things—how to box and how to swim. Thirty yards out, I dove, my throat threatening to clamp shut. Reached the bottom. Felt around till I found a clump of tangled vegetation where I anchored the package, then released to the surface, lungs pleading for air. Backstroked to shore, the yellow jasmine moon hanging in the sky above me, a darker shade of yellow, like an end-stage jaundice victim.

My teeth chattering, I opened Agresti's briefcase. Grabbed my spare jeans and tee-shirt and put them on. Ditto shoes and socks, then back through the parkland to the Honda. Got in the car and drove. Needed a cheap, out-of-the way motel. Not easy to find in the tony suburbs. By then, the ibuprofen was kicking in. Kept the heater on full blast until I stopped shivering.

Found a good place to pull over. Googled Motel 6. Found one in a place called Danvers, twenty-two miles north of downtown Boston. Took another forty-five minutes to get there. Checked in around ten p.m. Starving. Asked the deskman where I could still get food. He directed me to an Applebee's less than a mile down the road. I ordered a turkey club and sliced red potatoes.

Tough night, but with the help of the food and more painkillers, I finally managed to get some sleep. Had never killed a man with a knife before. I was shook. Badly, and it was no better in the morning. I was scheduled to meet Agresti at a North End café at five p.m. All I could do was tough it out until then.

CHAPTER NINETEEN

The North End café was three-quarters empty. Agresti, in jogging clothes and a Red Sox cap, was writing in his notebook. I walked over and sat down across from him. He greeted me with an inquiring look. I sketched out my story in broad brushstrokes. When I was finished, Agresti grinned, revealing his strong, even teeth. "Look on the bright side. That's one less domestic terrorist to worry about. You weren't eyeballed on the way here, were you?"

"I don't think so. But it's obvious that the bastards are all over me. Are you strapped?"

He nodded. "Just so happens I am, which is not my usual M.O."

I nodded. Agresti is more than capable with a sidearm, but likes to keep that particular talent under wraps. "Listen, Agresti, what have you found out?"

He warded off my question with an upraised hand. "Wait till the food arrives."

The roast beef was mouth-watering. I ate slowly, marveling as the strength poured back into me. Between bites, Agresti described his search engine efforts. After Adara moved to Washington, D.C. to study law at Georgetown, Mohammad had sold their house in the suburbs and relocated to the Back Bay, not far from Copley Square. Then he disappeared. "When you Google him, you draw a blank. I've even talked to my address people. Nada. I'd say it's a shade mysterious. Of course, I may have stumbled over him a few times while staggering out of McCoy's after watching Brady carry us home to yet another stirring victory. A group of well-heeled Arab businessmen, mostly Saudis and Iraqis, I believe, never miss game day there. They're big sports fans, and boy, do they love our Patriots."

I shrugged. "Diversity makes for strange bedfellows. The American way. At least it used to be...So how can we find Mohammad?"

"Good question. I'm sure he's around. Like I told you before, I have people I can talk to. I have a fairly good-sized clientele of wealthy Arab businessmen who keep me on retainer."

Damn, but Agresti was an operator. I must have raised an eyebrow. He explained that wealthy Middle Eastern fathers like to keep an eye on the escapades of their college-age sons and daughters. Precautionary measures. In case they get involved in bad romances or run up gambling debts in the casinos. "It's like an open tab. If the need arises, they know I'm only a phone call away."

I nodded, dipped a French fry in ketchup. "So now you'll call in a marker?"

Agresti's turn to nod. "Why not? I'm their fixer and their bagman. All modesty aside, I'm rather a valuable asset...But if I find Mohammad, what should I tell him? Why do you want to schedule an appointment with him?"

"Simple. Tell him I fear for his daughter Adara's safety and that she asked me to talk to him."

"That'll work...But listen. The Patriots are playing the Steelers tomorrow afternoon at one p.m. It's the first big home game of the year. I'll be at McCoy's, and so will the group of Arabs I was telling you about. Why not meet me there?"

"Not like I have anything else to do." I grimaced. "Except nurse my battered body."

"You'll live." Agresti sized me up. "That scumbag you killed had it coming." He dabbed at his forehead with a napkin. "So don't torture yourself…Listen, here's what I've found out about the bright boys."

It seemed QB Tragg had virtually no internet presence, but Baron Woodley was everywhere. He started out in the 2nd Marines and was decorated for his part in the liberation of Kuwait. Surfaced a few years later in federal prison for conspiring to sell firearms without a license while knowing full well they might be used for further crimes. A low security federal joint would've been cake for a guy like Baron, but he wasn't satisfied to simply do his time. Instead, he sang sweet music. Smart career move. A special hearing, smiles all around, and he was off to the School of the Americas in Fort Benning for counter-insurgency training. In 1997, he signed on with COMPSUP, Ltd., which, six years later, received a generous share of the spoils during and after Operation Iraqi Freedom. Their job was to handle logistics for paramilitary infrastructure companies like CBR during the rebuilding phase. "Or like somebody said," said Agresti, "you gotta burn down old bridges to build new bridges."

"I think that was Chairman Mao."

Agresti shrugged. "Whatever. I'm sure he wasn't the only one."

Baron Woodley may have met Amsterdam in Iraq. At some point, he returned home and resurfaced in Orange County, where COMPSUP had a satellite office. He resigned his post in 2008. After that, no more mention of him on the internet. And nothing on how he hooked up with Amsterdam. "But the real mystery," said Agresti, "is Amsterdam. I think it's a pseudonym. I've run searches of every paramilitary outfit in the country and plenty of other databases too. Nothing. My hunch, though, is that they both have military backgrounds, and they're both the bastard offspring of outfits like COMPSUP."

"Did you check the new para firms in Southern California?"

Agresti snapped his fingers. "I did, but I'll double check."

"What about Tami Wheat?"

"Ah yes. Ms. Wheat. She's definitely real, although the name Tami Wheat may be a pseudonym. According to her official biography, she went to George Mason University, where she studied political science. She married a much older man named Dick Crandall, I assume, for the money. He's the CEO of Crandall Coal & Oil International, Ltd. She mostly puts in appearances at political fundraisers." Agresti paused. Tried to smooth the wrinkles out of his forehead.

"What kind of fundraisers?"

"What kind do you think? Deregulate, deregulate, deregulate. She's apparently connected to the Roach consortium. The scary thing is she's reportedly a very effective public speaker."

I groaned. Based on Agresti's intel, it appeared Tami was not formally associated with any of the agencies, which made her all the more dangerous.

We drove back to Agresti's office building in separate cars. He had two assigned parking spaces, and I left the Civic in one of them. Handed him the keys. Went up to his office to retrieve my suitcase. The way we left it was we'd watch the Pats game on Sunday at McCoy's. In the meantime, he'd reach out to his Arab clients to try and get a lead on contacting Mohammad.

I checked into a suite on the third floor of the Harbor Inn, just off Beacon Street, half a mile from Agresti's office. Took off my clothes and lay down on the bed. Tried to sleep. Didn't work. Someone had murdered sleep. Within the last twenty-four hours, I had driven a four-inch Buck knife into a man's neck. As he lay dying, I had kicked him in the head. These facts ate at me. Finally, I got up and took a shower. My body was a sea of bruises from my neck to my solar plexus.

Phoned Bobby and Jack. Left messages. Got down on the floor and did four sets of pushups, jailhouse style. Got dressed and walked down to the lobby. Using an old Hotmail address, I sent out emails to Bobby, Jack, and Maleah. Asked them to phone me and gave them each different burner numbers.

Although it can be done with stingray-style interceptors, tracing burner calls is not easy.

Back upstairs, I ate chicken noodle soup and watched reruns of *Family Guy*. Even caught an hour's sleep. Woke up thirsty. A Middle Eastern cabbie dropped me off in front of a joint called Old Country on Tremont Street. I walked inside, noted the Americana décor, grabbed the only unoccupied seat at the bar, and started drinking.

Three hours later, I took the elevator back up to my third-floor room. Stretched out on the bed and watched the room spin slowly. Something was bothering me. Ever since my dream about Greg Thurston, he kept surfacing, and each time, it was harder to push him away. I knew my refusal to give him any high stakes work was eating at him.

"Listen, Nick. I'm sick of you blaming yourself. It's not fair to you and not fair to me. The whole thing was just bad luck, pure and simple. Our deal was you were going to bring me along. Well, you're not. I need to tackle something challenging 'cause without meaningful work…" He paused and glanced over at a 100-count bottle of 80 milligram SR OxyContin on his night table. "I mean it, Nick. I need something challenging. Seriously."

I lay there, my thoughts churning. Agresti was a damned good investigator and could charm the pants off damn near anyone, but he wasn't a hacker. I worked it every which way in my mind. Greg was right. But I was scared to pull the trigger. Finally, around two a.m., I got up, dressed, walked downstairs, and asked the night clerk where I could find a payphone. He directed me to an all-night restaurant on Tremont Street and was kind enough to scare up a taxi. When I got there, I ordered coffee to go and rang Greg.

It was midnight in California and he was awake. Gave him the same information I'd given Agresti. Get me intel on QB Tragg, aka Baron Woodley, and the elusive Miles Amsterdam. Not to mention Ms. Tami Wheat. As an afterthought, I threw in

Frank Constantine. Why not? Adara had said he and Amsterdam had been friends since childhood. Maybe the story made a bigger splash on the East Coast than in jaded old LA, where it was sold as just another deranged military shrink goes serial killer with nudity and public exposure thrown in to titillate the masses. I told Greg not to phone me, that I'd get back to him in a few days.

Back at the hotel, I put my barely touched coffee in the refrigerator, laid the Beretta on the nightstand, and faded into black.

CHAPTER TWENTY

In the morning, my burner was blinking. Two texts. Tony said, "Alive. Pissed," and Jack Snow said cryptically, "Greetings from LaLaLand." I got out of bed, dressed, and took some ibuprofen. Down to the lobby. Sampled the continental breakfast and wandered over to the business office. Sat down and logged on. Emails from Bobby, Jack, and Maleah. First Bobby. "Everything's good, Boss. Still waiting." Jack's message was identical to his voicemail. I deleted it. Then Maleah. "Hi Dad. You telling us to stay in England for a few days has turned out to be a good thing. I love the English countryside, especially the Lake Country. Mom is pretending to be furious, but she's actually enjoying herself. We might go to Ireland on the ferry. I love you." Brought a tear to my eye. I emailed back, "Everything's good. Thanks for being careful. I love you and will keep you posted. And don't worry...I know I owe you big time. Love, Dad." I logged off and went back up to my room, where I spent the morning sitting around in my boxers reading *The Deep Blue Good-by*.

When it was time, I walked to McCoy's, reading the engraved inscriptions at the historical sites along the way. Arrived at a quarter to one. Agresti was writing in his notepad and chewing distractedly on a hangnail. I sat down next to him. Could tell he was nervous, so I decided to fuck with him. "Good morning, Agresti. I trust you're rested and ready for the upcoming match."

"Game, not match, fucker. Actually, I'm nervous as shit. I hate the way Brady sometimes comes out of the gate plodding like an old plow horse. It takes him till the second quarter to get his rhythm." Agresti shook his head and went back to his hangnail.

The place filled up fast. Workingmen and young professionals and older couples and bikers, mostly the weekend variety, along with a few outlaw types. The Pats received the kickoff. As Agresti feared, Brady came out of the gate looking like a mastodon gumming itself to death, and the Steelers jumped off to a ten-point first quarter lead. "Fucker is old," said Agresti. Staring at the screen, he reached out automatically for his second tallboy.

Seven or eight well-heeled Arabs strolled in midway through the first quarter. No thawbs and keffiyehs for these guys; rather, expensive jeans with Vans and polo shirts, or in some cases, stylish jogging clothes. A muscular, young American with spiky blond hair stood up and greeted them. Then they all sat down together and ordered drinks.

A Pats drive stalled just before the end of the first quarter, and Belichick settled for a field goal. Agresti was livid. During the commercial break, he glared over at me. "You're not helping, fucker. You're probably rooting for the Steelers."

"I do not root. I watch and I marvel. To me, this game is like a violent ballet."

Agresti shook his head.

The Steelers ran the kickoff back to the 40-yard line, nearly breaking it and going all the way. The camera panned to Belichick. Cold stare, hands on hips. I was diverted, though, by a new arrival—a tall, elegant white guy with striking features, thin lips, and expensive workout clothes. He stepped crisply through the throng and approached the Arabs. When he reached their table, he held out his arms as if to embrace them all in unison.

"Gentlemen!"
"Francis!"
"Good afternoon, Francis!"
"Welcome, Francis. Sit down."

A chair materialized next to one of the older men. Francis and the gentleman kissed each other on both cheeks. Hard not to stare. Francis was a dead ringer for Miles Amsterdam, only twenty or thirty years younger and an inch or two taller. The same hard, drop-dead handsome look, the same thin lips, cold blue eyes, and deep tan.

In the second quarter, Brady woke up and the Pats began chewing up swaths of yardage. Agresti punctuated each completed pass with a fist pump and roar of approval.

But I was barely watching. Instead, I was feeling comfortable and drowsy. No unwanted attention, free to let my thoughts drift. Then I stopped feeling comfortable. Two tall, powerfully-built white boys with shaved heads, wearing jeans and white pocket tee-shirts, had separated themselves from the crowd at the bar and were eyeballing the Arabs with obvious distaste. I nudged Agresti, and he tore his eyes away from the screen.

The white boys peacocked over to the Arabs' table and stood there glaring at the backs of their heads. Brady hit Edelman with a strike in the back of the end zone. Ka-ching! A huge cheer went up. Agresti turned back to watch the replay.

"Hey, assholes!" said the first white boy.
"That means you!" said the second.

The younger Arabs turned around in their chairs while the older gentlemen kept their eyes on the big screen. A flicker of warning passed from the muscular blond guy to Francis, who gave a slight but definite nod. Blond Guy and Francis both stood up and advanced on the punks from either side.

"So," said Francis, screwing his hard, patrician features into a look of pure contempt, "it appears we have a problem."

"Only if you make it one," said the punk nearest him. "We don't like having these fuckin' camel jockeys taking up space here on game day."

"They probably feel the same way about you, but unlike you retards, they're too polite to say anything."

Misjudging Blond Guy for a mere hanger-on, the other punk ignored him completely and turned toward Francis, trying to stare him down. Big mistake. Blond Guy wrapped his right arm around the punk's throat and simultaneously shoved his right knee into the small of his back. Pressure in both directions. Hurt just watching. Even though the kid was an asshole, I felt bad for him.

"Should I break your spine?" said Blond Guy, "or have you had enough?"

"He's had enough," said his partner.

"Shut up!" said Francis. "No one asked you." He rammed a hard fist into the kid's gut. The kid staggered and clutched his belly. Francis clubbed him hard with a back elbow to the side of the head. The kid dropped. Blond Guy whirled his victim around in a half-circle and flung him toward his partner. The kid tripped over his fallen friend's body and crashed to the floor. Hard. He rolled over moaning, cradling his face. Blond Guy and Francis bumped fists.

By now, three or four of the outlaw bikers had advanced and formed a semi-circle just outside the danger zone. Francis turned to them. "Take them outside and dump them somewhere. But don't hurt them any worse than they're already hurt. They're freakin' retards, but they're still Americans. Have I made myself clear?"

"Clear as day, Boss," said one of the bikers. Within seconds, he and his friends had yanked the two young punks to their feet and were dragging them toward the rear exit. Francis and Blond Guy returned to their seats in time for the kickoff. The Steelers' return man was swarmed at the 12-yard line.

"Damn," said Agresti. Then he looked at me, a glint of wry amusement in his warm brown eyes. He spoke quietly, shielding his mouth. "As you can see, our cowboy friends believe in protecting their allies." He leaned closer. More than tipsy, less than drunk. Spoke. "Do you ever wish you were like them and could transform all the shades of grey into black and white and never look back?"

A helluva tough question. But pretty sure the answer was no.

CHAPTER TWENTY-ONE

It doesn't matter how good an investigator you are. Nor does it matter how tough, smart, valiant, determined, and courageous you are, or even how straight you shoot, unless you have one other quality, which is not really a quality at all. It's something that's given to you. Who knows where it comes from? A little thing called luck.

That night at the Harbor Inn, reading MacDonald and watching re-runs of *Family Guy*, I started thinking about how many times I'd already been lucky while maneuvering my way through my present shitstorm. QB Tragg visiting me alone that night in my cell at the black site. Bobby and his team arriving just in time. Hardbody and Peacoat in the men's room at Union Station, bitching about the train being late. My escape by Greyhound. Hardbody trying to take me alive in the Hawthorne College parking lot, which gave me the window of chance I needed to cut him down.

You can't help wondering if your luck is gonna run out. You hope it never does.

At ten p.m., my burner rang. Agresti. He told me to meet him in the hotel lounge in five minutes and to bring my suitcase. I walked downstairs to the bar and sat at a corner table. Agresti walked in sixty seconds later, sharp in pressed jeans, fedora, and brown velour blazer.

He was feeling good about the Pats' come-from-behind victory, but his mood changed when I brought up the one-sided battle we'd witnessed at McCoy's. "The government's men," he hesitated and ran a hand under his fedora, "are, shall we say, formidable."

"Plenty damned lethal." I shook my head slowly. The emptiness radiated from the pit of my stomach.

"But I've got good news," said Agresti. "Mohammad is on board." He extracted a plain white sheet of typing paper from an inside jacket pocket and handed it to me. "Read this. Carefully."

> You will meet your contact at ten a.m. at the southwest corner of the Boston University Sailing Pavilion on the Charles River Esplanade near the Boston University Bridge. He will be sipping a soft drink and wearing deck shoes, white linen trousers, and a white shirt with the sleeves rolled up. You will approach him while walking east, away from the B.U. Bridge. When you see him, nod three times and keep walking slowly east. Your contact will then start walking west toward the bridge and the old railroad crossing that runs underneath it. You will come to a stop, face the river, count to 100, reverse your course, and follow him. You will meet in a grove of hardwood trees on the west side of the railroad bridge. You'll be familiar with the area because your driver will have dropped you off close to the trees. You and your contact should talk for no more than twenty or thirty minutes. He is shadowed much of the time. He will have hopefully evaded surveillance before the meeting. Prepare your questions in advance and WATCH YOUR BACK! If you sense you are being surveilled, you should abort your mission, and your

driver, who will have your suitcase, will take you to a safe house where you will await further instructions from yours truly.

There was no signature. I turned to Agresti, who nodded with some satisfaction.

"Read it again and memorize it. Then tear it into pieces and hand them to me."

I did as I was told. Agresti stood up. "I'll be right back." Two minutes later he returned and sat down.

"So who's my driver?"

"A white guy I call Jet. You'll see why. He's a functioning junkie and one helluva driver. Make sure he stays in the immediate area while you talk to Mohammad. Jet's an old hand. He'll drive around in circles, act inconspicuous, and be there waiting when you're ready to leave. You'll like him. You'll be strapped, I assume?"

I nodded soberly. Agresti studied me. "Are you sure you're ready for this?"

"This is what I came here for."

"Good. So, to repeat, if anything feels wrong when you get there, abort. But if it works out and you get the information you need, Jet will drive you to a safe house in East Boston, where he'll switch cars before driving you to Hartford, Connecticut, where you'll catch the two p.m. Greyhound Express to Las Vegas. Have somebody meet you there. And pay Jet directly so that I'm out of the loop. You don't need to worry about him. He'd spend six months in the hole and still not roll over."

"Our kind of guy. I'll give him a stack if he gets me to Hartford in one piece."

Agresti let out a whistle. "He's gonna kiss you, Nick...Meet him at The Conscious Cup on Tremont at half-past nine. Wait inside, get two black coffees to go. He'll be driving a brown and yellow, two-tone Corolla."

That's Agresti. Not only had he found Mohammad, he'd set

up the entire play. I asked him how I could make it up to him.

"You don't owe me anything, Nick, unless this works out and you rescue Mohammad and his daughter. You pull that off, and I'll arrange, through my connections, for Mohammad to pay up big time. I think something in the high six figures would be reasonable. If he doesn't have it himself, he can take up a collection. This is obviously not your garden variety investigation. Depending on what else I have to do before the payoff, I'll take no more than a quarter or so at most. I think that's fair." Agresti had been unusually serious, but now his mobile face split into its customary broad smile. "I'm just thinking ahead. I believe Mohammad will do just about anything to rescue his daughter from these assholes."

"How did you get word to him?"

Agresti shrugged. "It was pretty simple, really. I checked my records and made some phone calls. A fella named Samar phoned me back a few hours later. We met in the Public Gardens near the lagoon, where he handed me a sheet of paper with the directions. I thanked him and we shook hands. Then he told me if either of his kids ever gets in trouble, I'll have to work pro bono. And he was serious. Boy, do those guys love to swing a deal. I went back to my office and typed up the directions. Then I called you."

"Jesus, Agresti, you're like a well-oiled machine."

"Just call me Brady."

I smiled. "Only if you insist."

Two minutes later, he stood up. "Good luck, Nick." I handed him my suitcase and we shook hands.

Back in my room, I stripped off my clothes and gave myself a thorough and deliberate sponge bath. My chest was many shades of red and purple. Then I got dressed. Walked downstairs and logged into my Hotmail account. No new emails. Fought off the urge to contact Maleah. Instead, I wandered through the lobby out to the street. The wind was blowing, and the sky was a palette of dark, roiling colors. I stoo7d in the lee of the building and watched the wind drive the day's debris against the brick walls. You could smell rain in the air.

Thirty-six years earlier, when I was sixteen, my father Adam, in the throes of delirium tremens, had tried to kill me in a fisherman's cabin on the shore of a northern Minnesota lake. Half-hearted effort, perhaps, but the shotgun was loaded and pointed straight at me. Adam hadn't even recognized me, which just made it worse. That was the first time I felt the cold that splits my skull, the same cold I felt in Nashua when Hardbody pointed his gun at me. That night in Minnesota I'd been carrying a drop point hunting knife, but I hadn't used it. Instead, I'd managed to deflect the barrel of Adam's shotgun with my bare hands. Then I'd tied him to a chair with fishing tackle so he couldn't hurt himself, turned, and walked away from my broken father and my childhood home. I'd been young and strong then and believed I could overcome anything. Now, I was still strong, but I was no longer young, and something inside me was breaking. It was Sunday night. I would not be meeting Maleah in San Francisco in three days to help her move into her new apartment. Instead, I'd be on the Greyhound, perhaps somewhere in Colorado, on my way to Vegas, where Bobby would meet me to bring me back to LA.

It began to rain, large distinct drops. The wind rose, the rain slanting under the streetlights. I stood there for a long time, watching. Then I turned and shouldered my way through the door back into the hotel. It was a long night.

CHAPTER TWENTY-TWO

Morning. A quick shower and shave. Checked out after nine a.m. No sun and a bone-chilling northeast wind. The rain had stopped, and I walked briskly east on Tremont to The Conscious Cup. Ordered two large black coffees to go. Then I stood near the door, taking occasional sips from mine while watching the street. Just after nine thirty, a two-toned, brown and yellow Toyota Corolla pulled up to the curb.

Jet could've been King Tut, and I would still have gotten in. Placed both coffees in the center divider and extended my hand. Jet's fingers were so hardened by decades of molecular destruction it felt like shaking hands with the Bionic Man. His face all bones and sharp angles. Greasy hair, dilated pupils. Junk sick. He called me Jack for some reason. We drove north on Berkeley toward Storrow Drive under a cloud cover so low it felt like we were in a dome.

"It's all good, Jack," said Jet. "Anthony said you're good people and you got the bread. That's all that matters. Me and the old lady got plans."

"No problem," I said. "I'll take care of you."

Jet stared at me until I told him to keep his damned eyes on the road. I could feel his junk hungry cells banging into each other.

Jet clover-leafed left onto Storrow, which fronts the Charles River Esplanade. We passed under the Massachusetts Avenue

Bridge and a series of elevated pedestrian walkways. Boston University on our left, the B.U. Bridge and the Grand Junction Railroad Bridge on our right. West of the bridges, Storrow Drive turns into Soldiers Field Road. When we got there, Jet pulled into the designated drop-off zone.

"All right, Jack. See that road?" He pointed toward a paved walkway that wound along the riverfront. "Agresti said you follow it east to the sailing pavilion. First you go through the tunnel, you'll see. Then you make a hard right and a left, and you're there. But be careful in the tunnel. A lot of shitheads hang around in there. Agresti said I should give you 'zactly thirty minutes. That means I gotta do the old loop-de-loop 'cause I can't sit here or I'll get cited." He reached past me into the glove compartment and pulled out an old-fashioned windup timer, which he set for thirty minutes. Then he held out his hand. I reached into my wallet and counted out five twenties, which he accepted without expression, his horn-hard fingers gripping the money like a cranked vise grips steel.

"Ten percent down, Jet. Don't leave me stranded. If you do, I'll hunt you down. I'm serious." For a moment, we stared at each other. Then he nodded. "I'm good people, Jack. You got nuttin' to worry about." My turn to nod.

I got out of the car. Low gray sky. The bitter wind felt even colder close to the river. On my left, shrubs growing along the riverbank. The path led through a copse of hardwood trees, their leaves beginning to turn. No one was in sight as I neared the tunnel.

Sudden whoosh of skateboards. Three teens, exulting in their speed and power. Two passed on my right, one on my left. I watched them vanish, swallowed up by the hardwood grove…A homeless man, half-in and half-out of his sleeping bag, had set up camp near the mouth of the tunnel. He stared at me, his eyes bright with fever. Then a broken-down woman wearing a babushka, sitting cross-legged, a begging cup between her knees. Her gaze was empty, and I shuddered as I dropped a few dollars into her cup.

Back into the bitter gray morning. A hard right, then left. Came to the pavilion. Passed within three feet of patient Mohammad on time and in place, clutching a large plastic drink cup, the sleeves of his white shirt rolled up to his elbows. I stopped, nodded three times, and started up the road past the sailboats and kayaks, walking slowly, counting off the seconds. In the near distance, three figures were coming toward me. Then they turned off the path and stood in a cluster, talking and laughing. When I reached one hundred, I turned around and started back, past the pavilion and into and out of the tunnel. There was Mohammad, waiting near the hardwood grove. He nodded and continued on to a vantage point that looked out over the river.

CHAPTER TWENTY-THREE

At first we stood there, side by side, looking out over the gray, choppy water. No handshake. No Arab kiss. Then we faced each other. He was of medium height. Dark complexion. Deep-set oval eyes and prominent Semitic nose. Looked to be in his mid-fifties. But what struck me was the singular sadness in his eyes.

"Mr. Crane." Like his daughter, he spoke cultured English. "I walk down to this park every morning around this time and look out over the river. My little break from my research in the university library. But this morning I'm here for a different reason." He smiled cautiously. "I'm told you have news about my daughter."

"Yes sir. My name is Nick Crane. I'm a private investigator." Handed him my license. He looked it over and handed it back. "I met your daughter, Adara, in Los Angeles ten days ago. She was frank with me. She says you're both controlled by a man named Miles Amsterdam. She gave me your name and told me to find you and talk to you. She said you would fill me in, give me background so I would have a better understanding of her situation and yours. By the way, I saw three men east of the pavilion. I assume they're your minders, right?"

Mohammad gave a long sigh. "That's right. I bribe them, and they give me half an hour alone here each morning. Then they come and get me...My daughter, is she all right?"

"She's fine physically. But, for obvious reasons, being on house arrest is weighing heavily on her mind. And she's worried about you." I repeated what Adara had told me at Abel's. That Amsterdam was an influential man with important friends, and that he had crazy ideas about loyalty. How Adara feared his violent streak might be turned against her. Not today or tomorrow, necessarily, but eventually. And that he held the threat of deportation over their heads. And how Adara said it would do no good to liberate one of them. They both needed to be rescued simultaneously.

"What I don't understand is why is Amsterdam treating you and your daughter in this manner? What is he trying to accomplish?"

Mohammad shrugged, a gentle lifting of his shoulders. "We'll get there, Mr. Crane. But I think I need to start from the beginning." He began speaking and didn't stop for quite a while. He explained he was a Ba'ath with good family connections, a distant relative of Saddam Hussein. His specialty had been the oil market. As a young man, even before Operation Desert Storm, he'd secretly dreamed of coming to America. Then the unthinkable happened. His wife Qamar was raped and murdered by a Shi'a servant named Daysam. The killer was arrested and hanged. Fair play, perhaps, but it led to bad blood between Mohammad and Daysam's family. He and Adara, who was ten, went into hiding.

"After that, I didn't care if I lived or died. All that mattered was bringing my daughter to safety. I put out careful feelers and was introduced to Thomas Quincey—the man you know as Miles Amsterdam. He was in his late thirties then, already a powerful man with powerful connections. He wore many hats—JAG, Marine Corps captain, and lobbyist with the State Department. He was on a first-name basis with his CIA friends, who, at that time, were covertly managing dirty tricks against Saddam's government. Because I existed on the fringes of Saddam's ruling clique, my defection would be considered a successful American intelligence coup."

Mohammad explained that after they'd come to an agreement, he'd transferred most of his money into several secure American bank accounts controlled by Quincey and his people. With Mohammad as a signatory on each account. "Those were the terms of the deal. Because of the sanctions, it was impossible for me to transfer my money out of Iraq on my own. That's why we couldn't take the normal refugee route; Adara and I would have arrived here nearly penniless. And it would have taken far too long. So in order to expedite things, I agreed, in writing, to work as a permanent asset to the United States. You might say I'm contractually bound. It was the devil's own bargain, but I felt it was the best choice, especially for my daughter. She had no future in Iraq."

Once the deal was finalized, Mohammad and Adara, disguised as peasants, were driven west through Al-Anbar province in a covered pickup truck, then south into Saudi Arabia.

"We were wrapped in quilts and covered with straw. Adara was ten years old. Like many Ba'aths, we are not religious. But there, under the straw, I prayed to Allah and to the Christian God and to the God of Moses and to any other gods I could think of. Somehow, we got across the border into Saudi Arabia. I dared to hope we would truly be free."

He paused and I felt a lacerating sympathy. Turned and surveyed the service road, east and west. No sign of his three minders.

"But then I imagine Quincey slowly tightened the screws in some kind of double-cross."

Mohammad nodded. "Exactly, Mr. Crane. In stages. Or, as we say in the old country, *whoever plays with a cat will find his claws.*"

At first it was just intelligence. Mohammad provided information about the Ba'ath Party and their political structure in both Iraq and Syria, and whatever information he had about the Shi'a opposition. At first, he felt deep gratitude and considered

Quincey a friend. But things were never quite right. Although they were allowed to live well, and Adara attended excellent private schools, Mohammad never regained complete control of his capital. Quincey discouraged him from investing his money as he saw fit. As early as 2000, he realized funds were being siphoned out of his accounts. After 9-11, the bleeding got worse.

Mohammad shook his head ruefully. "In the Middle East, we have another saying. *A chameleon does not leave one tree until he is sure of another.* In my desperation, I didn't follow that advice. I had never been sure about Quincey. You can't be absolutely sure about anyone in the intelligence game." Although his voice was steady, Mohammad was trembling from the cold, the black hair on his arms distinct against his skin.

"I've only met Mr. Quincey once. My experience was not a positive one. But listen, sir, we have to hurry." I looked around. Still no sign of the minders.

He nodded but continued to speak in the same deliberate fashion. "What are they going to do? Shoot me? Were it not for my daughter, I might not mind. But as long as I cooperate, or pretend to cooperate, I'm too valuable to execute…" He paused, shifted his gaze out over the river, but didn't stop talking. "If we were expatriated back to Iraq, the current Ba'ath opposition would kill us for being traitors. We would be hanged or beheaded or they might turn us over to al-Nusra Front or ISIS. And if the Shi'a got their hands on us, the blood feud would start all over again. They would kill me for being a Ba'ath, and my daughter would be raped and murdered or else sold into slavery."

A fleeting rage in his luminous brown eyes followed by unfathomable sadness. He paused and slowly rolled down his sleeves. Struggled with the buttons.

"So that's why you couldn't stop Quincey when he set his sights on your daughter."

"It killed me, sir. Unfortunately, Adara was swept off her

feet. She was young, a junior in college, and Thomas, like most fanatics, can be very persuasive. This happened in 2009, soon after Thomas returned from two tours of duty in Al-Anbar Province. Although marriage between an older man and a younger woman is common, practically *de riguer* in my native land, I was skeptical from the start. I did not think they were a good match. Thomas had always been rigid and controlling, while my daughter is very much a free spirit. Or at least she was a free spirit. Naturally, she wouldn't listen to me. She was in love, and they were married while she was still a senior at Hawthorne College. It was the saddest day of my life other than the day my wife was murdered. Thomas insisted Adara change her name to Amina to disguise the fact he was marrying my daughter. He pulled strings and got her new paperwork. On her marriage license, her name is Amina Hosseini."

Mohammad paused and rubbed his eyes. Looked past me. The river was almost calm now, and the sky to the north was an eerie brownish-orange. He fought to get control of himself. Rubbed his chest and took several deep breaths. Then he fixed me with his glittering brown eyes. "It didn't take long before Adara realized she'd made a terrible mistake. She was miserable. At one point, she lost fifteen pounds and shaved her head. The poor girl looked like a wraith or a cancer victim. Still, she completed law school. I was proud of her for that. But then it got worse, much worse. Thomas relocated to Southern California and took Adara with him."

I nodded and bit my lip. It got to me. We were two damaged souls on the edge of the slate-gray river. Small sailing craft in the distance, the burnt umber sky moving toward us.

"Okay," I said finally. "I think I understand. Your daughter is a prisoner in her own home. Thomas Quincey won't let her go. She's afraid of him. She didn't try to hide it. And deportation would be an utter disaster. But why is it necessary for Quincey to keep you under armed guard? Given Adara's situation, you're not going anywhere…"

"Precisely, Mr. Crane. It's sheerest overkill. That's Thomas's way of sending a message—to remind us it could always get worse—while at the same time reminding my daughter to cooperate and play the role of a good wife. Up till now, I'm pretty sure Thomas has never hit her. But that, of course, could change."

"Okay, now that I understand the situation, I need to ask you some questions, if I may?"

Mohammad nodded.

"Tell me what you can about Quincey's background. Where he started out and how he became what he is today."

CHAPTER TWENTY-FOUR

There on the edge of the broad gray river, shivering from the cold, Mohammad shook his head. "I don't like to even talk about Thomas, but I'll tell you what I know. As a young man, he was one of few among his peers who insisted arming and supporting the Mujahideen was a recipe for disaster. The neocons scoffed at him and told him he was a misguided liberal, out of touch with history."

"So, what changed him?"

Mohammad thought it over. "Several things, really. In 1999, soon after Adara and I arrived here, with the help of several of his Saudi sources, Quincey helped to foil an al-Qaeda plot to bomb the main branch of the New York Public Library. Right there in midtown Manhattan. It was hushed up at the time but gave him tremendous cachet with both the State Department and the intelligence agencies. After that, he was quite the rising young star."

"Then I guess he deserves some credit."

"For that? Undoubtedly."

"And then I suppose 9-11 drove him over the edge."

Mohammad nodded. "Indeed, it did. Quincey had always loathed the covert relationship between al-Qaeda and certain elements in the CIA. The *you scratch our back and we'll scratch yours* approach to covert statecraft. He thought it was not only traitorous but stupid and dangerous. But still, I'm sure he never believed anything like 9-11 could actually happen, not here in the U.S. It was a profound shock to him. After that, he became a hardliner focused on protecting American soil."

"Which means," I said, paraphrasing Agresti, "he's probably not above launching false flag operations to fan anti-Muslim hysteria."

Mohammad looked at me gravely. Then he gazed out over the water. "At this point, Thomas Quincey will stop at nothing to protect America in the manner he believes it needs to be protected. No matter how great the risk...And because of his high standing, he's been given carte blanche. At least up until now..." Mohammad paused, poker-faced. Awaiting my next question.

"You mentioned his military service in Iraq. How did that affect him?"

"Badly." Mohammad shivered. "It changed him dramatically. Thomas did two tours of duty in Afghanistan and four in Iraq, right up through the Al-Anbar Awakening. I rarely saw him during those years. Something happened while he was over there that shook him to the core, probably during his last tour of duty. Truthfully, I don't want to know the details. What I do know is he was different after he came back. Before, even after 9-11, he was usually polite, even while embezzling my money and limiting my freedom of movement. And putting me through periodic debriefings to remind me who the master was...But after he came back from Al-Anbar, everything was different. He changed his name, like he wanted to erase the past. Ideologically, he became a complete isolationist."

"When did the house arrest begin?"

Mohammad smiles ruefully. "I can tell you exactly, Mr. Crane. Three years, ten months, and eleven days ago."

"What triggered that, if you don't mind telling me?"

"Adara asked him for a divorce. It was as simple as that, and as a result, my daughter and I are prisoners. Everything we do is monitored. We are watched from morning to night, me by my minders and Adara by the minions at the ICE office where she works. She is required to carpool with one of the flunkies. This is all to get back at her for asking for a divorce. Thomas knows perfectly well Adara would never take flight as long as I'm a prisoner here, because she knows he would take it out on me. Like the proverb says, *she who has been bitten by a snake is scared of a rope on the ground.* We live in constant fear. When Adara and I talk, we don't actually talk because our calls are all recorded. I hear the despair in her voice, and I know she hears it in mine. I haven't seen her for nearly four years. Like I said, I don't care about myself. But my daughter, Mr. Crane, she is my only child."

Trembling from the cold, his voice broke and he bowed his head…

I wanted time to think. Ruminate. Sift through the possibilities. Compare alternatives. But no. The turkey was roasting and I had to say something definitive. "Okay, sir, here's how I see it. It's clear we need to rescue you and your daughter, and we need to do it soon. We will need to synchronize both your escapes. My job is to figure out how to accomplish that. Once we've liberated you, you will stay underground at first, and we will get you new temporary identities. After that, who knows? It's a risky proposition. If we can pull this off, you will want to bring all available cash with you. Once in hiding, you will probably not be able to access any of your bank accounts. For the record, I know several lawyers with impeccable credentials with whom you could place money in trust. It would be utterly safe, and you could draw upon it once you were underground. But I'm not going to kid you, sir. Going underground is an act of desperation. But I'm not sure you have any other choice."

I glanced back toward the tunnel. No one. Then it struck me. Something was still missing. I turned to him. "What I don't understand, though, is why is it still so important to Quincey to keep you under his thumb? Other than the money? 9-11 was seventeen years ago. You've been here for twenty years. What can you possibly have to offer at this point?"

Mohammad pondered. He turned and gazed out over the water, as if the answer lay somewhere between river and sky. Turned back toward me and spoke. "You're right, Mr. Crane. Other than the money, I don't have much to offer. The truth is, it's purely revenge because Thomas knows Adara doesn't love him." He coughed, cleared his throat, and looked me in the eye. "So that's it, Mr. Crane. That's the story. But I must ask you in all candor. Based on your meeting with her, how desperate do you think my daughter is?"

Didn't want to answer. Too much was riding on my reply. But I had no choice. "She's desperate enough to have retained me. She specifically sent me here to talk with you. She wants us to come up with a plan."

"I understand," said Mohammad. He moved closer, reached out, and gripped both my forearms. "I want you to do exactly what you described. I want you to engineer a dual escape for my daughter and me. You must take us somewhere safe where we can regroup while you wave the magic wand and get us new identities. Are you capable of that?"

I frowned. Acting. Just a bit. Hate to admit it, but the huge potential payday both Adara and Agresti had hinted at was very attractive. "Let me put it this way, sir. I am more capable than most operatives of my ilk. For one thing, I do not give up. Obtaining the IDs is not that hard. Naturally, the escape part is more of a challenge."

Mohammad nodded. "I want you to do everything you can. I am at your service, and you will be paid handsomely in the event you are able to bring this about." He paused. "I'm at the Boston University library, half a kilometer east of here, beyond the bridge and the sailing pavilion, every weekday morning at ten a.m. researching a book I'm writing about Mesopotamia and the history of the Tigris-Euphrates Basin. It's an innocuous project and Quincey has no objections. I have a dedicated email research account I use to communicate with other Middle

Eastern scholars. The address is Mesopotamia445@gmail.com. The M is capitalized. Can you remember that?"

"I better write it down." I produced a pen and a blank business card.

"Quincey believes this account is harmless and doesn't bother to have it monitored closely. My Praetorian Guard is at its laziest on Monday mornings, so that would be the best time to make a break. I want you to make this your top priority. You should get in the habit of sending me occasional historical links to maintain contact—anything archaeological about Mesopotamia, Sumeria, Babylon, or Assyria. But be careful not to send them from the same email account twice."

We agreed I would send him a link every few days once I was back in LA using email addresses like SumerianHistorian59@gmail.com. When it was time, I'd send two emails on consecutive days. Both links would reveal pictures of the big-eyed Sumerian gods. The first tagline would be two words. "Sumerian Gods." The second would read "A God for Every Day of the Week." I told him to be ready at all times. And that it might not be on a Monday. On the morning after the second email, we would meet at eleven a.m. near the loading zone where Jet had dropped me off. Adara would phone him the night before. She would say, "I had such a splitting headache; I wanted to cry," and he would know it was time.

Time to go. I held out my hand but instead of shaking it, Mohammad surprised me with an ardent Arab kiss on either cheek. I responded in kind. A mark of our mutual faith and goodwill. I happened to look back toward the bridge. The three men were now in plain sight on the trail, halfway between us and the hardwood grove. They were moving slowly, like they hadn't yet spotted us. "Go, Mohammad. Now. You can't be seen with me." I pushed him off the platform onto the trail and pointed him toward the bridge. Then I began walking casually toward the drop-off zone, which was about seventy-five yards from the river overlook. Mohammad began striding resolutely toward his minders.

They spotted him first and then me. Their casual pace quickened. Mohammad hesitated, then turned around, and without so much as a glance in my direction, started walking back toward the overlook. Buying time. I vaulted the barrier onto the shoulder of Soldiers Field Road. There was Jet, idling in the loading zone. I still had fifty yards to cover. The three skaters who had passed me earlier were now heading back toward the hardwood grove at breakneck speed, laughing and shouting. Mohammad stopped and stood there like a lone settler facing a buffalo stampede. The skaters streamed past him, one on his left, two on his right. They reached Mohammad's minders within seconds. No room to pass. No time for proper braking. The three boys flew forward off their boards, taking out two of Mohammad's guards. They all went down in a heap, while the third guard escaped by diving off the walkway. The first two jumped up, screaming at the boys who assessed the scene, grabbed their skateboards, and skedaddled. So did I.

CHAPTER TWENTY-FIVE

The Greyhound bus pulled into Cleveland after midnight. A bleak dead time in the bus stations of America. Faces tight and drawn. Only people moving are the janitors. My timing was bad. Last bus to Columbus had already left. The next didn't leave till five thirty in the morning.

Had a cabbie take me to a Best Western. Set the alarm on my phone and sacked out like a dead man. Caught the seven thirty Greyhound Express to Columbus. Even had time for breakfast. Reached Columbus before ten and caught a ten-thirty local to Athens, Ohio, which is where the bus turns around and heads back north.

South of Columbus feels like the South. The Klan was big here once, may still be. I pulled the bill of the John Deere cap I'd picked up in Columbus down over my eyes and dozed fitfully. In Athens, I would flag a taxi to Gallipolis, a quaint river town forty miles farther south. According to Tony, Roberto Diaz's daughter Gloria and her older sister Abrecia were being cared for by Hiram and Rosie Munson on their family farm a few miles north of Gallipolis.

Cost me fifty dollars, flat rate, to get from Athens to Gallipolis. Tip included. Once we'd settled, the driver barely said a word, which was all right with me. We passed well-maintained farms with large silver barns and lovely white farmhouses and beat-to-hell ramshackle spreads with the proverbial "cars-upon-blocks waiting for the parts to arrive" look. Cottonwoods and live oaks dotted the fencerows and cattle meandered across the hillsides. Postcard material, the pastoral beauty veiling the real lives of the inhabitants. When we reached Gallipolis, storm clouds were massing in the west.

Grabbed coffee at a greasy spoon. The server gave me directions to the law offices of Hammersford, Smith & Whitley. Second floor of the John Adams Building, a local landmark on First Avenue near the river. I took the staircase. The bannisters were worn smooth, the burgundy carpet threadbare.

The admin looked underdressed and underpaid, but sweet as pecan pie. Said her name was Cynthia. No sign of the firm's three founders, but the lawyer I needed, Lyndon Naismith, Esq. was standing in front of a filing cabinet studying a case file when Sylvia ushered me into his office. He wore a short-sleeved, pin-striped dress shirt and Dockers. Black lace-up dress shoes and longish, curly red hair. Impish looking. I flashed my bogus badge and told him I was Terry Fry, a Special Agent with ICE, and that I needed to talk to him about two of his clients, Gloria Diaz and Abrecia Eliade.

For a long moment, Lyndon said nothing. Just stood there staring at the document he was holding. Finally, he shot me an angry look and bit off the words, "What do you want to know about them?"

"Easy, man. This doesn't need to be a problem. Let's sit down and talk it over." Plunked my ass down in a worn leather armchair facing his desk. Which more or less forced him to sit down in his chair behind his desk. Told him I was in Gallipolis to investigate a report claiming Gloria and Abrecia were being abused at their foster home. Treated him to my most sincere look. Told him we were not all heartless at the agency. Lying with frightening ease. I said I wasn't there to harass him or the girls. Rather, I was there to help them, and I was hoping he would brief me before I headed out to the Munson farm to investigate the abuse claims.

Lyndon listened. Had to give him credit for that. "Hmm," he said finally. "I don't know about this. If I'm hearing you right, you're telling me you're not here to drag the girls off to some filthy Arizona tent city, correct?"

"That is correct. I'm only here to help. For the moment, ignore the fact I'm a federal agent. You and me, we're the two bookends tasked with protecting these two innocent children. So you've got to trust me, brother…"

He shook his head. "That's easier said than done. I've never seen a single instance of ICE agents giving a damn about the folks they take into custody. Frankly, they either treat them like dog shit or with complete indifference. Why should I think you're any different?" He folded his arms across his chest and sat up straight. Stony stare. Masterful. For an impish guy.

"Listen, Lyndon, sir, you've got me all wrong. Instead of getting all huffy, just listen for a minute. Why would I fly down here from Minneapolis unless it was important? If ICE wanted to transfer the girls to some hellhole, they'd send down a couple of agents from Columbus with orders to transfer them. But that's not the case here, Lyndon. That's not the case at all." I spoke gently but firmly. Heartfelt Crane.

We went around and around for the next ten minutes until Lyndon finally caved. Knew he would 'cause I had the moral high ground. "All right," he said at last. "Maybe you are on the level. So what the hell do you want?"

"Thank you, Lyndon. Thank you for being reasonable. I need you to take me out to the Munson place so I can do an inspection. This afternoon. I want to observe the little girls and their caregivers in action, from the moment the girls step off their school bus this afternoon until they're safely tucked into bed."

"You are one weird sonofabitch."

"Not at all. I'm just a public servant doing what public servants should do. Working to protect our citizens. The country needs more of us."

It was only one-thirty, and we still had a little over an hour to kill. Lyndon relaxed and pretty soon we were telling war stories, me substituting SA Terry Fry in place of the actual author of my (mis)deeds. He was plain old, rumpled Lyndon Naismith, Esq. fighting the good fight, doing his best to keep his men, women, and children safe here in the USA—where, though nothing was guaranteed, they might have a fighting chance of surviving and living good lives.

"'Cause all of us Americans are immigrants," said Lyndon later as we drank coffee (I paid) at an old-fashioned soda fountain a few doors down from the John Adams Building, "except for the Native Americans. And they say even they walked across from Siberia." He paused. Adjusted his glasses. "Yessir, Terry Fry, my heart goes out to these folks who come here seeking a better life. That's all. Just a better life." By now it was raining, not hard but steadily. Gray green gloom outside. Did not want Lyndon to get lugubrious, so I segued into a discussion of the current political scene. Wise choice. Sat back and listened to him rant.

CHAPTER TWENTY-SIX

When it was time, we drove out to the Munson place in Lyndon's 2016 Hyundai Elantra. Turned around in their driveway and parked along the county road, facing back toward town. By now the rain was lifting, the whole world an explosion of brown and green. We had a clear view of the Munson place. Ramshackle. By any standard. Not even an actual house. Just an old double-wide trailer in the middle of a half-circle of dilapidated out-buildings—corn cribs, pig sheds, chicken coops, and a machine shed with no doors. No barn. A rototiller rusting in the rain. Sort of place I might have hid out at as a kid while on the run from my father Adam.

Lyndon told me the Munsons farmed every inch of their eight acres. Truck croppers. "Pa Munson is a lazy SOB, but he's crafty. He puts all the kids to work while he walks around making lists."

"What does the law say about foster child labor?" I asked. Lyndon looked at me like I should know the answer, so I pretended I did. "I believe reasonable chores are permissible with an emphasis on reasonable."

"Correct," said Lyndon. "The school bus should be here any time now."

We got out of the car and walked across the street. Sunset Magazine material it was not. Hogs rooting around in the mud in the hog pen. Chickens pecking greedily, free to roam around the yard. Believe I even saw a raccoon in a cage, its clawed arm extending through the bars. But apparently no dogs. Walked over to look at the hogs. Their outdoor pen led into a dugout shelter no more than three feet high, built into a small hillside. Children could be eaten alive in there. But the fence looked sturdy. The doublewide was actually two single trailers back-to-back with about a foot of space between them. One bigger, one smaller. The left hand wouldn't know what the right hand was doing. Which worried me. We were about to knock on the door when the school bus pulled up.

"The girls know me," said Lyndon. "Let's go meet them." We watched the girls come around the front of the bus, one tall, one short, their backpacks dragging. They started toward us, recognized Lyndon, and ran toward him. He scooped them both up in his arms. Gave them each a hug and a kiss on the forehead and set them back down. "Hi girls! This is my friend Terry Fry. So tell me, what did you learn today?"

"I learned how to spell cookie," said the taller girl. "C-O-O-K-I-E. I'm going to teach my sister." She put her arm around Gloria, who seemed downcast.

"What did you learn, Gloria?" said Lyndon, crouching down to match her eye level.

"Alphabet," said Gloria. "I already knowed it 'cause my mother teached me. I had a bad day, Mister Lyndon. The kids were mean to me again. One of them hit me. Another one pulled my hair."

"Why don't you take us home with you, Mister Lyndon?" said Abrecia. "That would be better. You could homeschool us. Your wife could teach us."

Lyndon let out a long sigh. "I'd like that. I really would."

Could feel her sudden presence. I turned around just as Abrecia said, "There's Rosie." She had a broad red face and a large, formidable body. Wearing jeans and a flannel shirt, she smiled and walked up to Lyndon. "Hi, y'all. Lyndon, you ain't botherin' my girls again, are you?" Then all business. "Listen up, girls. Your snacks are on the kitchen table. You have ten minutes to eat, and make sure you finish your milk. Then you've got chores till five o'clock and homework till six. You know the rules. Now run along."

The girls hesitated, looked at Lyndon longingly, and trotted off toward the main trailer. Lyndon introduced me to Rosie. Said I was SA Terry Fry from ICE and that I needed to do an inspection. Said it was nothing to be concerned about.

"You got that right," said Rosie, sizing me up. "I know I have nothing to be concerned about. Everybody knows my husband Hiram and I run the cleanest foster home in all of southern Ohio. So go ahead and have a look-see, Agent Fry. Take your time. I'm here to answer any questions. I run a pretty tight ship, and Hiram is a right kindly genius at organizing the girls. They collect the eggs and work in the garden patch and Hiram rewards them with all the fresh fruit they can eat when it's in season. And let me tell you something, Mr. Fry, we grow some of the world's best berries. Red raspberries, black raspberries, and

my own special hybrid blueberry. I've been working on my blueberry strain since I was knee-high. But you don't care about that. You just wanna get on with your job. Those little girls you just met, they're good girls. The little one gets picked on at school, though. I reported it, but they don't do nothin'." She shook her head slowly, as if pondering the great sadness of life. She seemed okay. But don't jump to conclusions.

Over the next three hours, Rosie rarely stopped talking. She had six foster kids in all. We watched them eat (plain, healthy food), do their chores, and do their homework. Three white girls, one of whom seemed depressed, one cheerful black girl, and Gloria and Abrecia. No obvious cracks in Rosie's veneer. But still. Something churning in the pit of my stomach. Her husband Hiram finally emerged from his workshop, which stood behind the two trailers. To my surprise, he dressed like a country preacher—black frock coat, shirt and tie. Polite but careful, offered no information. I could tell he was proud of his wife. Not everybody had a partner who could rattle on like a can of marbles overturned on the kitchen floor, even if she was talking to a government official.

Their grownup son Roy, who worked as an auto mechanic, showed up around six. He said hello shyly, grabbed a PB&J off the table, and disappeared into his room, which was at one end of the main trailer. Rosie and Hiram slept in the big bedroom at the other end. The kitchen and living area were in the middle. Rosie explained their four foster girls and the two illegals lived two to a room in the small trailer. The living area had been converted into a third bedroom. The kitchen was intact, except for the gas stove, which was disconnected. "For obvious reasons," said Rosie. The girls had a small refrigerator where they kept their sodas and snacks.

"I keep the kids separate from my family at night out of respect for their privacy. I'm the only one who's allowed to go over there. From seven thirty to eight thirty, I go over their homework with them and listen to their complaints." She chuckled. "Then I check on them one more time around ten. I'm the only mother they have as long as they're here, bless their little hearts."

I'd heard enough. Eyes and ears told me she ran a clean ship.

"Everything looks good to me," I said as we were about to leave. "I can tell you work hard taking care of your girls. Do you ever get the chance to relax?"

"Not very often," said Rosie. "I do have one pastime. Walking in the rain at night. I love walking in the rain. Always have."

I nodded. Shook her weather-beaten hand and thanked her for her time.

CHAPTER TWENTY-SEVEN

Lyndon wanted to get rid of me. He'd humored me for the better part of an afternoon. Had even allowed us to bond to a degree, but enough was enough. We were silent on our way back to Gallipolis.

"Look, Lyndon," I said, as he pulled up in front of the John Adams Building, "I hate to break this to you, but the United States of America would be very appreciative if you would accommodate me a bit longer. Won't be much skin off your hide. The thing is, I still need to conduct nocturnal surveillance. I would be remiss if I didn't." Intoned with requisite severity. "So, I still need three things. Rain gear. Transportation back out to the Munson farm once it's good and dark. And finally, a ride back to town after I complete my surveillance."

Lyndon shook his head. Grimaced. He'd already gone beyond the call of duty. At least in his mind. "Respectfully, Agent Fry, I think you need to have your head examined." He tapped his noggin, then made the time-honored cuckoo circle with his index finger. Then a slow smile which expanded until it wreathed his face, like the full moon on amphetamine. "If you like, I can get you admitted on a seventy-two hour hold right over at Holzer Hospital. They have a brand-new state-of-the-art psych ward over there we're all quite proud of."

"Very funny, Lyndon. But if you don't want to help, where can I borrow or rent a car around here? I agree everything looks good out at the Munsons. Rosie appears to be a decent foster parent. But you gotta admit one thing. She talks too much. Which is a common occurrence among folks harboring unsavory secrets. So, I have to explore this a bit further." Nodded firmly and tapped my forehead. "It's the only moral approach."

"What the hell are you talking about? The bottom line is the Munsons run a good program. You saw it yourself."

"I'm sorry, Lyndon. I don't mean to be a pain in the ass. Maybe it's a hangup, but, man, I've got to finish my job. That's how I made my stripes, and that's how I'm going to keep 'em."

We went around and around. Till he broke. I knew he would.

Lyndon dropped me off with a resigned wave one hundred yards from the Munson farm. Ten after nine. I walked directly onto their property, a brown raincoat draped over my arm. If intercepted, I would simply say I had a few more questions that I would conjure up on the spot. Everyone was inside, the Munsons and their six wards. Made my way to a vantage point back in the shadows near the machine shed. There was decent outdoor lighting, and I had a clear view of the girls' trailer and anyone approaching from either direction.

Perched on a stack of pallets. Sussed the area. Night sounds. The whirring of hidden wings, bats perhaps, and the earthy grunts of the hogs settling down in their pen. Took out *The Deep Blue Good-by*. Just enough light to read by. In the story, a scoundrel named Junior Allen was giving Travis McGee a hard time.

Almost ten o'clock. Rosie was due for her bed check. She turned up two minutes early. A ponderous stride, like unseen forces weighed her down. In and out of the trailer in ten minutes. No surprise there. From what Jack Snow tells me, most deviants with a regular pattern like to strike late at night, generally after midnight. Not that I necessarily distrusted Rosie. But I wasn't sure. And I couldn't discount her husband Hiram in his peculiar country preacher attire. Or their son Roy, for that matter. The girls were vulnerable. I moved farther back into the shadows. Found a rock to sit on. Clear view of the road and the pathway to the girls' trailer. At a quarter to twelve, it began to drizzle. Pulled my rain hood over my head.

Rosie reappeared sometime after one a.m., wearing a bright orange parka and a floppy rain hat. She turned right onto the county road and headed away from town. I was drowsy now, the soft patter of light rain hypnotic. Dozed for a while and woke up with a start. One forty-seven. Cold and miserable. Had Rosie returned? Or was she still walking? I took some deep breaths and slapped myself a few times, trying to wake up.

Around two fifteen, Rosie finally returned. I was praying she'd head for *her* trailer. She didn't. Imagine a heart stopping. Mine. I watched—waves of mounting anguish—as she shadowed her way toward the girls' trailer. Her ponderous stride now refined into wary forward progress, stopping, looking around stealthily, advancing, stopping again. Every indication of a guilty conscience. A horrible eternity as she made her way to the single step leading up and into the girls' trailer. She stopped. If she went inside and didn't come right back out after a quick inspection, I'd have to act. Catch her in the act and turn her over to Lyndon. I felt sick to my stomach. Then what? I couldn't testify against her. Not without revealing to the world I wasn't really SA Terry Fry.

Rosie didn't go inside. Instead, she stood there, clearly uneasy, shifting her weight from foot to foot. Furtive glances back toward the road. Could almost hear her talking to herself. Nervous 'cause ICE had paid her a visit…I wondered which girl, or girls, were her victims. Maybe the depressed white girl. No way of knowing. After an eternity, Rosie decided tonight was not the night. She turned and walked away from the entrance. Felt like shooting her in the back with my throwaway Beretta.

Spent the next three hours fighting sleep. Rosie did not reappear, nor did Hiram or Roy. Every time I heard a strange sound, I started, convinced she was making her slow way back to the girls' trailer.

Lyndon picked me up shortly before dawn. Said I looked like I'd seen a ghost. I said it had been a long night. Told him what I'd seen and asked him to sit on it for a week. If I didn't return by then with a team to rescue the girls, as a prelude to shutting the Munsons down, he should take care of it himself, as a man of conscience.

Now he was really thrown. Did not like the idea of going to the police with what he considered insufficient evidence. "She might have left something in their trailer and then decided it could wait until morning 'cause she didn't want to wake the girls up."

I looked at him dubiously. Shook my head. "What are you, Rosie's defense attorney? You're supposed to be representing the little girls. We can't take any chances with their health and safety. They're completely vulnerable. You know that." I kept pressing him, and he finally agreed that maybe there should be some kind of investigation. But it clearly didn't rank high on his list of priorities. What he was curious about was what did I have in mind for Gloria and Abrecia?

"All we need to do is find them a good permanent home with a loving and legal Mexican American family. At that point, ICE will officially transfer them. But that can take time. And we're working to get their mother released."

Lyndon was dubious. Very. I was getting tired of him. "That makes no sense. ICE's job is to round up all the illegals and keep them detained until the courts decide their fate."

"True. But what people don't realize is that after we round them up, some of us try to find them good homes. In a subtle, off-the-books kind of way. Look, we're not all creeps at the agency. It's a beautiful thing, Lyndon. Rescuing folks in trouble by finding them good homes."

Lyndon looked at me. "Mr. Fry, you say all the right things, and I don't mean to be offensive. But for some reason, I just don't trust you. Maybe I'm wrong. I hope I'm wrong."

"You are wrong," I said.

That's where we left it.

PART THREE

CHAPTER TWENTY-EIGHT

On the way to Vegas (2100 miles by Greyhound), I did little other than eat, sleep, read, and think about my new clients. Never represented two little girls before. Refreshing. Spent considerable time mulling over various rescue possibilities. And then there were Adara and her father. A synchronized rescue mission was certainly possible, but unless we neutralized this Quincey bastard completely, escaping in the moment might be a pyrrhic victory. On the other hand, Adara and Mohammad *had* slipped out of Baghdad at night under straw in the back of a pickup truck when she was ten years old. And, their cultured natures notwithstanding, they had already shown some pluck by shaking their captors long enough to meet with me. And now, I was committed to their cause. Or at least to Mohammad's cause. Still a bit wary of charming Adara, given her close proximity to Thomas Quincey, but based on their history, maybe they were strong enough to wait patiently in a safe house while searching for a more permanent solution. The stakes could not be higher. If our initial strike succeeded, there could be no going back.

Like Adara had insisted that fateful night at Abel's, their

safety was my safety. As a group, we had to find a way to elude Quincey's foul shadow.

But how? Accidents are not my style. The simple way would be an arrest and conviction. On what grounds? Easy. False imprisonment of one Nick Crane. How could I make this happen without our theft of Constantine's torture records surfacing? I had no idea, but I was damned if I was going to go to prison for stealing the dead killer's torture log. Hell, I should have been given a medal. It was a conundrum. I batted it around in my mind, hour after hour, off and on, for three long days and nights.

Nervous about my burners. Made no phone calls except one quick message to Greg Thurston. Told him Amsterdam was actually a well-connected former Marine Corps captain and JAG named Thomas Quincey. Greg got it. Got excited. "Connect them, right?"

"Indeed."

The Greyhound reached Vegas at five a.m. on Thursday morning.

I met Bobby Moore in the Golden Nugget parking lot next door to the Greyhound station. Bobby is a specimen. Iron-gray beard, skintight shorts, thigh muscles bulging, Diet Coke in hand, prosthesis pink as a baby's ass. Standing next to a dark blue 2016 Chevy Camaro SS rental. I got in. Bobby flipped the hood and checked the engine block and the undercarriage behind the bumper. Scanning for tracking devices. Before leaving Vegas and driving north on U.S. 95, he ran through a series of evasive maneuvers, like a quarterback reading the defense. Operational security is a motherfucker.

I've known Bobby Moore for a long time. Met him in 1986 at the Bottom of the Hill Club on Potrero Hill in San Francisco. Bobby was rockabilly and I was rock 'n' roll, so naturally we hit it off. He'd been a sergeant and tunnel rat in Nam. Two complete tours of duty. Never made his men do anything he wouldn't do. A good soldier right up to the day he stepped on a

Dole pineapple mine one week before his second tour was up. Lost his left leg, amputated below the knee. Tough adjustment back in the States. No hero's welcome for Nam vets. Not in those days. The anti-war crowd was strong and relentless. Bobby grew bitter. Naturally. A decent young man with a bright future was transformed into one of God's angry men, his endless appetite for self-destruction in mortal combat with his true steady nature.

I was a good influence. At first. One drink for his three. Stayed away from the powders. Soon, however, I was introduced to the dragon, and for six months, I was playing with fire.

Then I met Cassady upstairs at the Paradise Lounge in SoMa. She was playing pool with a girlfriend, and I watched her—vibrant with her punked-out red hair, woman's curves, and that big cheerful grin I could never resist. I was game. Walked up and challenged her to a game of eight-ball. Let her beat me by scratching on a shot I could've made. "You bastard," she said. "I hate when guys do that. Let's play another game. But if you try any of that crap again, I'll beat your ass." I could tell she liked me. Beat her the next game and the one after that. Then we forgot about the game. Drove to Noe Valley, where she shared a flat with a roommate. We sat up in an all-night coffee house till we couldn't keep our eyes open. Went to her flat. I gallantly offered to sleep on the coach. She took me up on it. But then in the morning, she came out in her bra and panties, her red hair all tousled. Woke me up, grabbed me by the hand, and led me to her room. I never looked back till decades later, when it all came crashing down.

Bobby and I stayed friends. Always. He told me he was happy I'd straightened up and married Cassady. He meant it. He and Cassady were pals. When she and I moved to Los Angeles in 1990, Bobby helped Nick Crane & Associates get off the ground by loaning me some of his government disability money. Then he moved to LA and rented his house in City Terrace, where he watches the world with a wary eye. Bobby's deep...and dangerous. He's saved my life more than once and I've returned the favor.

For years, he wrestled with the powders. Then he finally got the upper hand, took whatever meds his psychiatrist prescribed, and started raising goats in his backyard. That was the turning point...

Once we were on the highway, Bobby held the Camaro at a steady eighty mph, listening as I ran through the high points of my unnerving tale...

"You stabbed Hardbody with a four-inch Buck knife?"

"Yep."

"Of course, he was trying to strangle you. Folks with that kind of anti-social agenda do need to be reprimanded. Before they do even more harm."

"Problem is—"

"—you never stabbed a man before, and it's got you all fucked up. I bayoneted a tunnel rat in Vietnam. Just one. That's all it takes. I never told you that. I still dream about it sometimes."

Long silence, which Bobby finally broke. "Let's move on. Meetings with remarkable men, Blaylock and Timberlake, that is. They're fucked. Timberlake lives in Torrance and is making frantic preparations to skip town. I've made 'em twice, once at Musso & Frank in Hollywood and once at The Roost in Los Feliz, which is my kind of place. Free popcorn with sitcom reruns on the big screen. On Tuesday, I picked up Timberlake at his office at Olympic and Sawtelle and followed him to The Roost. Transponders are a wonderful thing."

"As long as they're our transponders. What are they hooked up to?"

"My new iPhone."

I frowned and Bobby scowled. "Don't get your ass in a sling, Nick. The phone is for tracking only. I know what the fuck I'm doing...Anyway, when I got to The Roost, I hung around for a while. Those poor fools looked grim, especially Timberlake. It's not just alcohol. They're on something. Timberlake's head kept drooping and Blaylock wasn't far behind."

"Oxys."

"Maybe. That or the dragon."

We passed through Death Valley and drove south along the eastern slope of the Sierras. Somewhere near Olancha, after assuring myself Bobby was carrying at least three loaded and duly registered sidearms, including one of my 9mm Colt Commanders, I wiped the unused Beretta clean and buried it and the clips separately under some rocks near a dry wash one hundred yards off the highway.

CHAPTER TWENTY-NINE

Sometimes you get a hunch. Sometimes you follow it. Sometimes it works. Sometimes it doesn't. Sometimes it backfires completely. You never know. This time, outside of Lancaster, I phoned Stuart Tucker, a West Hollywood makeup and costume artist known for his work with the entertainment industry. Told him my name was Wayne, and I needed something eye-catching for an upcoming party. Stuart said he was open from ten to two and from six to ten. Booked me for nine o'clock. His salon was near the intersection of Santa Monica and La Cienega. When we got there, Bobby parked on the street half a block down, and we buzzed ourselves in.

Place was grand and glittery. Pedestal chairs for the clients. Portable makeup lights suction-cupped to walls and mirrors. A before-and-after of Marlon Brando as Don Vito Corleone looping on a big screen. They dedicated one wall to clothes and costumes, everything from tuxedos to Sheik of Araby silks and robes.

Tucker, sandy-haired with a plump, friendly face and lively brown eyes, greeted us. Like Bobby, he wore walking shorts displaying bulging calves and an LA tan.

"So," his eyes flickering from Bobby to me and back, "which one of you gentlemen needs a costume, or maybe you both do?"

"I'm the lucky one," I said. Stuart motioned for us both to sit down in his pedestal chairs. Then he moved closer and stared at me, as if consigning my features to memory before reassembling them in a different form. "So, Wayne, my friend, what'll it be?"

I shook my head. "I wish I knew. Maybe I should have a look at your costumes. Something might catch my eye."

"Very well, then." Stuart smiled and led me to the costume area.

It took a moment to get oriented...The striped Arabian robes were striking. Matching baggy trousers and various styles of traditional headgear. And then I remembered. *Three burly Middle Eastern types wearing Arab robes and headgear sandwiched me out of nowhere. Stuck a gun in my ribs and hustled me into an SUV. Muttering in English.* I wandered back to my pedestal chair and sat down. Bobby's eyes were closed—relaxing after his long drive.

"From what I've been told," talking as casual as could be, "some of the party guests are going as Arabs, so I was thinking maybe I would go as an Orthodox rabbi to balance things out. But then I saw your Arab costumes. Brother, those are sharp! All I'd need to go with one of them is an ordinary Zorro eyemask. And maybe I'll get one for my brother too..." Nodding in a self-satisfied way. Bobby got up from his pedestal chair and wandered toward the front of the salon. "Tell me something," I said. "Are the Arab costumes popular? I could swear I've seen guys wearing them around town."

"The Arab costumes are a smash," said Tucker. "Right now, I can only rent you one set. The other four sets are on reserve for a customer who's going to pick them up in the morning. I should have taken them off the rack."

"One set's better than none, I suppose, though my brother will be disappointed..."

"The funny thing is," said Stuart, "it's the same two or three gentlemen every time renting the Arab costumes."

"Gentlemen?" I said. I gave him a distinctly meaningful look and handed him my Investigator's license. He glanced at it and handed it back like it was hot.

"What's the matter?" He grabbed my arm, worried.

"Mr. Tucker," I began, stopped. Bobby was waving his arms. Had to hurry. "Those men are bad news."

"Oh, shit!" He recoiled in shock.

"What are their names? Quick, we've got to get out of here." He hesitated. "C'mon, Tucker." His mouth was trying to work. I hated to do it but I shouted, "C'mon!"

"All right. All right. What do you want to know? Just tell me. One guy is called Blink, the other is Sam. The third guy introduced me to Blink and Sam. I don't remember his name, but I think he's their boss. He's the one coming tomorrow to pick up the four sets. Blink and Sam are pretty rough-cut, not my usual customers. The third guy looked like any stylish Westside kind of guy. He was wearing expensive jeans and a long-sleeved Knit Seasons shirt."

"Did he rent an Arab costume?"

"Yeah, he did too."

"All right, thanks. C'mon, Bobby. We're out of here. Do you have a back exit?"

"Wait a minute!" Stuart shaking his head vehemently. "You can't spring this on me and then walk away."

"I'm afraid I have to. But listen. You'll be okay. Don't do anything out of the ordinary. Stick to business as usual. Don't let them know you're suspicious. Rent them their goddamned costumes, but keep track of their visits." I took one of his cards. "Oh yeah, one other thing. Whose name is on their credit card? I need you to check that."

"They don't use credit cards. They pay cash."

"Of course they do. Sonofabitch!"

CHAPTER THIRTY

No sign of surveillance outside Tucker's salon. We shot down La Cienega in the Camaro and headed east on Wilshire. The first motorcycle pulled in behind us just east of La Brea. "Shake that fucker." Bobby braked hard. The bike swerved, righted itself, and accelerated past us. A few blocks later, there it was in front of a 7-Eleven. Bobby pulled in next to it, muttering something about finding out what the fuck was going on. I didn't try to stop him. Sometimes, you've got to let Bobby freestyle. He went inside. Sixty seconds later, the biker, a young white guy in jeans, a football jersey, and a brown leather bomber jacket, came out, cell phone in one hand, helmet dangling from the other. Finished his call and put his helmet on. Got back on his bike but made no move to kick it over. Waiting. For what? Reinforcements? Bobby came out carrying two large coffees. He walked up to the kid and said something. The kid said something back. Bobby placed both coffees down on the curb. His shovel hook caught the kid on the point of his chin. Kid fell off bike, bike fell on top of him. Bobby rubbed his hand, pulled the bike off the kid, picked up both coffees, and walked back to the Camaro.

East on Wilshire. I asked Bobby why he hit the kid. He shrugged. "Young ones need it special."

Another bike picked us up east of Western. Same story. Bobby braked, bike swerved, righted itself, and accelerated. This one sounded English, a Norton or Triumph. At some point, the rider must've pulled over and let us pass. When we reached the Mayflower, the Triumph pulled in behind us and parked in the loading zone.

"Shit! I didn't hit him hard enough."

"That was the other guy."

"Whatever."

We drove around back and parked. We'd been made. I had given Stuart Tucker a false name on the phone, so it wasn't that. Bobby had checked the Camaro for tracking gear in Vegas. Yet they had tracked us to Tucker's salon. We had spent four restless hours at the Mayflower that afternoon before going to see Tucker. Plenty of time to slap a device behind Bobby's bumper. Which meant they knew he'd been staying at the Mayflower...

"They'll have the firepower here before long," said Bobby, turning it over in his mind. "Those clowns on bikes must be scouts, but it seems like the plan is to take us alive. Or at least to take you alive. I might be expendable."

"Not necessarily. They probably like you because you were a military man."

Bobby shrugged.

Upstairs in the Mayflower, I waited in the hall, mufflered Colt in hand, while Bobby grabbed his gear. Then we glided down the hallway, down the stairs, out the backdoor, and across the asphalt to Bobby's car. We each had two pistols with spare clips.

Screamed out of the parking lot, west on Wilshire. Nothing at first. Then the twin bikes pulled in behind us and snuggled up close. Bobby kept our speed steady. The bikers got bored and passed on either side. I had my gun out.

"Shoot the guy on the English bike."

"Why him?"

"I liked the other kid. The one I hit. He was wearing a Saints' jersey."

Bobby kept our speed steady. Concentrating. I put my gun away. Then I took it out again. The bikers were not the problem. The problem was the two dark-colored vans behind us, driving side-by-side. Bobby tapped the accelerator *one, two, three*. Exploded into a hard right followed by a quick left onto Sixth. Left on Vermont, heading south. Right on Eleventh. Down Arlington onto 10 West, jumping every light, the vans losing ground steadily. I thought we'd shaken them. Wrong. We were in the fast lane holding a steady eighty-five when Bobby grunted, "Take a look behind us." Different vans this time, brighter in color, side by side, closing ground.

Bobby went from eighty-five to one hundred and five in about forty seconds. Slowed to ninety, weaving in and out of traffic till he exited on La Cienega. South toward Baldwin Hills and the oil wells of Ladera Heights. Bobby was jazzed. Danger and a fast car can do that to a man. But he was worried too. "We're bugged. I know we are. I'll check it at the first stopping place. Hand me my coffee." I handed him his cup from the center console. Began drinking mine.

South on La Cienega, past Carl's Jr. and Louisiana Famous Fried Chicken at the Rodeo crossing. Bobby dropped his cup back into the divider and asked without ever taking his eyes off the road, "Where'd you say we're going?"

"I didn't. Let's shoot for View Park."

"Not a bad part of town." He retrieved his coffee. Past Blair Hills and Baldwin Hills and the State Park. Came to the power plants and the oil wells. LA is surpassingly strange. Oil wells pumping day and night smack in the middle of 469 square miles of Western urban paradise. Just past the Fairfax Drive overpass, Bobby exited and braked hard, coming to a stop in front of the locked gate of a SoCal Edison plant. Rammed it into park but did not cut the engine.

"Cover me, Nick." Bobby grabbed a flashlight and we both got out. He checked behind the rear bumper while I watched the road. No luck. Tried behind and under the front bumper.

Nothing. Resorted to the wheel wells. Took three tries. Sudden bellow of triumph. Bobby stood up straight, a transponder dangling between his fingers. Grinned, wound up, and chucked it over the fence into the Edison plant. We got back in the car. Bobby took a deep breath and gulped some coffee.

"Directions?"

"Hmm? What do you think?"

"I think we drive all over this fucking city. Drive and drink coffee. I want to hear more about this Mohammad dude."

Two hours later, Bobby and I checked into a two-bedroom suite at the Cradle Rest Motel on North Figueroa, not far from the Farmer's Market in Highland Park. Bobby would turn in his Camaro in the morning and I would retrieve my Chrysler.

CHAPTER THIRTY-ONE

Up early. A long shower to wash the Greyhound grime away. Thinking. Or trying to. Only thing I knew for sure was that Thomas Quincey, aka Miles Amsterdam, was intent on having me rounded up. The question was, why? So I could join his team of scumbags? So I could be shipped off to some foreign torture hole? So I could die painfully with Quincey and company watching? Lots of possibilities. Didn't like any of 'em.

At eight forty-five, we bought low-fat yogurt and fresh fruit at a café on Figueroa. Then Bobby drove over to West Hollywood to surveil Tucker's ten o'clock appointment, and I took a cab up to El Sereno. Picked up my Chrysler at a private lot where Bobby had cached it. Then I called Greg Thurston and told him to meet me in front of the Davies Memorial Building in Farnsworth Park in Altadena, a few blocks from his house.

Got there early and waited. A few minutes later, Greg comes whirring over in his electric wheelchair. Turns off his engine and sits there grinning. It feels totally wrong to be meeting him here in broad daylight, but this whole affair was off kilter. I stand up.

"Hi, Greg." Something catches in my throat. I stand back and gather myself. Then he speaks.

"Listen, Nick, I'm jazzed. You've finally put me on a real case. I love it. So stop second-guessing yourself. Suppose these international criminals you're chasing get to us before we get to them? Suppose they step out from behind that oak tree with their guns drawn?" He points. "What would you do? Something like this, right?" He reaches under his nylon windbreaker and whips out a .38 Smith & Wesson revolver. Draws the hammer back. Aims it at the oak tree. Sights down the barrel. Pretends to fire. Eases back the hammer and puts it away.

I make no move to stop him. In a way, I like it. Kid is sending a message.

"I'm glad to see you're a single-action guy." I laughed and clapped him on the back.

"I just happened to have it on hand." Gave me a serious look. "You'll be pleased to know I've put in my 3,000 hours and am now a fully licensed PI. I pinned my license to the wall next to my bed."

"What about your license to carry?"

"It's based on my condition." He gestured toward his legs…

This peculiar preamble out of the way, Greg briefed me on what he'd learned. First on Woodley/Tragg, then Quincey/Amsterdam. Like Agresti said, Baron Woodley served in the Kuwaiti theater. Went to prison for gunrunning. Sang. On to the School of the Americas. Worked for COMPSUP in Orange County. And so on. All as Baron Woodley. Greg said there were no Woodley entries after 2008 and nothing about QB Tragg, other than he was briefly active in the Los Angeles MMA scene, apparently training fighters for the Armenians.

Greg had unearthed plenty on Quincey. Born into an upper-crust, Anglo-American family in 1958, he attended Phillips Academy in Andover and majored in English and Poly Sci at Yale. On the crew team. Skull & Bones. From the crew team to the spook patrol. Went to Harvard Law and became a JAG. Commissioned as a Marine Corps captain. Little mention of him working as a JAG. Must have preferred combat duty. He had barely mustered out of Lebanon when 21,000 pounds of TNT leveled the 1st Battalion, 8th Marines headquarters, in 1983. He kept himself busy in Grenada and tried to capture

Noriega in Panama. Probably the best thing he did was helping with the Bangladeshi rescue efforts in 1991. After that, he left the Corps for a while and apparently consulted for the State Department on an informal basis.

By the mid-1990s, Quincey had developed solid spook connections. He bounced around from embassy to embassy. Russia. Germany. France. Egypt. Saudi Arabia. Turkey. In between times, he was back in the States. In 1999, Quincey not only foiled an attempt by a maverick Al-Qaeda offshoot to bomb the main Manhattan branch of the New York Public Library; he personally disarmed the bomber, Amir Kumari, on the steps of the building right in front of the Corinthian pillars. Swept his legs out from under him. They rolled down the steps like lovers in a shitstorm, whereupon Quincey beat Amir into submission. Or as Mohammad said: *"It was hushed up at the time but gave him tremendous cachet with both the State Department and the intelligence agencies. After that, he was quite the rising young star."*

Then, when the Bush and Cheney foreign wars broke out, Quincey mustered back into the Corps. That was where, according to Mohammad, he had changed. *"Something happened while he was over there that shook him to the core."*

Asked Greg how he'd learned so much. He grinned, almost bashfully. "I did it the modern way. I went straight to the dark web and purchased databases. You'd be surprised how cheap they are. Then I started digging. After his tours of duty in Afghanistan and Iraq, around 2009, Quincey vanishes. It's like he evaporates into thin air, and presto, Miles Amsterdam appears more or less simultaneously. He has no past, no history. If he did, I'd be able to dig stuff up. But there's nothing, not a trace. Q transitions smoothly into A. Pretty radical, huh?"

I nodded slowly. "It's really good intel, Greg. But there's another piece to this. Apparently, something really traumatic happened to Quincey in 'Raq, probably in Al-Anbar Province, in the 2006-2008 period. See what you can dig up."

Greg nodded. Deadpan.

"What about Quincey's more recent activities?"

"I haven't got there yet. But I will."

"And the divine Ms. Wheat?"

"Who? Oh, Ms. Wheat. I don't have much yet, other than she's very rich and is married to a CEO of a coal corporation. I'll keep looking. Mostly though, I focused on Quincey 'cause that seemed most important."

"Correct. What about Frank Constantine?"

"The same. I'm just scratching the surface."

"Okay. You know what to do. What do I owe you?"

Greg shrugged. "I put in about thirty hours. And $100 in expenses." I took out my wallet, peeled off $1,000 in cash, and handed it over. "That's too much."

"You just got a raise, kid. Now keep up the good work."

Greg tried to shrug it off, but he couldn't hide his delight. "So, are you going to tell me what this is all about?"

"Unless I miss my guess, you'll figure it out on your own."

A look of disappointment. Followed by steely-eyed determination. "I guess I still have to gain your complete trust."

"You're doing a damned good job of it." Walking away, I felt a surge of hope. Not a bad thing to have a dedicated young investigator with real curiosity and first-rate computer skills prowling the dark web.

CHAPTER THIRTY-TWO

Leo Perez owns two buildings tucked away at the end of a long, badly paved driveway in a crumbling East Los Angeles industrial park north of City Terrace. One building is used for paint and bodywork, the other for tune-ups and brake jobs.

When I got there, a catering truck was just leaving. I pulled over and waited till it passed. Drove into the parking lot and wedged my Chrysler between a yellow Mustang and a Chevy Blazer. Leo's body and paint men were clustered around the entrance to the body shop, enjoying their morning break.

I crossed the lot and wandered into the brake and tune-up building. Armed. Heavily. My Colt Commander snug in its nylon shoulder holster, my Walther secure in an ankle holster. My Buck knife sheathed to my belt under my jacket.

Leo keeps things casual. I found him talking to one of his mechanics, who was doing a brake job on an old Nissan pickup.

I waited. When Leo turned to me, he greeted me heartily but couldn't hide the concern in his weathered, red-rimmed eyes. "Señor Nicky, *mi amigo*, it's good to see you. I asked around, but no one seemed to know if you were back yet."

"I got in last night." We shook hands. Then I put my hand on his shoulder and gestured toward his office. Once inside, he uncapped a bottle of Buchanan's Red Seal 21, and we toasted each other's health and children. Then I asked him if he could store my Chrysler for a while.

"No problem, Señor Nicky. And, of course, you'll need a loaner." He paused. "So, what else can I do for you?"

I leaned forward and spoke quietly. "This is not easy, my friend. How well do you know Jared?"

"Jared?" He looked confused and rubbed his chin.

"Yeah, Jared. The guy in Salt Lake City. You gave me his number. I called him when I got there. We met at his house and I gave him the Acura."

"You must be mistaken." Leo frowned. "His name's not Jared. His name is Javier."

I shook my head. Vehemently. "*Mierda*, Leo! The fucker gave me up to the same people I was trying to shake. Almost got me killed." Leo stared at me, flinty-eyed, tapping his fingers on his desk blotter. Poured himself two more fingers of Buchanan's. Reached for my shot glass, but I waved him off. Ignored me, poured anyway. Drank, put his glass down, motioned for me to drink, and ran his fingers through his salt and pepper hair. First time in fifteen years I'd questioned the reliability of one of his people. It threw him. Finally, he spoke. "All right, Señor Nicky, tell me what happened."

I told him. Enough for him to get the picture. While speaking, I took out my Buck knife and held it to my throat. Leo stared at me, shaking his head. Then he put down his shot glass and dialed a number. Waited, then a burst of rapid-fire Spanish. He put down the phone. "*Un momento.*" He stood up, brushed past me, and walked out of the room. Fifteen minutes later, he returned, wearing a resolute look. "You may be right, *mi amigo*. There's been talk. I didn't know about this. Thank you for bringing this to my attention. I will deal with it. *Te doy mi palabra.*"

He offered me his hand and I shook it. "*Un momento, por favor.*" I reached into my wallet. Gave him five Franklins and a blank business card. He tried to refuse the money, but I insisted. Then I wrote down one of my burner numbers on the card and handed it to him. Five minutes later, I started up the long driveway in a forest green 2012 Camry XLE. By now, the October sun had dipped behind a cloud bank, and Leo's driveway was wreathed in shadows.

The driveway was fifty yards long, surrounded by heavy brush on both sides. I was twenty yards from the street when two burgundy-colored Dodge cargo vans pulled into the driveway.

I cut the ignition, flung open the door, and plunged into the heavy brush. Brief ominous pause, then the pock-pock of suppressed gunfire. Last night, Quincey wanted me taken alive. Today, the rules had apparently changed. I crouched in the underbrush. Multiple shots ripped past me. I fired two rounds in the general direction of the vans and crashed through the brush onto the grounds of an abandoned tannery. The crumbling shell of an old building faced the street. Behind it, ancient tanning vats full of debris and chemical sludge. I skirted a sinkhole filled with mud and oily brown water, mayflies and yellow jackets swarming, the yard so toxic I sucked in my breath. Took cover behind one of the taller vats, a gun in either hand. Nineteen live rounds and two spare clips.

A head poked through the underbrush. Middle Eastern headscarf. I fired. A man screamed. Three more heads. I fired twice into the brush at their feet. No more screams. The heads disappeared. Sick to my stomach. Shooting fish in a barrel. A long moment of silence, then bullets smashed into my vat, missing my head by inches. The top half of the vat exploded, and I hit the ground face first, covered in debris. Three gunmen appeared near the right rear corner of the building. Like phantoms in the foul air. They opened fire. Cement exploded all around me. I rolled to fresh cover behind another vat, switched hands, and came up firing. Two of my P22 high-velocity shells caromed off the side of the building; the third caught one of the shooters. His boys pulled him out of the line of fire. They rounded the corner and disappeared. Crouching like a primate, moving in spurts and bursts, I took cover behind the opposite corner of the building. Occasional bullets exploded into the vats.

The passageway to the street was choked with weeds, bricks, fallen mortar, and discarded lumber. I followed the water-stained wall. Dried feces and animal bones. Silence except for my pounding heart. Nearing the street, I paused. The cold gathered at the base of my spine. Three men came around the corner. I dove headlong into a bed of elephant ears, their bullets whining above my head. Seven shots left in my Walther. I used all seven. These men weren't dressed as Arabs. They looked like ordinary workmen. Bled that way too, a fact I couldn't escape as I kicked a semi-automatic out of a wounded man's hand. Then I spewed against the water-stained wall. Wiped my mouth with my sleeve and loaded a fresh clip into my Walther.

Again the cold, this time in my chest. Peered around the front of the building. No one. Then I heard clambering on the roof. The cold turned to utter terror. I broke and ran out the front gate and up the road, weaving and scrambling in and out of brickworks and scrap metal yards, past industrial lots and foundries, cement factories and auto wreckers.

I don't think anyone followed me. If they had, I would have defended myself till the bitter end. My obit would have read, "Shot Down Like a Junkyard Dog." In a kind of delirium, I lost all sense of time. I do remember several forks in the road. Weaving left and right, I passed through several abandoned nopales groves, until finally, with my last remaining strength, I climbed a burned-over hillside where I collapsed behind the charred trunk of a California live oak.

I must have passed out. When I came to, I felt deep gratitude that Greg Thurston hadn't been there to witness his boss in survival mode. I phoned Tony. Couldn't tell him exactly where I was, but I described where my odyssey had begun. Then I signed off and waited.

CHAPTER THIRTY-THREE

Thirty minutes and several phone calls later, Tony arrived, accompanied by a trim Latino gentleman in a crisp blue blazer and open-necked white shirt. My cop sonar alerted. Tony was in his stakeout clothes—distressed jeans, nondescript tee-shirt under unbuttoned flannel shirt, and bandana headband. He pulled me to my feet. "What the hell happened?"

"I'm doing a whole lot better than the other fuckheads." We hugged and then stood there, both unaccountably shy. He was still the same rakish undercover detective, strapped and riding in the Mexican car—but something was different. Maybe it was one or two fresh worry lines carving his forehead, or maybe it was the unyielding look in his eyes. Roberto's death had torn him up, and I'd been doing the dirty boogie all around the killing floor.

"Nick Crane," said Tony finally, "meet Diego Smith. LASD. He's the lead homicide detective investigating Roberto's death."

"Mr. Crane." Diego offered me his hand, which I shook.

"We went to Leo's shop first," said Tony. "The place is in an uproar. Nobody seems to know quite what happened. And there's no sign of your assailants, other than the shell casings."

"Figures. Those guys are cleaners."

Diego nodded. He knew. Sophisticated criminal organizations clean up their carnage. Erase all traces whenever possible. "So, what the hell did happen?"

I told them how I'd been driving up Leo's driveway in a loaner car when I'd been ambushed by anywhere from twelve to fifteen gunmen, some dressed like Arabs, others like ordinary workmen. Explained how they'd jumped out of twin burgundy-colored Dodge cargo vans and pursued me onto the grounds of the deserted tannery next door to Leo's. Said it was entirely possible these men were part of the same organization that had murdered Roberto Diaz, but said nothing about Tony's earlier encounter at the U.S. Attorney's Office or my ordeal at Thomas Quincey's black site.

"Was anybody injured?"

I looked at Diego. Nodded. "Oh yeah! They sure were. Maybe one or two casualties, I'm not sure. It was pure hell, Officer. It's lucky I can shoot straight. Otherwise, I'd be dead."

"How did you get from the auto body shop to here?"

"Very good question. I ran like hell. I panicked when I heard the guys up on the roof of the tannery. That's when I broke and ran."

Diego, who was scribbling notes rapidly, nodded. At that moment, it hit me. Why hadn't they followed me when I ran? Something about the left hand and the right hand?

"And I assume you're licensed to carry?"

"Of course."

"And you probably didn't have the opportunity to get a license plate off either of the vans, did you?"

I frowned. "This isn't the first time their vans have been on my ass. I never seem to get a license plate number, though." Grim chuckle. Diego joined in. He seemed all right.

"We'll put out an APB…So, if you don't mind me asking an obvious question, why did they try to kill you?"

"I'm not trying to be facetious, but sometimes they don't. Some days, they want to abduct me. Other days, they want to whack me."

"Who are they?"

I pondered. "Like I told you, I'm ninety percent sure they're the same people who murdered Roberto Diaz." I looked at Tony, whose gaze flickered from me to Diego and back. Then he spoke. "I filled Diego in on how this all started. Without putting words in his mouth, I think he agrees Roberto's death was not just an ordinary informant whack job, but rather part of something larger we don't yet understand."

"I'm leaning that way." Diego frowned. "Let's ride."

We got in his Ford Explorer and drove back toward Leo's. Surprised to discover that in my frenzy, I'd covered nearly a mile before collapsing behind the oak tree. Forensics was hard at work when we got there. Yellow tape, like a guilty conscience, circled Leo's property and the tannery. Diego got out of the car. Conferred briefly with the technicians. Got back in behind the wheel. "It's like we thought. The killers didn't leave anything behind except for blood stains and shell casings, which are mostly from S&W .40 semi-automatics." He paused for a second, thinking. "Okay, Mr. Crane, I'll get a more complete statement from you later. Let's take a ride over to where Tony and I were headed when you phoned this in."

Diego drove us over to Ramboz Drive in City Terrace, where Roberto's body had been found thirteen days earlier. I phoned Bobby and told him to meet us there.

Diego parked at the base of a large hillside about the size of a football field, covered with matted brown grass and a few straggling trees. Roberto's body had been found near the top of the hill with a dog collar around his neck. A teenage girl who lived across the street had come forward on Wednesday. She had witnessed the abduction while waiting for a late-night rendezvous with her boyfriend. Recorded it on her smartphone. Roberto had arrived in his F-150 at about two a.m. A late model dark blue Dodge cargo van pulled in behind him a few minutes later. Three men wearing headscarves got out of the van. Roberto moved to greet them. Then the double cross. Two of them pointed their guns at him, and the third guy looped a chain around his neck and stuck something in his mouth. Then they dragged him up the hillside. One of the assailants came back down, unloaded some camera equipment from the van, and carried it up the hill.

"This kid is streetwise," said Diego. "She knew Diaz was going to die. She phoned her boyfriend and told him to stay away. But she didn't go back in her house. Instead, she watched from her steps, which lead up to the street. She couldn't see much, just dark forms up on the hillside. She said they were up there for about half an hour. When they finally did come down, they were laughing and high-fiving each other. Then they got in their van and drove away."

"Brave kid," I said.

Diego nodded thoughtfully. "Of course, it would've been nice if she'd phoned it in right away, but you know how that goes."

"They appear to have this thing for cargo vans."

"The funny thing is—and I've discussed this with your friend here," Diego hooked a thumb toward Tony, "something about this doesn't add up. Because it was dark and that area is poorly lit, even with the witness's video, it's hard to make out the faces and clothes of the killers. We had forensics blow up the pictures, and we looked at them under different lightings and at different resolutions.

"The killers don't appear to be Mexicans or Central Americans. They don't look like Southsiders or paisas. They're not black, but they could be white. I don't think they're Asian. They're well-dressed like they were out for a night on the town. So what are they? Or rather, who are they? Our forensics expert, Ms. Kindergrave, thinks they could be Middle Eastern, but she's going by their headscarves, which do look like something Arabs might wear."

Diego stopped. He frowned and reached into his shirt pocket as if searching for something. "Oh yeah, I forgot. I don't smoke anymore. The missus'll kick my ass." He smiled. "After talking to Ms. Kindergrave, I thought it didn't make sense. Why would three Middle Eastern guys, flashy types out for a good time, execute an LAPD drug informant? While wearing headscarves to draw attention to themselves? Sure, it's possible, but it seems unlikely. Middle Eastern guys traffic drugs like everybody else, but it hasn't been a big problem here in LA except for opium, and that's usually limited to the Persians. And in speaking to Tony here, I learned every single trafficker Roberto set up was Mexican and had cartel connections. This Arab thing doesn't smell right...unless Diaz owed them money, which Tony says is unlikely. And the funny thing is, after it was over, they didn't even bother to search his truck. They just got in their van and drove away."

I looked at Tony and he nodded. Then he spoke. "When I told Diego about us meeting Tami Wheat, I also told him about Blaylock ordering me to lay off Roberto and the part about certain federal agencies investigating human smuggling and narco-terrorism, whatever the fuck that is. I also told Diego about our trip to Culiacán."

"Tony has been very forthcoming," said Diego. His phone pinged and he checked his email. "Hmm, this is interesting. My office emailed me a video they just received. It was dropped off by a messenger service and addressed to Homicide, LASD." He smiled grimly. "That's me. Let's have a look." He was about to click on the link when Bobby drove up in his Dodge Charger. Diego paused. Bobby got out and Tony introduced him to Diego, who was kind enough to summarize what he'd told me about Roberto's murder. I gave Bobby the bare-bones version of my recent City Terrace shootout.

"Dangerous world," he said dryly. "It sounds like you did pretty good considering the odds...which doesn't surprise me. You've always been a capable bastard." Short chuckle. Then he addressed everyone. "So do any of you—especially considering the fact Nick just shot it out with half-a-dozen pretend Arabs and half-a-dozen run-of-the-mill workmen carrying semi-automatic handguns—believe actual followers of Islam had anything whatsoever to do with Roberto's death?"

"Funny you should ask," said Diego. "Let's see if this video sheds any light. We're going to have to do this two at a time." Law enforcement went first. By the halfway point, Tony was stricken. Toughed it out till the end. Then Bobby and me. Also stricken. The slaying of Roberto Diaz edited down to four minutes. A gloating man wearing a keffiyeh plunged a syringe into Roberto's right shoulder. A second man, also wearing a headscarf, planted one foot firmly on his chest. Once Roberto was unconscious, his sleeve was rolled up and tied off with a phlebotomist's cord. The first man slowly and carefully inserted a second syringe into his vein. Diego paused the video. "That's probably the potassium phosphate." The heart of the video showed Roberto in various stages of agony. At one point, the knockout shot had apparently worn off, and he seemed fully conscious, writhing around on the ground. He couldn't scream because of the gag. The "Arabs" were having a grand time, laughing and high fiving, slapping each other on the back. From there, the film panned in on the first Arab's headscarf, which appeared to be a fishnet keffiyeh, not unlike what Yasser Arafat wore back in the 1970s. As death came for Roberto, his limbs grew rigid, his head wrenched off to one side. The final shot was of a three-quarter moon, which seemed to be retreating behind the cloud cover.

Bobby was the first to speak. "ISIS loves to record their beheadings, right?"

Diego nodded and Bobby continued. "What's the tone of those ISIS abominations?"

"Over the top but somber," I said. "Ceremonial. Like a ritual slaying from a horror film."

"Exactly," said Bobby. "Sick fuckers think they're doing God's work. Or they're pretending they do. But in this video, these fools are clowning. Why?"

"You tell me," said Diego.

"I don't know why. Maybe 'cause they're amateurs. Maybe

'cause they're on drugs. Maybe 'cause they're ex-cons working for a sophisticated criminal organization. But it definitely doesn't smell right."

"You have a point there." Diego ran a hand through his thick brush cut hair. His phone rang. He answered. Spoke quietly into the mouthpiece. Hung up and faced us. "I've just been told the killers released this video to the news services. It'll be all over the internet in a few hours...Mr. Crane, I think I already know what your answer will be, but I have a legal obligation here. Given that you seem to be a primary target, do you have any interest in going into our witness protection program?"

"Nice of you to ask." I meant it. Diego seemed okay, and I suspected Tony and Bobby felt the same way. "I think I'll take my chances for the time being."

"Your call. But let me know if you change your mind."

"I will."

"Okay, men, I can't say this hasn't been interesting. Ciao, Tony, I'll be in touch."

CHAPTER THIRTY-FOUR

After Diego left, we held a war council. Of the three of us, Tony was the most visibly shaken. Naturally. It was his friend who had died in agony. He looked at me and he looked at Bobby. Then his face darkened. He shuddered. Caught himself. Waited for me to speak. When I told him Roberto's last target, Javier Fincus, was the same guy who had dimed me in Salt Lake City, he swore softly and pounded his fist into his palm. When I got to the part about stabbing Hardbody in the neck with the Buck knife, he turned away. Profound sigh and then silence. For the first time I could remember, he didn't want to meet my eye.

"Listen, Tony, we've been cocky sons of bitches for a long time. Maybe we've been too cocky. And we've been lucky as hell. But it feels different this time. This whole thing feels wrong. Spooky. We gotta figure it out. And we will...But listen, man, you were right there with me on the Constantine matter. You were vital. I couldn't have done it without you. This time around, you asked me to ride along, so I said sure. I chose to go with you to Culiacán. You didn't twist my arm. I was glad to get away for a day." I laughed, trying to cheer him up. Didn't work. "Tony, listen to me, goddamnit! I'm the one to blame for what happened at LAX. I was asleep at the wheel. Bad form. And I chose to meet with you and Tami Wheat at the Bar & Grill. And, as I believe Bobby may have mentioned, I chose to meet my new client Amina, whose real name is Adara Ghaffari, later on that evening. Now, I've gotta help her and her father Mohammad." Paused for a second. "The good news is, I've got pretty solid intel on Gloria and her sister."

Tony perked up immediately. "Yeah? What kind of intel?"

I filled him in. It was a tough call, but I said nothing about Rosie likely being dirty. Didn't want to inflame him and have him go off half-cocked. So instead, I praised Lyndon's competence and told him that with the lawyer's help, I'd checked out the foster home carefully, and the girls seemed okay. I thought, though, given their precarious immigration status, we needed to rescue them as soon as possible.

"I agree. So how in fuck are we gonna do it?"

I smiled. "Shouldn't be too hard. I've got an idea, but I've still gotta work out the details. I'll let you know as soon as I'm a little farther along."

That did the trick. Tony snapped out of his funk. We powwowed. Decided Tony would continue working with Diego without saying anything about Quincey yet. Our knowledge of the demented patrician spook was still far too nebulous. We had nothing solid at present to charge him with other than the false imprisonment of one Nick Crane. Which wasn't going to happen. No way was I going to testify at a probable cause hearing about how a gang of criminals with a loose affiliation to ICE had abducted me and locked me up in a black site because I stole Frank Constantine's federally protected "gentler, kinder" torture records back in 2011.

"Bobby, did Tucker's a.m. appointment show up to pick up the Arab costumes?"

"He did. I watched him walk out of the salon with a stack of garment bags folded over his arm. I was able to Velcro a transponder behind the left rear bumper of his Dodge cargo van while he was inside. My plan is to follow his movements with great interest."

"Hah! I bet you will. What did this joker look like?"

"Like an aristocrat wearing cool westside clothes."

"That's him. Just like Tucker said. Good work, buddy."
It was.

CHAPTER THIRTY-FIVE

Bobby and I dropped Tony off near the East LA Sheriff's Station to pick up his truck and drove back to the Cradle Rest. We stopped in Eagle Rock, where, inspired by Lyndon, I rented a Hyundai Elantra. Back at the motel, Bobby started fiddling with his tracking devices. I lay down and tossed and turned. Body exhausted, mind racing. Useless. Got up, wandered out to our "living room," and sat down facing the big screen. *Law and Order, SVU*, was on, which got me thinking about the little girls in the Munson family's single-wide trailer. My goal was simple. Liberate them. That would be hard enough. But *how* and *what* to do with them once they were in my custody? Shaking my head, I watched the TV idly. An attractive redhead was testifying in a crowded courtroom. Reminded me of someone. Yeah, Caroline Best. Only younger. Hmm...I told Bobby I was going out for a while. Didn't say why. He looked up at me. Nodded distractedly. Went back to his devices.

Caroline Best lives in a seven bedroom, seven bath house, in a posh section of Pasadena. A ten-minute drive from the Cradle Rest. Took a while to get past her Palace Guard, but she finally materialized, her long and curiously unkempt red hair hanging past her shoulders.

I met Caroline in 2011 when she hired me to find her schizophrenic son Peter's best friend, a fellow mental patient named Lou Hernandez. This was the start of the clusterfuck that led to

Frank Constantine's death and my perhaps fatal error—stealing his torture records. Caroline is a little younger than me, probably in her late forties. Her husband Walter died of leukemia three years ago after fighting it for more than a decade. It took Caroline a long time to recover, but lately (we talk every few months), she's been more chipper. She seemed happy to see me, the light playing in her warm green eyes.

She ushered me into one of her many parlors. We sat down on an antique sofa with curved back and arms and amazing gold cushions. A servant appeared with a bottle of Coppola's pinot noir and accoutrements. Poured us both glasses and left the room. Caroline razzed me about my shaved head. I shrugged. Said no sacrifice is too great for the client. That got her interest, but I steered her away from my current nightmare. Focused instead on the little girls in Ohio and how I'd recced their foster home. And how I had to rescue them before they were moved to some horrible tent city down on the border…as a preamble to something much worse.

She asked me how I planned on doing that, and I said it was a trade secret, unless she wanted to help. "And how would I do that?" She smiled but did not seem disinterested, so I told her. In broad brush strokes. She stared at me. Drank some wine. Put her glass down, picked it back up, and drank some more. Mulling it over. I sat back casually and sipped my wine. Knew this would be no easy sell. She finally spoke. "I realize you follow a different drummer than most of us, Nick, but this is absolutely crazy. I can't believe you would actually do that. Well, maybe I do believe it. And you want me to help? Jesus! I don't know whether to be flattered or terrified."

"Your choice," I said, laughing. "But this is nothing, really, compared to the moxie you showed when you escaped from Frank Constantine."

"You know what's funny?" she said, a moment later. "The most scared I ever was during my whole encounter with Frank, including all the time he had me locked up in his underground bunker, was out in the dry wash after I escaped. It must've been about three a.m. I saw something move up ahead of me, and I almost peed my pants. In fact, I did, a little." Couldn't tell if she blushed or if she was just flushed from the vino. "It was a fucking coyote, Nick, a big one with a big bushy tail. Ohmigod, it's a good thing I have a strong heart."

My chance. I pounced. "You also have a kind heart. Very. And you're a fuckin' trouper."

"My, my," said Caroline. "Such passion. I guess you really feel strongly about this."

"I do. And you would, too, if you'd been with me when I met the little girls."

"Maybe so," she said lightly. "Let me think about it."

I drained the dregs of my wine, and Caroline poured me a second glass. Time to segue. I asked her about her son Peter and his friend Lou Hernandez and their friend Charles Lenoir. My mentally challenged friends, who'd been so stalwart during the pursuit of Frank Constantine. We talked and drank slowly, Caroline's green eyes bright with reminiscence. Then she gave me a curious look—slightly glazed, fond, smiling. Or maybe I was slightly glazed. She put her wineglass down, reached out, took my right hand in both of hers. Brought it up to her mouth.

She didn't take me to her bedroom, for which I was grateful. The splendor might have killed me. The guest bedroom was fine. Persian rug on the fine old hardwood floor. Comfortable bed, snowy white quilts piled high. Caroline disappeared for a minute. I stripped down to my boxers. Got in under the top quilt. She reappeared in her bra and panties, a big, voluptuous woman with wild red hair. Everything natural. Large lovely breasts and...I won't even try to describe her ass. Not every billionaire goes in for reconstruction.

I moved toward her. She stopped me. Whispered, "Start out gentle, okay, Nick?"

Not sure what it would have been like if we hadn't been drinking. But we had been, and gentle quickly turned into a kind of controlled frenzy as we devoured each other with our mouths. Her bra fell away and her breasts tumbled into my hands. Soft, full, and oh so pleasing. I ran my tongue across her left nipple. "Harder." Obliging Crane. Obliging Caroline. It was slow and sensual and never seemed to end. She came the first time before I got inside her. Then she burst into tears, wiped her eyes, and enveloped me completely. Womanliness, thy name is Caroline.

Afterwards, I lay with my head between her breasts. Asked her what the tears were about.

She hesitated. Murmured an answer. "'Cause you're the first guy since Walter died."

I let that sink in. Murmured back that I was honored. Then I came up for air and we kissed again. This time we really were gentle…

Later, she saw me out to my car. I told her I would supply the private pilot for our flight to Ohio. I didn't want to put any of her people at risk. She regarded me skeptically. "But you're willing to put me at risk." Her sanity had returned.

"There's always risk." My prepared remarks. "I took a risk coming here and asking you for help. You could have easily said no."

"I almost did."

"I'm glad you didn't."

That's how we left it.

Back at the Cradle Rest. Bobby awash in his cyber world. "C'mere, Nick. This is fascinating." Our new target, who Bobby called AG, simply because of the Arab garb, had been busy. First NOHO, then Frogtown and the Spoke Bicycle Café on the LA River, then the Westside.

"What about Motor Avenue?"

"Negative."

Like many Nam vets, Bobby has been a news junkie for as

long as I've known him. I was starting to think about food when he turned the box on. It was all there. First, Roberto's murder. In gory detail. With some video. His death was now being referred to as the LAKS murder (the LA Keffiyeh Slaying). Then, to our utter shock, the camera panned in on Stan Timberlake's Torrance neighborhood. White vans and yellow crime tape surrounded his house. A technician disappeared into the house, and a newswoman appeared on the screen.

"This peaceful Torrance neighborhood is convulsed with shock. Today, around noon, Stanley Timberlake, a Los Angeles criminal defense lawyer and former Assistant United States Attorney, was found dead in his study. The preliminary indication is drugs may have been involved. Although the police suspect an overdose, they have not ruled out the possibility of murder. Back to you, Marvin..."

Back in the NBC studio, news anchor Marvin Kemper frowned at the camera. His colleague Stacy Yen, comely and properly subdued, stared straight ahead. "We've just been informed," said Marvin, "that the deceased lawyer, Stanley Timberlake, is the same man who left the U.S. Attorney's Office five years ago under questionable circumstances. A spokesperson, who asked not to be identified, reports law enforcement is taking this very seriously...And now, in Echo Park..."

"Damn, Nick, that's cold. Suicide or a hot shot, either way, he's dead."

CHAPTER THIRTY-SIX

Dinner at a burrito house. Then Bobby drove to City Terrace to check on his goats, and I made my way to an internet café on Green Street near the skating rink in Old Town Pasadena. There, I mined Google Images till I found a Sumerian cuneiform describing how to brew beer: *Soak grain in water and a seed begins to sprout. Dry out that tiny protoplant, or acrospire, roast it, and you've got malt—the basis for fermenting beer.* Saved the link. Created an email address: SumerianHistorian59@gmail.com. Logged on and sent the link to Mohammad. A kind of cyber therapy. Out into the clear, cool October night, feeling strangely lucid...

Back at the Cradle Rest, I sketched out a rough map on a fresh piece of whiteboard. Motor Avenue was point #1, Ramboz Street in East LA #2, Tucker's salon #3, and so on. I added numbers for Leo's auto body shop, the Spring Street courthouse, and Torrance. Then I drew a line pointing east. Salt Lake City was #7, Chicago #8, Boston #9, and Nashua #10. Skipped southern Ohio. Unrelated to the Quincey matter. I sat there committing the numbers and coordinates to memory.

My thoughts strayed to Timberlake. Murder or suicide? Either way, like Bobby said, he was dead. I emailed Tony and asked him to call me on Bobby's cell in the morning.

One of my burners chirped. Audrey. Parked outside. Dressed in jeans and a knitted pullover sweater. And her chic leather vest. I helped her carry stuff in. Clothes and supplies. Two M26C Taser guns and a couple of spandex hoods she'd retrieved from one of our storage lockers. Could not survive without Audrey. She's the only one who knows where we keep all our hardware. After we'd unloaded, we sat down with cold Heinekens.

"Tell me the truth, Nick. Things are bad, aren't they?"

I shrugged. "Nothing Bobby and I can't handle."

"That's all you're going to tell me? You drive me crazy. I have nightmares in which I try to figure out what's going on."

I smiled. For ten years, I've been protecting Audrey from the dark side. "I tell you what I can…and what you need to know. Let's talk about *your* work."

Bingo! Audrey loves talking about her adultery cases—the suffering the wronged ladies endure (can go the other way, of course) and the sweaty gymnastics of the illicit lovers cavorting behind drawn motel shades. The horrible moment of truth when they realize they've been filmed and exposed. The frenzied pleas to make a deal. Their outrage because the deal is always bad. I let Audrey talk till she'd finished her beer and gently steered her toward the door.

Sixty seconds later, Jack Snow's dedicated burner chirped.

"Hello, Jack."

"Good, Nick! Glad I got you. We need to talk."

He sounded excited. Rare for Jack.

"I've been saying that for years. Where do you want to meet?"

"I don't care. Anywhere. I just left MDC. They threw me out at closing time."

We decided on an independent coffee shop named Clyde's Beans near the corner of Pasadena and Figueroa south of Highland Park. Open till midnight on Fridays. When I arrived, I found Jack in a booth, staring at a yellow legal pad. He'd put in his usual monster week. Didn't matter. He was bright-eyed and perky as ever.

"It's been quite a day, my friend."

I nodded. "Every day lately, it seems."

"So what's this about you and Bobby being on the DL?"

"Stopgap measure. I hope it won't be for very long. I love the big guy, but he gets on my nerves with his electronics obsession." I grimaced. "So what gives, Jack? What do you know that I don't know that I need to know?"

Jack smiled, revealing strong, square-blocked yellow teeth. He glanced around. Sipped his coffee. Then he spoke in a quiet voice. "Remember when you stopped in at my office on Friday night two weeks ago, and we discussed a couple of legal stalwarts who just might be on a pad?"

"I do remember. I was envious of your admin's brilliantly organized database."

"For good reason. But listen, some things have come down you need to know about. Stanley Timberlake was found dead at his house. Apparently, from a heroin overdose."

"I saw that on the news. Maybe a suicide."

"That's what they're saying. But there's more to it than that."

"There usually is."

Jack explained that based on Timberlake's death by overdose, Sam Blaylock, his alleged drug supplier, was facing a potential second-degree murder charge and was already under arrest for taking bribes and money laundering. With a possible RICO charge in the offing.

"So I guess somebody's been watching Blaylock for a while?"

"So it appears," said Jack. "An independent AUSA, I imagine. Timberlake's death was the smoking gun they'd been waiting for."

Out of curiosity, Jack had stopped by MDC to talk to Blaylock. To find out what he could about Blaylock and Timberlake's unholy union. Maybe even get retained. When he got there, Blaylock was already down in a visiting room talking to an AUSA named Charles Landis.

"Sam was graveyard pale," said Jack. "He looked awful. Landis, who's a RICO and Public Corruption guy, looked totally bored. I told Sam I was there to see him when Landis was through. Then, I waited in one of the visiting rooms."

"And then?" Hearing about other people's problems always makes me feel better.

"You know how these things work." Jack smiled. "Hope springs eternal in the heart of the felon. For starters, Sam wants to get out on bond. He says he didn't tell Landis 'a goddamned thing.' I don't suppose you'd have time to help me put together his bail motion?"

I smiled. "Of course. Though my assistant Audrey will do most of the heavy lifting. She writes good bail reports. I'll have her contact you in the morning. Who's the judge?"

"The Honorable Cynthia Charles. Could be worse. Is ten enough to cover it?"

Ten stacks is nearly always enough for a bail report, but I pretended to consider. "Sure. Make the check out to Nick Crane & Associates, or better yet, wire it straight into my account."

"I will. As soon as I'm officially retained…So Sam and I are sitting there, and the first thing he tells me is he's got to get out on bond quickly because he's strung out on heroin…"

"So I've heard," I said slowly.

Jack gave me a 'how do you know' look. "Have you ever seen a junkie in the midst of withdrawals?"

I shook my head. "Only in the movies."

"It's a pathetic sight. Fortunately, the MDC staff was prepared. They'd given Sam his own personal puke bucket…Sam and Timberlake have been on the edge for a long time now. Sam said it started when they went on the pad five years ago. Right from day one, the traffickers started lobbing boatloads of drugs at them."

"Why heroin?"

"Why not? It gets you high. Then the traffickers cut them off when they realized they were getting strung out. Though they kept doing business otherwise. Strange as it sounds, for the last three years, Sam has been scoring seven-dollar bags of lightly stepped-on Mexican brown from an El Salvadorean parking lot attendant near Fourth and Broadway."

"Makes sense. Keep it in the neighborhood."

"Sam's been passing on half of his stash to Timberlake. Thus, the pending capital charges."

"Hmm…Can they make that stick? Timberlake's a big boy."

"Correction. Timberlake *was* a big boy. At the very least, they can use it as a bargaining chip in plea negotiations. Though it might not be admissible at trial if Sam fights the bribery and money laundering charges." Jack explained that with the help of some serious hand-holding, he'd slowly extracted Sam's story. Five years ago, the DEA took down a coke dealer named Javier Fincus. Javier's people retained Timberlake and offered a six-figure bonus on top of a $100,000 retainer if they could work something out. Timberlake turned to Sam, who, by fate or circumstance, was assigned to the case. In return for some bullshit cooperation, Mr. Fincus got time served.

"Which was how long?"

"Umm," Jack ran a hand through his spiky hair, "no more than two or three months."

"And, of course, the government didn't appeal."

"Bastards couldn't be bothered," said Jack with a grin.

"When the devil taps you on the shoulder," I said, "a bright boy kicks him in the balls…Just so you know, I'm acquainted with Mr. Fincus, and I can state without reservation, the guy is a scumbag."

"Not a *bon homme* guy," said Jack drily. "But something is definitely rotten. There's no way an AUSA would recommend a twelve-week, time-served deal for twenty kilos and negligible cooperation unless he was on a serious pad."

"Hmm. How much money are we talking about? Total?"

"The government is claiming the bribes totaled well over one million dollars, but Sam insists it's less than half of that. Even so, he'll be facing seventy months under the sentencing guidelines unless we can come up with some powerful factors in mitigation. This is where your office comes in. I suppose that'll cost another ten?"

I shrugged. "That sounds about right. Maybe a little more. I'm not against gouging a corrupt AUSA now and then. But let's wait till you get retained. Then we can talk about it...By the way, did Blaylock mention a man named Miles Amsterdam?"

"No. Should he have?"

"Possibly. Wait till he's out on bond. Gain his trust. Then you follow the smell...Last question. Does Sam know who Javier's people are?"

Jack hesitated. Thought about it. "I think he does, but we haven't got there yet."

"You will."

That's where we left it.

CHAPTER THIRTY-SEVEN

Back to the Cradle Rest. Bobby in black jeans and a dark blue sweatshirt, striding from room to room, iPhone in hand, riveted to his readout. Looked my way, frowned. Back to his screen. Thirty seconds later, he spoke, "C'mere, Nick. You're gonna like this."

I grunted something sour and he told me to fuck off. I shaped up and listened as—with the help of the readout—Bobby described AG's recent wanderings. Fifteen minutes later, we were driving west on the Santa Monica Freeway in Bobby's recently rented Altima. The night was clear and luminous. Bobby goosed the accelerator, vying with the caravan of high-end rides and designer SUV's nightcrawling toward the ocean.

We were carrying four sidearms, two Tasers, two spandex hoods, and two brand new G700 military flashlights. North on 405, west on Sunset, right on Capri, winding up into Pacific Palisades, Bobby driving with one hand, fingering his tracking device with the other. He finally pulled over to the side of the road. "Look, Nick. Check this out. He hasn't moved." There on the illuminated screen, a dark-colored cargo van was parked along what appeared to be a rutted road at the bottom of a canyon.

"God knows why AG is skulking around the old World War II Rustic Canyon Nazi encampment." A note of triumph in Bobby's voice. "Maybe you're like me and would like to find out why."

"I am like you."

"We've got two choices. We can try to drive in, but if we hit a locked gate, we're screwed. We won't even be able to turn around. I say we hike it."

Which meant walking up a pitted, one-lane asphalt road. The residential streetlights faded into nothingness and the wind kicked up. Glad to be wearing one of my thigh-length, flannel-lined jean jackets over a sweatshirt over a denim shirt. Had my sidearms and two spandex hoods folded up in my right jacket pocket. Bobby carried the Tasers and his pistols. We each carried our own flashlight. Bobby was in his element. He had been tracking AG for twelve solid hours. But we were careful. Nothing about us 'closing in.' No jinx. A half-mile up the road, we came to an unlocked orange gate, which marked the actual entrance to the canyon.

"AG's not too careful, is he?" said Bobby. "We could have driven in."

"Probably better this way. Harder to spot us."

More rugged and closer to the ocean than Laurel and Benedict Canyons, Rustic Canyon is mostly undeveloped. Just the Nazi camp, a Boy Scout camp farther in, and occasional eccentric dwellings. We stopped at an overlook that sighted south and west toward Santa Monica and the ocean.

"Damn," said Bobby. "Right about now, I could do with some seafood. Abalone sounds good, with horseradish and olive oil. And a hint of lime." He laughed and punched me in the shoulder. We stood on the promontory trying to pick out the coastal landmarks. 100 Wilshire, the twenty-one-story high-rise on the corner of Wilshire and Ocean. Farther south, the Santa Monica pier. Venice Beach farther still. But the sky was too bright, the air too cold. I shivered. Folded my arms across my chest. Shivered some more. Bobby felt it too. We were silent for a long time.

"Listen, Nick," said Bobby finally, "I hate to admit it, but this whole affair has got me spooked. It was bad to start with, but then that detective had to go and show us that snuff film." I looked at him. His face half-hooded in darkness. I wanted to say something. But didn't know what. This case had nothing to do with Bobby. Nothing in it for him. He should walk away. But I knew he wouldn't. Not now. Not ever. So I told him how happy I'd been to see him standing there at five a.m. in the Golden Nugget parking lot in Vegas, scaring the crap out of the locals. "You looked like goddamned Hercules."

"Felt like him too. 'Cause I was driving a rocket." Bobby grimaced, teeth brown from decades of hard living. "Took me three cups of coffee and a lot of bad country music to make it from Baker to Vegas." He grimaced again, like his teeth were hurting. "Let's go, Nick. Our West LA buddy doesn't know it yet, but we're crashing his costume party."

Bobby filled me in as we hustled up the trail. The camp had been built by an American Nazi named Schmidt back in the 1930s. With the help of four or five million dollars ponied up by fellow travelers, Schmidt built a series of concrete and wooden structures deep in the canyon, along with a massive reservoir, fuel tanks, multiple cisterns, and two brick smokehouses. The Feds allegedly shut it down right after Pearl Harbor.

There were three ways in. Through the worn brass gates that mark the formal entrance or down either of two steeply pitched, concrete staircases that drop hundreds of feet from the road to the canyon floor. When we came to the first staircase, visible through a break in the chain-link fence, Bobby stopped and checked his readout. "The van hasn't moved." He looked at me. "It's go time."

Our flashlights on low, we started down. With extreme caution. The angle was steep and every second or third step was crumbling. Heavy brush on either side of us. Took me right back to the murderous assault on Leo's driveway. My heart racing, I took several deep breaths. Tried to count the steps and kept losing track, but it calmed me down…

There was a second asphalt road at the bottom of the staircase. "Either way," said Bobby, "this road loops into the main compound. Don't move. I'll be right back." He turned right and faded into the darkness. In his mind, he was back in the Vietnamese highlands, leading his men across treacherous terrain, Charlie in the shadows, the fear palpable under the ancient hardwood trees. And those were the good days. I waited patiently. Ten minutes later, Bobby reappeared, a broad, crouching gargoyle of a man. He gestured and we headed left down the road.

We came to the powerhouse, a dark, abandoned two-story building layered in graffiti. I waited in the shadows across the road while Bobby did a perfunctory search.

"Empty. For a long time. Ditto the bomb shelter in back."

The next structure was hardly a structure, just a haphazard pile of rusted machinery inside the skeletal remains of a machine shed. The Dodge van was parked off to the right. Bobby started toward it, stopped, shot me a glance. I shook my head. First, AG. We walked past the ruined shed and came to a chain link barricade with a No Trespassing sign and a cutaway area to allow for foot traffic.

"That's why he parked back there." I gestured back toward the ruined shed. "You can't drive in any farther."

Bobby nodded, his eyes hooded. Shouldered his way through the opening. The road turned into a trail. Then we heard it—a rumble in the near distance that sounded like a piece of machinery. The trail narrowed and the sound grew louder. We passed the rusted husk of an old automobile. Rounded a bend and came to the source of the sound, a generator, dimly lit by crude outdoor lighting. Beyond it rose a sharply pitched, red-brick smokehouse, perhaps fifteen feet tall.

We crossed the clearing, clicked off our flashlights, and waited in the gloom under a brace of sycamores. Ten minutes stretched into twenty. No one came or went. The noise of the generator, at first so jarring, seemed to realign itself into a loud but comforting hum. Bobby started to nod off. I let him doze for a while, then reached out and nudged him back awake.

"Shit, Nick. What'd you do that for? I was having a good dream." He yawned. "For all we know, he's asleep in there." Bobby gestured toward the smokehouse.

"Cheap rent."

"Very funny, asshole. That's where they keep the prisoners."

Bobby was itching to get moving, but I wanted to wait till AG tipped his hand. "C'mon, Bobby. You got us here. 'Cause you're a brilliant investigator. But now, we can't rush things. Why don't you go back and search the van? I'll give you a hood in case you run into AG. If you do, use your own judgment."

I extracted a spandex hood from my jean jacket pocket and held it out to him. He snatched it out of the air and stumped back up the trail. Bobby's irritability is legendary among us, the few and the lucky who know him well. He is not necessarily the kind of guy you bring home to mother. But he knows a few things worth knowing, and I knew I could count on him. Fast as I am, and even though I can street fight and box, I would never want to go up against Bobby *mano a mano*.

He was gone a full thirty minutes but finally reappeared, wreathed in shadows, angling toward me. Now his mood was different. "Real interesting, Nick. Better than I expected. Not quite search and destroy. More like penetrate and analyze. The van just happened to be unlocked. The back is hollowed out—a big flat space with storage cabinets along the sides. It's registered to a company called Fletcher Moss, Ltd. out of La Jolla. I wrote it all down." Teeth stained dark in the half-light.

"Keep going." I sensed the best was still to come.

"First, I searched the storage cabinets. Lots of tools—wrenches, hammers, hacksaws, screwdrivers—and several boxes of S&W cartridges. And, of course, Clejuso handcuffs and leg irons, which is about what you'd expect from these Nazis. But the best part was a box of syringes pre-packed with Versed. I copped a dozen. When the cortisol becomes unbearable, there are few things better than a shot of Versed to take the edge off. But the big surprise was the garbage bags. On the floor..." Bobby paused. Quantum shift. A bright part of my brain dropped into darkness.

"The garbage bags," said Bobby slowly, "are full of women's clothes—cheap designer labels, jeans, dresses, lingerie, teddies with peek-a-boo cutouts, hot stuff if you catch my drift..."

"I can see you made a study of this..."

"Naturally. But that's not the point. The point is: Why are half the items too small for full-grown women?"

Again, the quantum shift. Could swear another part of my brain went black.

"We're back," said Bobby. "Church of the poisoned mind..."

We stared at each other there in the half-light. Somehow, given the dark possibilities I'd witnessed at the Munson farm, I wasn't totally surprised. I told him we'd wait ten more minutes. Then if AG didn't appear, we'd hit the smokehouse.

Five minutes later, AG came strolling down the road, a high-powered flashlight in his right hand. Wearing a keffiyeh and a white and blue striped tunic, courtesy of Tucker's salon, his left hand firmly grasping the hand of a dark-haired girl in a loose, short-sleeved blouse and tight jeans...that showed off her half-formed curves.

A kind of growl erupted in Bobby's throat. He started towards them and I yanked him back. He pivoted and shoved me hard. I stumbled and righted myself. He stood there staring, his eyes so full of pain I could hardly stand it. "C'mon, Nick! We can't let him take her in there." His hoarse whisper was chilling.

The steady hum of the generator muffled Bobby's voice, and AG never looked our way. "Relax. The damage is already done. He's dropping her off. We'll arrest him on his way out. I don't want the little girl to see it. It'll scare her even more. But remember, he's got intel. We gotta be careful."

Bobby snorted, hating me for implying he might screw things up. Hating himself, too, for hating me. But more than anything, he hated the tall white man in the keffiyeh. Which I understood completely. You shadow someone with the intention of taking him down. You usually have a pretty good idea what his crimes are—both the mortal and the venial. But this was a shocker.

We watched AG lead the girl around to the back of the smokehouse. Barely audible rasp of a metal gate or grille. Two minutes later, we skirted the tree line and took up a position directly behind the smokehouse. The gate, backlit from inside and partly illuminated by the crude outdoor lighting, was about four feet tall. Made of strips of steel welded to a rectangular steel frame. Unlatched and half-ajar. A smaller gate, large enough for a mid-sized child, was hinged to the grille. Behind the gate, a full-sized metal door, closed. We waited, flattening ourselves against the brickwork on either side of the gate...

CHAPTER THIRTY-EIGHT

AG had his keys out and was about to lock the gate when I slipped the hood over his head. Bobby hit him hard, straight shot to the midsection. AG crumpled and I held him down. Bobby plunged a syringe of Versed into his shoulder. Big nurse delivering a most emphatic flu shot. AG thrashed about for sixty seconds, then lay still. We searched him. Nothing much. Just a .40 caliber S&W standard issue semi-automatic and a couple of Ka-Bar hunting knives in their stock leather sheaths, along with keys, two smart phones, and a wallet.

Popped the clip out of the gun and stuffed everything into my inner jacket pockets. Tried the inner door to the smokehouse. The knob turned easily. Found myself staring into darkness. Flicked on my flashlight. A sharp intake of breath. Furtive eyes blinking and looking away. Others staring like burning coals. Looking into such a private place was not for heathens such as me. I closed the door. Relief and guilt in equal measure. Bobby locked the gate and we conferred. A hellish decision, but Bobby agreed. Wrong as it felt to leave the females there, rescuing them at this point would be premature. First, we needed intel. We helped our half-comatose captive to his feet and marched him up the trail. No resistance from AG. He tripped once but I grabbed him on the way down. Back at the van, we trussed him up in his own Clejuso cuffs and leg irons and laid him down amidst the bags of women's clothing. Then we got in, Bobby behind the wheel, me in back, keeping an eye on our new companion.

Ninety minutes later at around four a.m., we began interrogating AG in our own "black site," a bare bones office in an old, deserted hay barn off Brown Mountain Truck Road in the foothills north of Altadena. The place had once belonged to Frank Constantine. This is where Frank's double-dealing lieutenant, Henry Taylor, shot him from the trees with a Ruger SR9 while Tony and Bobby and I watched. Frank was waving a pipe bomb, and I was pleading with him to surrender, to opt for the insanity defense. It might have worked. Frank had pedigree. But he was beyond reason. So Henry Taylor shot him, which probably saved all of our lives. Frank's estate has been deserted ever since. The two-story faux Colonial house at the end of the long driveway was boarded up, and the barn and corral have become a refuge for small animal life…and very occasional interrogations…like the one we were about to conduct.

We propped our chained and hooded captive up in a rickety chair and sat across from him—Bobby in a sprung office chair, me on top of a battered teakwood desk. Behind AG a single casement window sighted off into the gloom.

"This could get ugly, podna." Bobby's melodious drawl belied the menace in his words. "But it doesn't need to. I'm Jack and this here's my partner Grant. We have questions. You better have answers. First, why are you fools running around disguised as Arabs? This is not an Errol Flynn movie. Second, why did you murder Roberto Diaz? He was a family man. End of story. Third, what were you doing with that young girl up at the Nazi encampment? And last, who the fuck are you?"

"You needn't be so rude," said AG calmly in the cultured tones of someone who had grown up with a polo pony cropping grass outside his bedroom window. "I'll answer your questions, but only if you take this hood off. I suffer from claustrophobia, and I'm right on the verge of a panic attack."

A captive man usually looks small under a hood. AG was no exception. "Taking your hood off is not out of the question," I said. "If and when we come to an understanding. So first, why the Arab disguises?"

"Isn't it obvious? Certain zealots are conducting false flag operations to fan the fear of Muslim terrorists while deeply offending the real jihadists. It's not a bad tactic. Of course, you have to be insane to do it." He paused. "I'm dead set against it. But what you need to understand is I'm working undercover investigating these guys. And you're interfering with my work. It's called obstruction of justice, which, if I'm not mistaken, is both a state and federal offense. Next question…"

"By certain zealots, you mean Thomas Quincey."

"True, but he's not the only one."

Interesting. Moving on. "Why did Quincey order the murder of Roberto Diaz?"

"I don't recognize the name. Who's Roberto Diaz?"

"Maybe this will help you remember." Bobby jumped off the desk, set himself, and delivered a reminder to the man's midsection. AG groaned and doubled up in his chair.

"Love taps, podna. Now answer the question."

AG moaned, tried to straighten up, failed, and waited, tensing himself for another blow. I shook my head and Bobby sat back down.

"Where do you get the girls?"

"You have to promise not to hit me again. I'm sixty-two years old. I haven't done anything to you. Why are you using me as a punching bag?"

"You haven't seen Jack go really berserk," I said. "It's not a pretty sight. Where do you get the girls?"

"Where do you think? They're illegals, detained by ICE at the border. By law, if you don't have proper paperwork, ICE takes you into custody. You have the right to seek political asylum, and some illegals do obtain permanent residency. But that's pretty rare. Most detainees are deported."

"Yeah, I get that. But aren't the girls supposed to be housed at a federal detention facility?"

"Of course. They are at a federal detention center. ICE has the legal authority to set up temporary facilities to combat overcrowding. Would you rather they were held in some overcrowded and understaffed hellhole down on the border?"

"You're a real politician, ain'tcha?" said Bobby.

"What were you doing with that young girl you took into the smokehouse?"

"Smokehouse?" AG clasped his cuffed hands together. "There's no smokehouse. Oh, you mean that red brick building? For your information, I dropped the girl off with her mother. And just so you know, no one is being gassed, burned, or tortured. That little girl, who's very smart for her age, is delighted to be safe in that shelter with her mother. The girls and mothers are supposed to be kept separate for interrogation purposes."

"Fuck you and your interrogation purpose bullshit," Bobby burst in. Beside himself. Literally jumping up and down. "You piece of shit. You piece of pure shit." I slid in between AG and Bobby, who smacked one huge fist into the other and sat back down.

"You probably missed the other shelter on your way in," said AG calmly. "The small one is for the girls. Because I have a heart, I bend the rules for the sake of the children."

"And because I have a heart, I'm keeping my partner from beating you to death. Now that I understand how the girls came to be there in your prison compound, perhaps you could explain what you do with them."

"Certainly. I feed them and clothe them. And try to comfort them when they're sad or lonely."

"So you're their minder, right?"

"You could say that."

"How many under-aged girls?"

"Four. Dolores, Teresa, Tamara, and Amy Li Kong. They're really nice girls. I have to force myself not to get attached to them. Dolores is Colombian and Teresa is the younger member of a mother-daughter team from Guadalajara. Tamara is Ukrainian. Her mother wants to marry an American man. Amy Li is Korean. And so it goes. Everyone has a story in the theater of poverty and despair. Teresa is the girl I was walking with."

"So your job, then," said Bobby, "when you're not feeding and dressing or comforting the girls, is to pimp them out to fat cats."

AG threw up his cuffed hands. "Ridiculous! That's so insulting. I would never be part of anything so loathsome." Aggrieved. To a fault.

"Glad to hear it. Only one problem. Why did my partner find children's lingerie among the women's clothes in the back of your van?"

"That's news to me," said AG quickly. He shook his head under the hood. Pulled himself fully upright and spoke firmly. "Maybe they like to play dress-up. Although I was driving that van, I didn't load it. The supplies are purchased at closeouts by one of the shoppers."

"You fuckhead! You absolute fuckhead!" Bobby jumped to his feet. Again, I had to slide in between him and AG.

"Look, fool, my partner and I think you and Tragg and this Thomas Quincey-Miles Amsterdam prick are pimping out those children. You're right in the middle of it. The facilitator." It hit me hard and my throat tightened.

I looked at Bobby and motioned toward the door. We stepped out of the office into the barn, which was an explosion of rusted machinery, moldy hay bales, burlap sacks of undetermined content, and animal droppings.

I took a deep breath. Then another. Had to slow my heart rate down. "Don't worry, Bobby. These pricks are going down."

"Yeah? How?"

I hesitated. I knew this thing about the children was killing Bobby. Full disclosure is just another word for terror.

"Listen, Bobby. We'll figure it out. But our timing has to be right." I shivered. Something my deceased DOJ friend Hec Green told me while we were on the hunt for Frank Constantine. *The higher up the food chain you go, the better people get at concealing their actual intentions. And the harder it is to know when they're lying.*

"I know," said Bobby, "you're the surprise attack guy and I'm the berserker."

"All I know is we've got to take it slow and read this guy. Listen to his lies and figure out what he's not telling us."

We went back into the interrogation room.

CHAPTER THIRTY-NINE

"Did you miss us?" said Bobby cheerfully.

"I missed you, Bobby Moore," said AG calmly, "but not your snakehead partner. We know you served our country bravely. Though I do wish you would stop hitting me every time you don't get your way. Nonetheless, there is something engaging about you. Perhaps it's your lack of guile and the fact your brand of violence is not that of a programmed killer. We would prefer to let you go your own way. It's your bad luck, though, to be tangled up with Mr. Crane, your own personal albatross. He's the man with the big X on his back. He's the man who led the lynch mob that harried poor Frank to his grave…"

He had made us. Maybe while driving over to the old hay barn? Or maybe during the interrogation, based on the nature of our questions?

AG had a wonderful ability to spin the facts of Frank Constantine's death. The truth was, Frank died because his trusted assistant, Henry Taylor, had the presence of mind to shoot him through the head from his vantage point in the trees when Frank was about to blow us all, including himself, to kingdom come with a pipe bomb. A weapon that, oddly enough, Henry had built for Frank in the first place.

So AG spun. Spin and spill. Spill and spin. He talked, we listened. He said his name was James Franklin Rowe. He said we had a few friends among the principals, but we had far more enemies. And that Hec Green, who'd pulled strings to locate Frank Constantine's foothill hideaway, had been much-loved by both moderates and hardliners. And how Hec's last act before his fatal heart attack a few weeks after Frank's death had been to arrange for Frank's torture records to be returned to the military forthwith and as discreetly as possible. The unidentified agency with the brown cargo vans had arrived first, however.

But as with any story with too many tellers, as it made the rounds, the actual facts devolved. In one alarming version, I was the one who procured Frank's female victims, the proverbial lambs for slaughter. Frank's murderous rampage would never have happened without Crane supplying the bait.

But what really caught my attention was this. James Franklin Rowe said my recent gun battle at Leo's auto repair shop had been a kind of initiation. One or more of the principals were responsible. And one of them, at the last possible moment, had told the men on the roof to stand down. Which was why I was still alive. "I have tremendous respect for my colleague, who will remain unnamed," said Rowe. Oddly, he compared my initiation to that of a Spartan youth sent out into the countryside at age thirteen to survive for three days by tooth and claw before being allowed back into the barracks.

I didn't believe Rowe. Not really. Hard to believe anyone could have timed the battle so precisely. Maybe the guys on the roof were lookouts? But that, too, seemed unlikely...

"Now, Mr. Crane, I do want to make one thing clear. I did not sign off on the attack. In fact, I vigorously opposed it. You could easily have been killed, and I'm surprised you weren't. But you did demonstrate a certain pluck. Much as we find your lack of patriotism distasteful and, frankly, a tad alarming, based on what you've shown us so far, we're ready to discuss you coming on board in some capacity. And in this age of accelerating disorder with the Constitution in peril, I don't recommend waiting a day longer than necessary."

Quincey all over again. Recruitment pitch. Smooth and brazen like a master jewel thief or cool jazz on heroin. Despite being shackled with a hood over his head. Then came the next peculiar revelation. Charges were to be brought against Thomas Quincey, the man now calling himself Miles Amsterdam. Rowe was there to help build the case against him. In his zeal to protect America, bitter truths, which came as no surprise to more cynical or worldly men, had demoralized Quincey. He had become increasingly unstable, which caused much head-scratching. The practical men who keep the ship afloat were well aware that complex circumstances sometimes call for the ability to step out of the line of fire and think things through. Which Quincey had not been able to do. A good soldier who served four tours of duty in Iraq, it had been a rugged road, and Quincey had become unhinged.

Off-the-book escapades require money. Quincey had turned to drug trafficking and money laundering. Rowe believed the case against him would be airtight. A slam dunk in federal court. Quincey would have no choice other than to cooperate and plead guilty to conspiracy to traffic cocaine and methamphetamine. He'd serve a few years in a protected federal facility. Since he had never been officially a part of any government agency, he could be prosecuted like any ordinary felon. His unsanctioned hijinks would recede into memory like the remnants of a guilty conscience. While Frank Constantine was still seen as a good and patriotic soul who had been undone by inner demons, Quincey, a man of great courage and resolve, was thought to be fatally flawed, in the end a slave to his own stubborn pride.

"Very few people could have done what Thomas did," said Rowe sadly. "He averted the deaths of hundreds of Americans and saved the beautiful library from extreme damage when he wrestled the suicide bomber into submission. But damnation, man, now he's gone over the edge. And can you please take off this hood?"

"We're almost there. First, tell me what you're leaving out."

A long silence. Bobby yawned, and Rowe finally shook his head. "I don't know what you're talking about."

"Well, then, let me put it this way. What happened to Quincey in 'Raq? Why did he come back unhinged?"

Another long silence. When Rowe spoke, I could hear real sorrow in his voice. "That's what we all ask ourselves. We know that mistakes were made, but of the kind that could happen to anyone."

"What sort of mistakes?"

"I'm not privy to the details."

Rage. I stood up. Started toward him. Stopped. Sat back down. Perhaps Rowe got the message. He spoke in a wheedling tone. "What I do know is when Quincey returned from Al-Anbar Province, he had turned into a fanatical isolationist. He insisted we had no business in the Middle East. None, the oil notwithstanding. His primary focus became keeping America safe from terrorists here at home. This, in turn, became a kind of megalomania. The man is on the brink of madness."

"Poor baby. This is the man who ordered the murder of Roberto Diaz."

"I already told you," said Rowe. "I don't recognize the name."

Bobby let out his breath. Time to change gears. He said, "But if your job is to build a case against Quincey, how come you're working for him up at the Nazi compound?"

"Fair question. Thomas got a call from a certain ranking principal. He was told to put me to work. We already knew each other from our State Department work in the nineties. At a certain point, Thomas asked me to take over monitoring the female detainees. His everyday thugs were incapable of handling them with even a modicum of decency. For a while, Tami Wheat was getting called in daily to put out fires."

"Tami" again. Interesting. So Rowe undoubtedly knew about my black site abduction, which meant he probably knew about Roberto's murder. "I like Tami. The way you like a retrovirus. But just out of curiosity, where is Quincey's office?"

"When I first got here, it was at One World Trade Center in Long Beach. Thomas still rents it, but it's mostly empty now..."

"So I suppose the black site on Motor Avenue is his real office now?"

Rowe hesitated. We waited as he gathered his thoughts. "I wouldn't say it's his office. I think he only uses it for interrogations. Wasn't that your experience, Mr. Crane?" He laughed. Shade of sarcasm. But no bite. He fell silent. He'd done a lot of talking. We'd done a lot of listening. Bobby stood up and walked over to the window behind Rowe's chair. Stared out into the half-light. Dawn bathing the foothills to the east.

"One more question. Where does Quincey live?"

"That's a tough one. He lives nowhere and everywhere. I think he stays with friends, mostly on the Westside, and he may have a place of his own. We communicate by phone and meet in public places—restaurants, bars, sometimes in parks. Thomas is a bit of a health nut..."

I nodded to Bobby and we stepped outside. Stood shoulder to shoulder, gazing at the rock outcroppings at the top of the hill behind Frank's house. The obvious decision was to release and monitor Rowe. Better than dragging him around with us or locking him up in a safe house. Better to have him in the field. Bobby counted off our goals in no particular order on his thick stubby fingers: liberate the girls and women, including the two little girls in Southern Ohio; liberate Adara and Mohammad; bring Roberto Diaz's murderers to justice; and finally, neutralize or liquidate Quincey, Tragg, and Tami Wheat. This is where it got tricky, mining the inscrutable layers of the principals' agenda. Connecting the pieces. The who's, why's, and wherefore's of the steadily expanding chess match...I sighed and Bobby grunted. We returned to the barn to fetch our new asset.

CHAPTER FORTY

The October dawn cut purple runners in the sky behind us as we drove west on 210. I rode in back next to Rowe, Bobby behind the wheel, slapping himself to stay awake, belting out scraps of Nirvana in his raspy baritone.

One of Rowe's phones trilled just after we'd turned north off Sunset onto Capri. "Answer it," I said. "Put it on speaker."

Rowe frowned and elbowed himself to a sitting position. "Good morning, Blink. I trust you slept well."

"Good enough, I guess. Had me some freakoid dreams." Blink's voice was flat and bored. "I'm fifteen minutes from camp. I'll meet you there."

"Sounds good. You've got the day's supplies, right?"

"'Course I do. Breakfast, lunch, and dinner. And plenty of water. Why wouldn't I have them?"

"Just following through. I'll see you in a few minutes." Rowe signed off.

When we came to Casale, where we'd left the Altima the night before, Bobby turned right, flipped a U-ey, and parked. "Okay, Rowe," I said. "We're gonna cut you loose." We wrote down his cell numbers and dialed them. They checked out. I unlocked his handcuffs and leg irons and gave him back his stuff. The deal was we'd check in twice a day. Eleven a.m., eleven p.m. His job, among other things, was to get us intel on Tragg and Quincey's whereabouts. And Tami Wheat for good measure. But our main goal for the moment was to liberate the girls and women and close down the Nazi camp. Had to be. Of course, we didn't tell Rowe that. We told him if he tried to shake us, we'd hunt him down and execute him Red Chinese style. A single bullet to the back of the skull.

Rowe made one last pitch. Told us to step back into the shadows and wait. Told us if we would be patient, Quincey would be in federal detention before Thanksgiving. I told him no thanks. We got out of the van and watched as Rowe climbed slowly out of the back seat and into the front. Then we got in Bobby's car and pretended to drive away. Circled the block and watched Rowe pull slowly away from the curb. Three minutes later, a second dark blue cargo van trundled up the roadway toward the compound.

No need to speak. We knew what we had to do. Back on the trail, we checked our weapons. Bobby produced a brace of granola bars. A blotchy, overcast morning, the sun simmering behind a cloud bank. We hustled and were dripping sweat by the time we reached the staircase. The five hundred steps dropping to the canyon floor were surreal in the early morning light, the sky a bruise of brown and gray. Scrub oak and manzanita. Occasional wildlife scuttling through the heavy brush. When we reached the bottom, we turned right and looped around to the main road, then left into the compound.

The first strange thing was the dog. As we approached the power station, a border collie came bounding toward us. Saw us. Stopped dead as if throated by an iron chain and slunk away into the underbrush. Bobby shook his head. "Motherfucker better not be rabid."

The vans were parked side-by-side, their noses nearly touching the rusted debris spilling out of the ruined machine shed. Bobby looked at me. I nodded. He walked briskly to the second van and planted a bug inside the left rear bumper.

Then the second strange thing. A young girl with long blonde hair came walking toward us, a bowl of rice cradled against her chest. She wore a pink nightgown and had apparently just passed through the hole in the chain-link fence. When she saw us, she stopped and stood there, hanging her head.

"Talk to her, Nick. You're better at this than I am."

Yeah. And I was about to lose my mind. No matter. Bobby was right. "Okay. Cover me."

Bobby blew on the barrel of his Ruger SR9. I slipped my Colt into my right-side pocket and walked casually toward the child. As I came closer, she cringed and covered her mouth with her right hand, balancing the bowl precariously with her left.

I stopped about a yard from her. The terror in her eyes was chilling. "I'm Nick. Don't be afraid. I won't hurt you. We're gonna rescue you." She shook her head, and I realized she didn't speak English. Or was too freaked out to talk.

"Is your mother here?" This time she understood and pointed deeper into the compound toward the smokehouse. "Who is the food for?" Again, she shook her head. "For the other girls?" She nodded. "Where are they?" She hesitated for a long moment. Uncovered her mouth and pointed with a trembling right forefinger in the direction of the bushes where the collie had vanished.

It seemed cruel but I knew I had to ask. "Are they hurting you?"

Her face fell and her eyes clouded with tears. Then she nodded slowly and pointed toward her pelvis. The red curtain of rage split my forehead. It came in waves, and I had to fight to steady myself. The child's trembling seemed to spread throughout her thin frame. I thought she might collapse and reached out to take the rice bowl. She seemed to understand and released it. Then she began to sob quietly, large tears flowing down both her thin cheeks. I wanted to hug her but feared it would only make things worse. Waited. She fought to compose herself. Rubbed her eyes with both fists.

Once she was calm, I spoke. Gently. "Come with me. My friend and I will walk with you."

She seemed to understand. When we reached Bobby, she showed no fear. Maybe she realized the only thing Bobby loves more than his goats are children. She led us up the road past the powerhouse. There, a barely marked dirt trail led back into the brush.

The third strange thing was waiting fifty yards down the trail. A second smokehouse, smaller than the first, was tucked under sycamores at the edge of a clearing, its entrance shielded from the road. In front of it, in what appeared to be a work area, a plank was stretched across two sawhorses. A man lay strapped across the plank, blindfolded, pinioned at the ankles, waist, and throat. Rowe.

The child gasped, and I clapped my free hand over her mouth. Led her back down the trail. Told her to walk back to the other smokehouse and pushed her in that general direction. Then I joined Bobby. By now, two men wearing Middle Eastern headscarves and tunics were hovering over Rowe. One shoved wooden blocks up against either side of his head. He tightened them in place by looping a belt-like mechanism under the plank and across his blindfold before cinching it tight with a locking clasp. Immobilized, Rowe spoke to the other man, who was holding a gallon jug of water in his right hand and a plastic funnel in his left. "Listen Blink, this is crazy. I'll tell you whatever you want to know."

"You got things a little out of order, Mistuh Rowe. First, we waterboard you, then you flap your gums. Mistuh Tragg wants to know who you're working for, who you report to, how much you're being paid, and where you're stashing the cash. I'll record your confession and my partner will film it." Blink patted his shirt pocket with the heel of his left hand.

"But Amsterdam already knows everything."

"Who the hell is Amsterdam? I report to Mr. Tragg and his instructions are clear." Blink spat expertly, his lunger splashing across Rowe's mouth and chin, where it hesitated before sliding down his throat.

"You bastard!"

"You got that right."

"Can the bullshit," said the other guy, who was punching numbers into his phone. "I don't feel too good about this, so let's just get it over with."

"C'mon, Sam. I'm not sayin' this is fun, but it sure beats Ironwood."

"What do you want?" said Rowe. "My people will take care of it. I can offer you a much better deal than Tragg."

Blink was unimpressed. "Say your prayers, baby."

Bobby looked at me and I shook my head. Whispered. "One or two rounds before we stop 'em."

"That's torture, Nick."

"I know." My jaw set, I shook my head. "We need the overt act for evidence. You should record it on your phone." Bobby looked at me and nodded grimly. Stepped back into the brush to film covertly.

Blink moved forward. He wrenched Rowe's mouth open and inserted a rubber mouth prop. Covered his face with a cloth. Then held the funnel over the cloth and began to drip the water slowly and deliberately. At first, no response from Rowe. Blink increased the flow rate. When the water reached Rowe's bronchioles, he gagged and began sneezing uncontrollably. His entire frame spasmed like a man in the jaws of a grand mal seizure. It was horrible to witness, but Blink clearly enjoyed it. He stepped back to observe his handiwork while the gentler, kinder Sam stepped up and reached for the locking mechanism.

"Not yet, baby. Let him drown awhile."

Sam hesitated. "C'mon, man. This is nasty."

"That's the idea. It's supposed to be nasty." Blink began dripping another full funnel of water onto the cloth and into Rowe's nose and mouth. Muffled screams. Retching. Gagging. It was sick. I was riveted. With a huge effort, I wrenched myself out of my own private torture mode. I nodded toward Bobby and motioned. Go time.

Guns drawn, we eased into the clearing, first me, then Bobby. A mistake. A third phony Arab, this one wearing a fishnet keffiyeh, had apparently been watching from around the corner of the smokehouse. The Taser darts struck inches below my solar plexus. A split-second of confusion. Then I pitched forward onto the ground. Somewhere in the back of my mind, I knew Bobby had faded back into the brush. Spasms. Neuromuscular incapacitation. The ripple effect spread through my nerves and muscles like a stone dropped into water. Pure fetal agony. Keffiyeh Man stepped up, yanked me to a sitting position, and smashed me twice in the face.

CHAPTER FORTY-ONE

When I came to, my head was pounding, my jaw throbbing. Burning on the outside, hollow on the inside. Aching everywhere. A heavy weight across my legs. Tried to buck it off. Failed. Tried again. This time Rowe slid off me, moaning. No sign of Bobby. I'd been tased and punched out, not a stroll down Park Avenue, but it hardly compared to being waterboarded.

"Rowe? Are you alright?"

"Peachy." The words grated in his throat, triggering a fresh coughing spasm.

"Where are we?"

Rowe coughed instead of answering. I forced myself to a sitting position. We were inside the small smokehouse. A thin stream of early morning light filtered through a skylight. No sign of the girls. The Taser darts, still attached to their guide wires, were burning at their point of entry. I took a deep breath, grabbed one dart between my thumb and forefinger, and yanked it straight out. Repeat performance with the other. Get a tetanus shot.

Minus his keffiyeh, Rowe looked the perfect patrician. Even-featured, long nosed, middle-aged finishing school product in need of a shave. Got to my feet. Slowly. Legs wobbly. Took a deep breath. Another. We were in a brick room with a gently sloping ceiling, the top cut away to allow for a skylight. The interior brickwork was painted white. A plastic curtain cordoned off one side of the room. Sleeping bags lay neatly stacked against the opposite wall next to a pile of backpacks and half-a-dozen one-gallon plastic water jugs. Children's pictures, including a crayon drawing of a ferocious-looking dinosaur, were taped haphazardly to the walls. No chairs.

I took a quick look behind the curtain. A plastic utility sink and chemical camp toilet. I grabbed a sleeping bag from the stack and threw a second one at Rowe. Sat down with my back against the wall, muscles expanding and contracting. Vaguely aware of something hard in the sleeping bag. Kneading my calves and thighs, I treated myself to a long self-pitying sigh and stared at Rowe, whose features telegraphed purest misery.

"So what do you think, Rowe? Should waterboarding remain part of our torture arsenal? Thumbs up or down?"

"Fuck you." He stared at me. "Why didn't you and Moore stop them? You must have seen the whole thing…"

I shrugged, which set off tremors in my chest and shoulders. "I figured we needed a round of waterboarding as evidence. Bobby has it on his phone. Too bad you had to be the guinea pig. Of course, as a spook, you really should experience what you dole out. My mistake was I hadn't reckoned on the third guy with the Taser."

"That was Javier Fincus. How could you be so stupid? Didn't you know those three operate as a team? And what about Moore? Why did he run away with his tail between his legs? I expected better from him."

I shrugged. Broke it down in my mind. "Probably didn't want to risk a shot with me rolling around on the ground. If something went wrong, I might've been killed."

Rowe didn't give two damns about Bobby's concern for my longevity. "So where the hell is he?"

I shrugged. "He's around somewhere. Unless they jacked him, which I doubt."

"Shit, Crane. Why are you so passive? Do you realize what's

going to happen when Tragg arrives?"

I gave him a hard look. "Actually, I do. He's going to try and beat me to death with his bare hands. Like he's wanted to do all along. But he won't kill you. You're too connected. Too many friends in high places. Maybe he'll give you another round of waterboarding, though. Unless, of course, you've already confessed to everything."

"I've admitted nothing. I have nothing to confess. After you showed up, the goons lost all interest in me other than batting me around while they were dumping us in here."

"Fuckheads are probably ADHD. Like half the criminals in America. Once they saw me, they probably couldn't even remember why they were waterboarding you." I stood up. Chuckled mirthlessly. "C'mon, Rowe. Stop whining. We could be in Pelican Bay or someplace really nasty. This is no supermax. More like a boy scout camp."

I patted myself down. Nothing. No guns, knives, or phones. Although I refused to show fear, I was plenty worried. Out of all the creeps, Tragg was the most volatile and hated me out of pure cussedness. Rowe had said the principals were serious about recruiting me, but he had also given the strong impression that there were many different versions of moonlight worming around in the shit-for-brains of the shot callers. The fact the attack at Leo's was being sold as an initiation seemed a cruel whimsy, like boys tormenting a wounded animal or a cold god paring his fingernails, his victim pinned and wriggling. The fact I might have mere hours to live was just that, a fact—cold, hard, real. But I didn't want to die without saying goodbye to my daughter. I turned to Rowe. "Do you have a phone?"

He felt his pockets and shook his head. "They took everything."

"I have to phone my daughter."

He chuckled sarcastically, and I almost got up and slapped him. "What about knives or guns?"

Again, he shook his head.

"Didn't your mother ever tell you it pays to be prepared?" I got up, crossed the room. Looked behind the curtain. The chemical toilet was built into a wooden frame. Freestanding, sitting on the cement floor, a single enclosed unit with no outside access. My gaze shifted to the utility sink. Black plastic tubing ran from its base through a ragged, two-inch hole cut in the brickwork. It was screwed to a two-by-four fastened to the wall with wall dogs.

I stood there staring, a black sphere of destructive desire gathering at the base of my brain. Took a deep breath, grabbed the rim of the sink, and began jerking it away from the wall. The wall dogs rasped but would not give way. My fury grew. I released the sink, turned, and ripped the plastic curtain down. Threw it across the room, spat on my hands, and went back to work. More methodically this time. Finally, it came free, the two-by-four dragging behind it. I shoved it out toward the middle of the room. Jimmied my hand through the hole in the brickwork. Pure futility. No tools. I cursed and turned back toward Rowe, who was now on his feet, eyeing me warily. "You're making too much noise. What's the matter? You got a death wish?"

"That's right, motherfucker. C'mere, gimme a hand." I centered the sink under the skylight. Climbed up into it, using Rowe's shoulder for balance. Fully extended with one foot on the rim, I could touch the skylight but couldn't get any leverage to bust it out.

I jumped down. Needed something hard. The inner door to the smokehouse opened from the inside, but the welded hatch was locked. The smaller children's panel was latched with an old-fashioned hook and eye lock. Got down on my knees, unhooked it and reached outside, feeling for the lock, hoping for a twist knob. No luck. A keyhole. That was it. I yanked my arm back inside and stood up.

"C'mon, Rowe. Help me out here. We need something hard to bust out the skylight." Fat chance. Rowe's deck shoes were even softer than my cross trainers. I took a deep breath and tried to think. Had to be missing something. Searched through the stack of sleeping bags. Crayons, magic markers, even a poster of an idyllic Asian nature scene with stylized flowers, brooks, and bridges, but nothing hard. Had to hurry. Assholes capable of anything. Death, torture, castration, a one-way ticket to a Polish dungeon. Then it hit me. Walked back over to the wall, crouched down, and reached inside the sleeping bag I'd removed from the stack.

It had been there all along. A set of hand-painted Russian nesting dolls. Must belong to the Ukrainian girl. I unscrewed the outside doll, which was about twelve inches high, and removed the inside dolls. Then I mined the plastic water jugs for precious H_2O and managed to fill the base of the big doll up to where the top half connected. I screwed it back together and faced Rowe.

"C'mon Rowe, let's get out of here." With him bracing the utility sink, I stood with one foot on the rim, the other in the basin. I gripped the smaller cylindrical end of the doll, narrowed my eyes to protect them from falling glass, and used it as a battering ram. Three precise blows and the skylight cracked. Two more and it shattered like a car window crushed by a rock. Glass poured everywhere, a hard-edged waterfall. Rowe held the sink steady.

"Progress, buddy." I methodically broke the remaining glass away from the grooves that held the pane in place. Tossed the Russian doll back onto the sleeping bag and stepped back down into the basin. Gave Rowe a hand and pulled him up into the sink next to me. Lovebirds in a shitstorm. He was agile for an old guy.

"Okay, I'm going up first. Brace me and give me a boost when I climb out." With both feet straddling the rim of the sink, the top of my head was still six inches below the opening. The trick was to get my elbows above the roofline. Would be cake after that. We were not a well-oiled machine. Rowe's boost was feeble. I growled at him. Shook him off. Quick crouch and I leapt as high as I could. It worked. Got my shoulders above the roofline and braced myself with my forearms against the tiles. Pulled myself out.

Looked around. No one in sight. Uneasy morning sun filtering through the cloud cover. The trail to the asphalt road vanished in the trees.

"Okay, Rowe. Your turn. Give me your hand and brace both your feet on the rim. I'll pull you out." His hand was soft and moist with long slim fingers. I pulled hard with one hand, anchoring myself with the other. Prick was an acrobat. And light as a feather. Up he came, and for a long moment, the two of us just sat there in wonder.

"Good job, Rowe. I told you this was a boy scout camp. Now, let's get out of here." It was an eight-foot drop. Hang. Release. We brushed ourselves off and started up the path. Complete silence. Except for our breath and our footsteps. We were halfway up the path when the dull pop of suppressed semi-automatic rifle fire sounded from the road.

CHAPTER FORTY-TWO

You never want to see your partner pinned down. It's something you live in fear of, not because you doubt your own nerve or his nerve, but because all the nerve in the world will not save your partner if his time is up.

Our escape energized Rowe. I was shifting. Reptilian mode. Cold in the front of my head. Black ball of destructive desire at the base of my brain. I told Rowe to stay back. He refused. Up the trail toward the asphalt road. Fast. A shot every four or five seconds. Nearing the road, we raced across an abandoned garden, heading toward the shots.

Came to Blink and Sam, crumpled in a heap. Grizzled white guys, veterans of many dark and lawless campaigns. Headscarves missing, unconscious, but still breathing. They were not the problem. Bobby was the problem. He was pinned down near the far edge of the garden, ninety feet away. Fincus stood in the middle of the road, cradling an M16. He aimed low and fired. The slug seemed to skip along the ground. Bobby jerked back. Fincus laughed and moved closer. "Hands on your head, *maricón*." He fired again. This time, the bullet came much closer. Bobby barely jerked. I knew he was steeling himself, hoping one shot would finish him. Death more dignified that way.

Hard to explain what happened next. I streaked across the garden, tripped once, kept my balance, low and lean like a sprinter. Rowe followed suit, but at a graceful, rapid lope. Thirty yards to cover. Five seconds from take-off to impact. Up close and personal, the pop of an M16 sounds hollow. Rowe screamed and I slammed into Fincus. Bastard put up a good fight, but I rarely lose a first-strike advantage. I kneed him into submission while Bobby joined in to finish the job.

Meanwhile, Rowe was bleeding to death. Chest ripped open by the M16 slug. By the time we got to him, he could only mutter a few words. I held him in my arms as he shook and gagged. Just when it seemed he was done for, he choked, coughed, shivered, and repeated the cycle. Then he really was dead. I laid his head down gently and climbed to my feet. Stripped off my denim jacket and covered him.

Bobby and I stood there, staring at the dead man. Then we turned away and he briefed me. When he was reasonably sure Fincus and his team weren't going to kill me, at least not immediately, Bobby had pulled back and waited. Blink was the first to appear. Bobby ambushed him with a set of Taser darts before putting him to sleep with one-and-a-half doses of Versed. Then Sam. Bobby got off two clean Taser shots, but Sam was either the bionic man or wore a protective vest. He staggered slightly on impact, shook it off, and righted himself, gun in hand. Caught napping, Bobby had thrown up his hands.

"Bad form. Either I didn't take the fool seriously, or I was too slow...But once he had me covered, lulling him to sleep was the right play. He would've shot me if I'd gone for my gun."

Bobby had handed over his weapons and waited for his chance. "I could tell he was one of those guys who could shoot you without blinking at a distance but would hesitate up close. And I figured his orders were to take me alive. Soon as I saw an angle, I swept his legs out from under him. The rest was cake. Since he was immune to electricity, I gave him two doses of Versed."

Bobby had been reaching for his guns when a slug from Javier's M16 buried itself in the dirt next to him. After that,

Fincus had toyed with him, spraying enough bullets between Bobby and his weapons to keep him from making a desperate dive. The rest of the time, Fincus fanned bullets around him in a circle. To make him dance. Was moving in for the kill when Rowe and I attacked. "I had the feeling he didn't give a damn about any orders and was gonna cut me in half. But only when he was good and ready. First, he wanted to conduct his little sadistic ritual." Bobby pointed at Rowe. "But this guy deserves a warrior's funeral."

"He's the reason you and I are still alive."

"Poor sonofabitch died a hero. I'm sorry I hit him back at the barn."

Courage is a funny animal. You never know where you're going to find it. Rowe had surprised us. But then we remembered the girls. He had been their minder. It left us sad and speechless.

We locked Sam and Blink and Fincus in the large smokehouse, trussed up in handcuffs and leg irons. That was the easy part. The hard part was convincing the girls and women to come with us. I spoke to them gently, then, when that didn't work, quietly and firmly, gesturing with my hands. Then an idea. During his call with Rowe, while we were still down on Casale Street, Blink had said he was bringing the day's supplies—breakfast, lunch, and dinner. But no sign of fresh food in either smokehouse. I walked over to Blink's van. Looked inside. Jackpot. Together, Bobby and I carried shopping bags filled with cartons of Chinese takeout and boxes of burritos over to Rowe's van and stacked them up on the ground next to it. Carrying a single carton of egg rolls and potstickers, I walked back over to the females. Popped half an eggroll in my mouth. Chewed solemnly. Popped the other half in. Chewed some more. Pointed to Rowe's van. Popped another eggroll into my mouth. Food. The women thought it over. Finally, as if of one mind, the mother and daughter teams walked over to the van, loaded the food into the back, and climbed in after it.

Before we left the compound, we collected our captives' weapons, handcuffs, keys, phones, drugs, and sundry supplies and dumped them into a plastic garbage bag we stashed under a rusted wheelbarrow in the tumble-down machine shed. The only exceptions were the keys to the smokehouses, which we cached near the large smokehouse door. As a precaution, we each kept a handcuff key. You never know. When everything was ready, for the second time in the last eight hours, we drove up the winding road leading to the gate.

CHAPTER FORTY-THREE

Back on Casale Street, Bobby jumped out of the van. Removed the tracking device from behind the bumper. Stuck it in his pocket and headed for his car, eager to get back to the Cradle Rest. With a pit stop for food along the way. Which left me in the van with the refugees.

I drove slowly east on Sunset, my mind racing like the proverbial hamster trapped in a roundabout. Nagging thought that unless I liberated the little girls in Ohio quickly, they could end up like these poor children. A bad feeling. Began wondering if Rowe had a pint of something strong stashed in the glove compartment. Even took a look. No luck.

A few miles from the ocean, Sunset passes under 405, which connects Orange County to the San Fernando Valley. On automatic pilot, I rounded the cloverleaf and headed north on 405. Relatively light traffic. Sailing along at a steady sixty-five, my mind slowed down. I had two possible safe houses: the barn at Frank Constantine's old place or Caroline Best's horse ranch up in the Valley. The barn was too nasty. The girls might try to run away, and genteel Audrey, who would be tasked with caring for them, might vomit at the sight of it.

This left only Caroline's place—twenty acres of rugged hillside in Granada Hills, half a mile north of the Ronald Reagan Freeway. Place had a well-maintained corral and a habitable bunkhouse. But how in hell could I ask Caroline to hide the eight refugees there when she'd already agreed to help me out in Ohio? While drumming up the courage to call her, I rang Tony.

First, I told him Bobby and I had captured Roberto's killers, including their boss, the despicable Javier Fincus, and had left them trussed up in leg irons in the main smokehouse at the Nazi encampment in Rustic Canyon. Tony shouted YES so loud I fumbled my phone and caught it in midair. Moved on to the enigmatic James Franklin Rowe, explaining that while under interrogation, he had claimed Thomas Quincey would soon be facing federal drug charges. Then, I described how Bobby and I had released Rowe and tailed him back to the canyon, where we found Roberto's killers—Javier at the helm—waterboarding him.

"Bobby videoed the waterboarding, but I got caught napping. Took a couple of Taser darts and ended up in a miniature smokehouse with Rowe. I had to MacGyver our way out. Then we found Bobby, who had been ambushed by Javier. The sonofabitch was toying with him, moving in for the kill. Rowe and I charged him. Javier shot Rowe, cut him in half with an M16 slug. He bled out right in front of us. Bobby would be dead if it wasn't for Rowe. I might be too."

"Damn." Tony's voice was flat, matter of fact. "So that's why they killed Roberto. Javier was running coke and meth for Quincey. Quincey was using his profits to finance his sicko operation. And Roberto had Javier in his sights. Someone tipped off Javier…or he figured it out on his own…"

"Yep. Just an ordinary narco-style rub-out disguised as a false flag terrorist killing. Javier is the guy wearing the keffiyeh in the video Diego Smith showed us. Jack Snow told me Javier got a twelve-week, time-served sentence five years ago in a twenty-kilo coke case. That's when Blaylock and Timberlake first went on the pad."

"So what does Quincey use the money for?"

"According to Rowe, Quincey uses the money to finance

false flag operations like Roberto's murder. To stir up anti-Muslim feelings here at home. It's all part of his 'keep America safe' campaign. But I'm just scratching the surface. Scary thing is, these fucking geniuses killed two birds with one execution. They whacked Roberto, thus protecting their little cartel, while undoubtedly stirring up anti-Muslim sentiment, which is their overriding goal."

"So, you might say they killed Roberto in the name of national security," said Tony. "Domestic terrorists led by a maniac." Expelled his breath scornfully. "That's narco-terrorism. That's where this all began."

"Something like that." Long silence. "Okay," I said finally. "You've got to get up to the camp and take those fools into custody before Tragg gets there. And don't kill Javier. We're going to need him as a witness against Thomas Quincey."

"I won't kill him. But he's going to wish he was dead."

That's where I wanted to leave it. But I couldn't. So I told Tony about the four women and their four daughters and our belief that Quincey's crew of domestic terrorists had been pimping the little girls out to fat cats. Tony became unglued. He cursed, then I heard a crash, and then he really cursed. "Fuck! I almost broke my hand!"

"Tony. Don't. Stay calm. Is your hand okay?"

Another long silence. "Yeah. Barely."

"Good. Here's what we gotta do. I'm going to convince Caroline Best to let me harbor the refugees at her ranch in the foothills. They've got a decent bunkhouse there. I'll have Audrey stay with them while we decide what to do...So that's part of it. But here's the other part. We've got to rescue Gloria and her sister sooner, not later. What if their minders *are* dirty? I didn't want to tell you on top of everything else, but I don't trust the wife Rosie." Didn't give him any details. He was worried enough already.

"I agree," said Tony. "How do we do it?"

"I'll handle it. You can't get involved because of your official status. What I need you to do is find a home for them. Where they truly will be safe. Why don't you contact Raymundo and see if he can talk to the Señora on the ranchero in El Tamarindo? She probably knows all about them. And she's got the *dinero* to support them. If we keep them here in country, they'll always be in jeopardy."

Silence. Then. "I'll see what I can do."

That's where we left it. I phoned Audrey, who was on her way out the door to interview Sam Blaylock at MDC. She didn't like being waylaid. I gave her directions to the stable and told her to meet me there ASAP.

"Why? What's going on, Nick?"

"Classified. Operational security. You'll see when you get there. Bring children's toys and books. Anything you can get your hands on for kids."

My very human cargo was restless. I drove carefully. Didn't want to get pulled over. Turned off the Ronald Reagan Freeway and drove through the brown hills, getting drowsy, slowing down, slapping myself to stay awake. A series of turns and I came to Caroline's driveway, hidden away under a canopy of deodar and eucalyptus. Giant black cottonwoods at the end of the driveway. The brown-shingled stable on the left, the tar-papered bunkhouse on the right. No vehicles. Caroline's hostler, Eduardo, had apparently finished his day's work.

Stopped at the foot of the driveway and phoned Caroline. Left a message. Told her it was important, but something different, not the Ohio matter. Drove up to the bunkhouse. Parked and climbed out of the van. Opened the sliding door. The women and girls tumbled out and stood there, trying to take it all in. I motioned for them to follow me. Opened the door to the bunkhouse, stepped inside, and turned on the lights. Basic. Unfinished floor and walls and an all-purpose picnic table. Bunk beds, microwave, water cooler, gas range. Big upgrade over the smokehouse. My new guests unloaded their scant belongings and sat down at the table. I joined them. We dug into the cartons of Chinese takeout.

By the time I'd devoured two helpings of chicken l'orange, the little girls were bouncing from bunk bed to bunk bed. The women were looking at me curiously. Was I a savior or just another predator? I knew they knew that this, at best, was an interlude. Stolen moments of solace in their hard and often brutal lives. Somehow, this reminded me of the people I hadn't been able to help—my alcoholic father and my shadowy mother, who had pulled out right after my younger brother Rafer was born. It hit me hard. Pushed back my plate and was nearly out the door when my burner rang...

CHAPTER FORTY-FOUR

"Hi Caroline."

"Hi Nick. What's going on, my intense friend?"

"Not what I expected. Something peculiar has happened." I filled her in, concluding with the fact that the eight refugees were now enjoying her bunkhouse and acreage, and I would be grateful if she would drive up to Granada Hills so we could talk it over.

Expected her to scream. Instead, she spoke calmly.

"Sorry, Nick. You're crazy, and I'm on the way to my yoga class, which starts in exactly seven minutes. I want you to get them off my property immediately."

"Caroline, please! I don't mean to be a pain in the ass, but I don't have any other place to take them."

"Oh, poor baby... You're pretty damned helpless for such a big, strong man."

"Aw, c'mon, Caroline. I'm desperate. Couldn't you drive up here after your class is over? So we could at least talk about it? I would be very grateful."

She didn't say yes and she didn't say no. Said she would have to think about it. And signed off before I could say anything else.

Wandered over to the corral. Trying to empty my crowded mind. Bright October sunshine, horses ambling their way through the afternoon. Time seemed to stop, and then it started again when Audrey's Prius came skidding past the black cottonwoods on three wheels.

She parked, got out. Spotted me, came racing over. In overalls and a flannel shirt—quite a departure for my normally chic assistant. "All right, boss, what the hell is going on? Like I said, I was virtually out the door, on my way over to MDC, when you called."

"It's a long story." I gestured toward the bunkhouse. "Take a look. It'll clear things up." She gave me a dubious look. Shook her head, but did as I'd suggested. Came running back.

"Holy shit, Nick, they look like refugees. What are they doing here?"

"They are refugees. Bobby and I rescued them from their minders, who are, without exception, the worst of the worst."

"Oh, Nick. Oh my God!" Her eyes filled with tears. I put my hand on her shoulder and squeezed gently. Audrey and I rarely touch, but this was not an ordinary moment. We walked over to the bunkhouse. Nervous moment introducing Audrey to the females. Scared she might shrink from these pariahs at close quarters. Wrong. She walked around introducing herself. Like it was an everyday occurrence. Then she went back to her car and brought back toys and coloring books. Proud of her and told her so. Took her aside afterwards and told her the place belonged to Caroline Best, who was expected in an hour or so. Said I was exhausted and had to sleep. Naturally, Audrey wanted to know what the plan was. Naturally, I shook my head. Said I'd tell her as soon as I knew myself.

Collapsed in a chair by the corral. Warm now, but the cool autumn evening was not far off. Dozed and was roused by the sound of the little girls' voices. Then came Caroline, channeling Audrey, skidding around the corner into the barnyard in her black Range Rover. She slammed on the brakes at the sight of the girls, who were retreating hastily into the bunkhouse.

The hustle, the play, the feint, the maneuver—all part of the repertoire. But nothing in the tank this time. I was scared, identifying with the refugees. Their pure need. I've spent a lifetime feeling it, fighting it. Safe harbor for many years with Cassady and Maleah. The litany of tender moments filled my heart. But then Constantine wreaked havoc and Cassady fled...

Caroline got out of her truck. Two of the little girls, Tamara and Teresa, were peeking out of the bunkhouse. I didn't say anything. Simply pointed. She walked over. Said hello to the little girls and looked inside. Came back two shades paler, Tamara trailing behind her.

"I see you made a friend." I smiled and she tried to scowl. Didn't work.

She stared at me for a while, her lower lip trembling slightly. Then she spoke. "I'm testing my compassion meter." Her voice trailed off.

"And?" I guided her over toward the barn, Tamara right behind us.

"And what? All I've got to say is you're out of your fucking mind!" Another attempt at a scowl. Still didn't work. "Okay, how long do I need to keep them here? And just so you know, this is going on your tab. Room and board and a whopping inconvenience fee. I'm not kidding, Nick." This coming from a woman who had paid me $300,000 for liberating Lou Hernandez, three-quarters of which was a bonus.

"Thank you, Soul Sister. You're the kindest woman I know."

She shrugged. "Where did you find them?"

My turn to shrug. "Bobby and I liberated them from a gang of neo-fascists. Oddly enough, the fascists are Frank Constantine's bosom buddies."

"Jesus." She looked around carefully, like the wrong person might be watching. "Tell me the truth, Nick. If I do this, am I in danger?"

Answer a question with a question. "Didn't you once tell me you were an actor? In high school and college?"

She nodded. "Sure. I had a few good roles. What does that have to do with the price of tea in China?"

I chuckled. "You'll see. Here's our play. It may require a little acting on your part. You've got lawyers you trust, right?" She nodded. "You tell them eight female refugees showed up on your land in Granada Hills. You have no idea how they got there. Tell your lawyers to stall. Do nothing for one week. That'll be long enough. You'll be protected because you will have disclosed the situation. Nobody's going to reproach you or your white shoe boys for sitting on a small refugee crisis for a week. Not with so much other major refugee stuff going on."

She pondered. I moved closer and put my arm around her. Brotherly. "Sorry, Caroline. I wouldn't ask you to help if I had anyone else. Somehow, fate has blown you into the eye of the hurricane."

"Fate," she said, "or a man named Nick Crane."

The way we left it was Audrey would be the main caretaker, but Caroline would spell her. I would check in regularly by burner.

Just before I drove away, I took Audrey aside. "I'm counting on you, Audrey. This is the most important job I've ever put you on. Nobody but you and Caroline know the refugees are here, so you should be fine. But don't breathe a word to anyone. And don't worry about the bail report. I'll give it to Greg."

"Greg? He's never done one."

"Well, he's going to."

She shrugged. "Okay, Nick. I appreciate your trust."

I wasn't sure what to say, so I said nothing. Saluted her and Caroline instead. Got back in the van and drove south on 405 and east on 210.

PART FOUR

CHAPTER FORTY-FIVE

Considered the gas-can-with-shop-rag-fuse-approach to destroying paramilitary equipment but fought off the impulse. Wiped Rowe's van instead and dumped it at a Caltrans lot on Foothill Boulevard in Lake View Terrace. Took a taxi back to town. Drifting off in the backseat when the first call came in. Audrey, intense and energized. Said Caroline was a sweetheart, and they had everything under control. Said the Korean refugee, Soon Lin, sat apart from the other women and kept muttering, 'The river, the river.' I told her to dig. Drifting back to sleep when Bobby phoned. Nothing new. He was at the motel. Told him everything was stable, and I'd be there in a couple of hours.

The third call floored me. At first it was good. Tony said he and Diego Smith and his LASD team had arrested the Fincus trio without a hitch. No sign of Quincey or QB Tragg. The presumptive killers were in protective custody. Diego would present evidence at their arraignment on Monday, and Tony was confident they'd be bound over for trial with no colorable immunity issues.

Then the monkey wrench. Diego had fielded a call from West Hollywood LASD. A well-known make-up and costume artist named Stuart Tucker had been found at his salon. Shot through the head with a hollow point bullet. One of his legs amputated mid-thigh. The killer or killers had written ALLAHU AKBAR across the main mirror in lurid red lipstick. Beneath it, small purple letters announced: DEATH TO HOMOSEXUALS. Quincey and his crew had struck again.

One moment I was breathing, the next all the air was sucked out of me. I started shaking. The lines on the freeway began to waver. The driver sensed it. Watched me in the rearview mirror. "I'm okay." My voice cracked. "Please, just drive."

The pain in my voice was unmistakable. The driver looked away. Tucker's tip concerning the sudden run on Arab costumes had been a key clue leading to the arrest of Fincus and his soldiers. And now the poor guy was dead. The motorcycle lads had slipped Tucker the black spot…by reporting that Bobby and I had met with him. Now, thirty-six hours later, Tucker and Rowe were both dead. Javier and his crew were in custody. The unconscionable hand of fate mixed with my own volition—our little fact-finding tour at Tucker's salon—had kick-started this horrifying chain of events.

Paid off the cabbie a block from the Cradle Rest. Picked up a watermelon *agua de fresa* and a bean and beef burrito at a neighborhood bodega. Then a pit stop at the motel to change clothes. Bobby was asleep in his room. I locked up, got in my rented Elantra, and drove to a payphone on Eastern Avenue…

Thirty minutes later, I met Greg in Farnsworth Park near the tennis courts. Getting dark. Greg was energized. His hair was damp and he rocked nervously in his wheelchair. "Nick!" He motioned me over. "I'm glad you called." He leaned toward me and started talking in a low, rapid tone. He'd punched through the glass into a world that—despite its elegance and hypnotic sheen—was fraught with peril and its own distinctive darkness.

The first revelation was that Frank Constantine and Thomas Quincey had grown up together in the picturesque town of Red Hook in Dutchess County along the Hudson River—Frank with a Chris-Craft tied to the dock behind his palatial mansion, Thomas in a more modest colonial home. Same schools, same teams. Thomas was a star athlete; Frank, one year younger and a grade behind, was even better. They boarded together at Phillips Academy, joining such illustrious alumni as Levi Hutchins, a fifer in the Massachusetts Revolutionary Militia, Humphrey Bogart, and the House of Bush. Greg had found a written history extolling some of the Academy's most accomplished students during the 1970s. Frank and Thomas were featured.

"They were both voted most likely to succeed. As a senior, Thomas was starting varsity quarterback. He threw touchdown passes to Frank, who played split end. The following year, Frank sacrificed himself for the good of the team. He took over at quarterback, which cost him an all-league berth and possibly an Ivy League football scholarship. Not that it mattered. His family was loaded."

What Greg found strange was that after following Thomas to Yale, Frank—who was the more obvious candidate based on his pedigree—refused to join Skull & Bones. Said he wasn't interested. After Yale, he went to medical school at Georgetown, where he specialized in psychiatry. Cut his spurs in private practice treating trauma victims. Then he was recruited as a military psychiatrist and entered the Marines as a captain.

"Did he serve in 'Raq?"

Greg smiled. "Does a leopard have spots?"

"Where?"

"Camp Cupcake at the Al-Asad Airbase. II MEF. Very likely, he and Thomas Quincey served together. According to some reports, it was Frank's work with traumatized soldiers that led him to torture research. He was known for his empathy for both his patients and the Iraqi prisoners. He saw everyone as a victim. This was the key to his epiphany." Greg paused dramatically.

"Which was what, exactly?"

"You already know the answer. That gentler, kinder torture techniques would greatly aid intelligence gathering." Greg paused and nodded. "This, in turn, would shorten wars and reduce suffering."

"A great humanitarian."

Greg gave me a puzzled look, which I ignored.

"What about Quincey? What happened to him in 'Raq?"

"That's the really interesting part." Greg smiled. Brushed his forelock out of his eyes. "Here's what I found. Five or six of his rifle teams ate it on a reconnaissance mission on the eastside of the Euphrates, a few miles north of Hīt. They were apparently the victims of bad intel. I couldn't find any other details."

"Whose bad intel?"

"I dunno."

"Anything on how they died? Suicide bomber? IEDs?"

"Probably IEDs. I'll keep looking."

"Good. Do that. It's important. What about Quincey's personal life?"

Greg shrugged. "He's been married three times, or rather Thomas Quincey has been married two times and Miles Amsterdam one time. His most recent wedding was in February of 2010, shortly after he changed his name. Oddly enough, Frank was his best man. This was about six months before Frank ate it."

"The old boy got around. What is Quincey's wife's name?"

"Amina Hosseini. She's an Iraqi refugee. There's nothing about her in the databases except one picture of them at the altar. At the Old South Church in Boston. She's wearing a white dress and veil."

At that moment, my phone rang. Jack. Told me something had come up and he had to see me. As soon as possible. His voice sounded strange. Or maybe it was my imagination. I asked him if everything was okay, and he said everything was fine. I told him I'd meet him at his office in forty-five minutes.

"So what about Quincey later on? After he turns into Miles Amsterdam?"

"There's very little. All I've got so far is his Boston wedding and a single appearance at an Obama fundraiser here in LA during the 2012 presidential campaign. That's it. Almost like he's trying to stay out of the spotlight."

"That doesn't surprise me. What about him and QB Tragg?"

"Nothing about them interacting, but I've got more on Tragg. He's right there in plain sight on the deep web. After returning home from Iraq in 2007, he worked for that Orange County para firm, COMPSUP, for about eighteen months. Then he signed on with a couple more firms. Briefly."

Then came the tidbit I was waiting for. Tragg, a highly touted amateur club boxer, worked Sunday afternoons as a volunteer firearms instructor at the Beaver Bend Gunnery Range in San Bernardino National Forest. "That sounds like him," I said. "Never trust a guy who prefers guns to the NFL. Probably figures he's helping to arm the good folk of California in case we have to secede from the union. Good work, Greg. What about email addresses?"

"I've hacked into various defunct email accounts belonging to Tragg, Quincey, and Amsterdam. Some of them are fairly recent, but all content has been deleted. Unfortunately, I don't have the technology to dig it out of the trash."

"Keep trying. Anything more on Tami Wheat?"

"You betcha, Nick. Her real name is Marguerite Ferguson. She was student body president at George Mason University. People describe her as a born leader, not only ambitious but effective. For the past few years, she's given talks to various conservative organizations connected to..." He paused and looked at his notes. "...the Roach brothers. You know, those super-rich mining guys. Her husband, who looks twenty years older, is a bit of a mystery. He does something with coal...Wait, there was something else." Greg shuffled through his notes. "Here it is. Marguerite also gives talks to law enforcement groups and gun groups with names like First American Freedom and Arm, Protect and Serve."

"You've done fantastic work." I smiled and wrapped an affectionate right arm around his shoulders. "Great stuff. Keep digging. Try to connect Marguerite to DEA and ICE and the Los Angeles U.S. Attorney's Office. Hell, even the FBI or DIA. I know she's working with Thomas Quincey in some capacity. Get her email. I don't care how you do it. Just don't leave any traces. Her email record could break this wide open." Could also save my life, though I didn't tell the kid that. All this valuable intel was scaring the hell out of me. Here I was up against these powerful, entitled superpatriots determined to wreak havoc...while taking me down in the process.

But I was not without assets. Had my wits, martial skills, and loyal companions. And, strangely, LASD homicide detective Diego Smith was solidly in our camp. Or so it seemed. Told myself it could be worse.

Time to go. I remembered Sam Blaylock's bail report. Told Greg what I needed and said we had samples in our company file. Told him it was important.

"Which comes first?" said Greg. "Quincey and Marguerite, right?"

"They all come first. They're all part of this case. But right at this moment, Quincey and Marguerite pose a clear and present threat, while Blaylock is in custody. You're gonna have to prioritize."

Then I knew. It was time. Greg had to be able to reach me on his own. I gave him a burner number and he wrote it down. "You know how to use this number, right?"

He looked puzzled. I cleared it up for him. "Very sparingly."

On my way to Jack's office, I called Bobby. No answer. I left a message and he called back five minutes later. I told him Greg Thurston had learned that QB Tragg was a Sunday afternoon firearms instructor at the Beaver Bend shooting range.

"So, what's our plan? Another citizen's arrest?"

"More of a let's slap on the transponder."

Bobby thought it over. "Then it's a one-man job. We're in no position to waste manpower. I'll take care of it. And I'll keep you posted."

"Good." Then it hit me. Just a feeling but... "Listen, Bobby, let's reconnoiter at the office tomorrow afternoon after you get back from the gunnery range. But between now and then, do me a favor. Track me on my GPS. I want big brother watching."

"Gotcha, Nick. I'll track you and this QB moron." Bobby, jazzed, excited by this new tracking venture.

"And don't walk into any traps." Either Bobby had hung up or the signal got dropped. Fuckin' cell phones. I called back. No answer. Left a message. Told him to be careful.

The number I'd given Greg was for an unused burner. He would be my only contact on that phone. When I got to Jack's building in Monterey Park, I left it in the glove compartment. Got out and took a good look around. Nothing out of the ordinary. Parking lot almost empty, no purple or maroon vans. No vans at all. Just Jack's Buick and a few nondescript cars. I started up the stairs.

CHAPTER FORTY-SIX

Ever since I've wondered...Why did I fuck up so badly? Exhaustion, the most dangerous state of all? Later on, I realized that the van that got up on my ass and honked—just before I turned onto Jack's street the night this whole clusterfuck began—was part of Quincey's crew, which meant they had Jack on their radar all along...Jack's door was unlocked. No surprise there. I stepped into his waiting room. Called out his name. Silence. Jack often dictates with his headphones on, so I walked down the hallway to his office door, which was half open. I pushed it the rest of the way. Someone shoved me from behind, and I stumbled into the office. Jack sat in his chair, but his chair wasn't where it was supposed to be. It was out in the middle of the room. His law library was scattered all over the floor, his filing cabinets trashed. His hands were cuffed. Blood dripped from a slice wound across one cheek.

Two men wearing Satanist hoods and robes hovered over him. One man, whose rolled-up sleeves revealed thick tattooed forearms, breathed heavily, an open switchblade in his right hand. Tragg. The other man pointed a gun at Jack's head. A third masked figure trained an S&W .40 at my mid-section.

"Look what the cat dragged in." The voice came from behind me. I pivoted. The man wore a hood and robe, but his warm, soothing enema of a voice was unmistakable. Quincey also held an S&W .40, pointed at my face.

"Mr. Crane. It's been a while. I can't say I've missed you, but it has been interesting. The ball's in your court now. You can come with us peacefully or you can protest, in which case my medics will slice your friend's testicles right down the middle. You know what that means. I take a scientific interest in examining a man's seminiferous tubules. It's one of my little quirks."

"Okay, prick." I didn't hesitate. "Let him go."

"You heard the man," said Quincey. "Give Mr. Snow some Versed to keep him quiet. Then cut him loose."

"Fuck," said Tragg. "I was gonna enjoy this." He pivoted and swung. His fist caught me square in my right kidney. Huge pain. I staggered toward Quincey, who side-stepped and swept my legs out from under me. I fell sideways and landed hard on my left shoulder. More pain, though not as bad as the kidney shot. I lay there, covering my face and hands. Then I was injected, hooded, dragged downstairs, and thrown into a vehicle. I would fade, wake up, and fade again. Finally, the vehicle stopped. More dragging, banging, bumping, and a cold wet crossing. Then the wet was gone but the cold remained. The quick jab of another injection. Then nothing at all…

CHAPTER FORTY-SEVEN

Dark shapes, patterns, masses. My head resting on...something cold and hard. Shoulder aching, kidney throbbing. Hands cuffed under each thigh. Plastic gag in my mouth. I shuddered and opened my eyes. Black and cold. The chain around my neck triggered a cold burn that rose into my jaw and down into my chest. *Jack Snow cuffed and bleeding in his office chair. James Franklin Rowe bleeding out in my arms. Bobby pinned down in the ruined garden. The child in a pink nightgown carrying a rice bowl. The crumbling staircase. The tanning vats exploding around me. Bobby at dawn in the Golden Nugget parking lot. The three skateboarders skimming over the ground. The grief in Mohammad Ghaffari's eyes. He and Adara crossing the desert, huddled under straw in the back of a pickup truck. Hardbody bleeding out on the ground. The sage and fashionable Agresti. The Union Station men's room. Rosie Munson hesitating at the trailer door. The Red Rock country at dawn. Barry Camus, bare-chested and quick to anger. QB Tragg dropping like a stone. Dust devils in Mexico. Raymundo drinking Buchanan's Red Seal 21. Roberto in agony on the East LA hillside, dead as a forgotten cause.*

Rolled over on my side and maneuvered myself into a sitting position. Slowly. In stages...Leaned forward, testing the chain until it was tight against my throat. A heavy-duty bicycle chain, wound steel encased in plastic, unbreakable by human hands.

My handcuff key was taped to the inside of my waistband. Could not reach it. My new GPS device was still intact, velcroed to the inside of my jeans. Closed my eyes and breathed slowly. At least Jack was alive. That was something. I was a single die marooned on the cold, hard earth. Weary beyond measure. Last thing I remember was slumping over on my side...

I eased my eyes open. It was getting light outside. My gag was pro deluxe, soft and pliable. The inside of my mouth felt like it had haired over.

I was in a low rectangular building, little more than a shack. Apparently built in stages. Perhaps fourteen feet wide by twenty feet long. Dirt floor. The ceiling—rough boards, bark, and thatching material—was no more than five feet off the ground. Plywood walls to my left and right with a crude sliding door halfway down on the left. The far wall little more than sandbags and a wood scaffolding. Water pooling under the sandbags. In a heavy rain, the shack would flood. The only solid thing was a cement block wall behind me. It anchored a metal plate attached to the linked steel chain that was looped around my throat. A chemical camp toilet stood against the wall. My body ached like I'd been beaten with a two-by four. Closed my eyes and waited...

Voices and the sound of approaching footsteps. The door to the shack slid open, and Thomas Quincey, carrying a sport bag and a large thermos, eased his tall frame through the opening and closed it behind him. He ducked to avoid hitting his head. Came over and crouched down in front of me.

Appeared unchanged since our first encounter—same tall aristocratic bearing. Same pale, flat eyes. Same knife cut mouth. Same well-cut, dark blond hair. Something of the eagle's brow, feral and deadly. Hip-length wading boots. In casual workout clothes. My frayed nerve endings twitched, but more than that, I felt a sudden huge interest. Death on the horizon can do that to a man. I decided to play this bastard. Why not? Could hardly make things worse.

He didn't speak. Not at first. Instead, he glared at me for at least sixty seconds. Overwrought fascist stare. Gagged and trussed, my hands locked under my thighs, I was at a disadvantage, but I didn't care. The fool was damaged. So was I, but I still had my humanity. At least I liked to think so…Quincey finally took out his phone and sent a text. Sixty seconds later, the hatch slid open, and a man stuck his head in. "Ready?"

"Come in."

Quincey moved to one side. The new guy was beetle-browed and bearded with a shaved head, squat and powerful, the back of his skull tatted with swastikas, the sort of cretin you don't want walking up behind you on the prison yard. He was also carrying a thermos…

"Everything shipshape, Emery?"

"Right as rain." Emery's voice was deceptively soft and slightly high-pitched, surprising in a Neanderthal.

"Uncuff this guy and take out his gag. He needs to eat. If he tries anything, break his face." Amsterdam produced an S&W .40, adjusted the suppressor, and blew on the barrel.

"Ten-four." Emery came closer. Kneeled beside me. "Open wide, friendo." He yanked the gag out of my mouth, regarded it with disgust, and chucked it toward the pooled water at the far end of the shack. Then he unlocked my cuffs, his movements quick and certain. Grabbed my hands and started kneading them to jump-start my circulation. Tickled my palm for good measure.

I flinched. Emery chuckled. "Feels good, don't it, baby? Never knock a little stolen pleasure. You know what they say? Be grateful for what comes your way. I'm a fuckin' poet." He smirked, his teeth a catch-alive trap of stains and wires.

It hit me. The Korean woman, who could only stare and

mumble about *the river*, had probably been held prisoner here before being transferred to the Nazi camp. Quincey gave his thermos to Emery, who uncapped it and handed it to me. "Beef bouillon. Good mojo, baby."

Raised it to my lips. Hot and salty. Purest ambrosia. I forced myself to drink slowly. After a few minutes, I set the thermos down. "What's in the other one?" The sound of my own voice startled me.

"Oh baby," said Emery. "You're gonna love this. Beef stew with potatoes and carrots and onions and all kind'a good shit. Cooked in a crock pot with extra virgin olive oil."

"Emery cooked it just for you," said Quincey matter-of-factly. "When QB hired him, we had no idea he was such a good cook."

"Fringe benefits, baby. I worked in the kitchen at Soledad. When I wasn't gettin' slob on my knob." Emery uncapped the second thermos and set it on the floor between my knees. Then he produced an over-sized plastic spoon and handed it to me. "Bombs away, baby. And there's more where this came from."

I bent over the thermos, dipped in, and carefully brought a spoonful to my lips. Emery had shredded the beef and chopped everything super-small, resulting in a thick and thoroughly delicious soup. Keeping my head down, slowly, deliberately, I spooned the life-giving mixture into my mouth.

While I ate, Quincey stepped outside, leaving me with Emery, who kept up a steady stream of jailhouse chatter. The more I ate, the hungrier I got. Finally, I put the thermos down and reached for what was left of the bouillon. Quincey returned, his waders wet up to his knees. He then collected the empty thermoses while Emery re-cuffed me, hands behind my back, but loosely, giving me some range of motion. Emery then exchanged a few gibes with Quincey and ducked out through the sliding door, leaving me alone with my nemesis...

CHAPTER FORTY-EIGHT

This time, Quincey dispensed with the bullshit stare. He sat back and crossed his legs in modified yoga style, his pistol dangling idly from his right hand. When he finally spoke, his tone was dreamy, like intestines awash in post-fecal reverie. "There was a time, Mr. Crane, when the king and his army mattered. Working together, they were a tower of strength, a bulwark against the heathen. A man in good conscience could set aside his pride and yoke himself to the chariot. The rewards were clear and simple. Wine and women and a good sleep after every victory. Are you with me, Mr. Crane?"

"Lay it on me, baby. I'm just soaking it in." It's always wise to let the morally entangled spew. But I couldn't bear not getting the dig in.

"Fuck you, Crane. Shut up and listen."

I smiled. "Sorry, Tom. I couldn't resist. You're so sensitive."

He ignored me. Went on. "It took two thousand years of years of suffering, but the Republic finally overcame the old aristocracy. This was a good thing. The Republic, flawed though it undoubtedly was, stood for a new kind of justice. It still lived off the bent backs of the downtrodden, but it didn't pound them nearly so far into the ground. There was art and science and music and a healthy rebellious spirit, which led to growth and progress. Then came the shots heard round the world. JFK and RFK and Martin Luther King were cut down in their prime, only to be replaced by heathens. It was a bleak time. Many believed the Republic was doomed, but I still followed my family's ideal of service. I believed in our country and that good will and honor would return."

I started to speak. Stopped. Clapped my cuffed hands over my mouth. Dramatically. I was provoking him and he knew it. Still, he kept up his monomaniacal rap.

"Then came the end of the world as we knew it. The Iranian hostage crisis set the stage for Reagan. The Soviet Union fell. We grew in power, but as we grew, we fostered the worst in ourselves and the worst in our cut-throat allies. We took on the traits of those we despised. And the Republic crumbled, replaced by Empire."

This made sense. *The worst are full of passionate intensity.* One of the few lines of poetry I remember.

"I was a good soldier. There was corruption all around me, but there were also good men. Frank Constantine was one of those good men. A man you may meet someday, Desmond Cole, was another. I thought James Franklin Rowe was a good man, but he betrayed me in the end."

Quincey's voice faltered. He caught himself quickly. "So let me ask you, Mr. Crane, what should one do when the ideal has been shattered and can't be repaired? How does one go on? Like you—a spineless hedonist stroking himself and preening in front of the mirror, congratulating himself for hating America—or like me, a patriot, wracked by heartache and loss but still crawling through the wreckage, fighting for the ghost of the Republic.

"And what does all of this have to do to you, you ask? It's very simple. We all admired Frank Constantine. He was strong and focused, kind, gentle when appropriate, but never weak, cut from a pragmatic bolt of cloth. For a man of his humane disposition to accept that some form of torture, much as we all hate the idea, is necessary, was an act of pure courage. Frank never failed to take the high, hard road, and he never lost sight of the greater truth..."

Amsterdam's eyes glittered. His voice reached a crescendo and fell away. The knife line of his mouth seemed to disappear. He stared past me at the blank cement wall...

During those terrible moments before Henry Taylor shot Frank, I witnessed the humanity in Frank's anguished gaze. I pleaded with him to surrender, to claim insanity, which, because it was an accurate diagnosis and because he was Frank Constantine, might have worked.

Time for a tactical change. Keep this fool guessing. I spoke quietly. "I know Frank had a noble soul. It was obvious. I told him to surrender. Hell, I begged him. It didn't work. He was determined to die."

Amsterdam's gaze shifted back to me. His eyes were frozen blue ice. "Aren't we all, Mr. Crane? Aren't we all?" Very slowly, he raised his pistol, pointed it at me, and sighed deeply. "It's a simple thing, Mr. Crane, to pull the trigger."

Fuck you. "Go ahead, my friend. I'm ready but I don't think you are." It was a risk, but I took it.

"Oh, I'm ready, Mr. Crane. Readier than you'll ever be. And if I don't kill you, someone else will. And it will happen soon. But first things first." Casually, he lowered the gun. Put it down on the floor in front of him. Spoke. "There used to be rules to live by. Things like honor your mother and father. Let the other guy merge in front of you on the freeway. And don't fuck your best friend's wife. Now, though, there are only two rules left that actually matter. The first is to stay alive at all costs. The second is to honor the ghost of the Republic, which brings us back to why we're here. You entered Frank's world and my world and Desmond Cole's world and James Franklin Rowe's world. Your soldiers killed Frank. I know you didn't kill him personally, and I know you didn't want him to die, but nonetheless, he died on your watch. And you stole his torture records—a thief in the night.

"There's been much talk of having you killed. Some would

say the ambush at the auto body shop was attempted murder, and I don't disagree. I know neither Desmond Cole nor I ordered that fiasco, which makes me think it could have been Rowe. But we don't know for sure. I know it wasn't our resident roughneck, QB Tragg; he doesn't have nearly enough juice. But it really doesn't matter. You surviving against all odds has quenched any lingering doubts about your competence, which, in turn, brings us to my main point. I think it's fair to let Frank choose your punishment..."

What the hell! Pure looney tunes. Next thing I knew, we'd be sitting down at a séance.

"You protest, Mr. Crane. You insist Frank is dead. True. So tragically true. But Dee Cole and I know perfectly well what Frank would say if he could speak to us from beyond the grave. First, he would thank you for setting him free from his demons. Second, he would want you to help us carry on his work." Quincey paused for a long moment. "Which is why we've decided to bring you into the fold."

Yeah, right. This madman was going to bring me into the fold? "And if I don't agree?"

Quincey shrugged expansively. "You do have the option of being ass-raped nightly by Emery until we decide whether to kill you or send you to Poland for other kinds of persuasion." He smiled, his flat lips hideous. "The word is he has a very big dong. So, if that's what you'd prefer..."

I shook my head and laughed. That's what it always comes down to in good old America. Ass rape and golden showers. The Christian right's favorite obsessions. And if that fails, torture. I gave the slightest of nods. "Okay, Tom. I get it."

"Good. What I need is a first lieutenant to recruit soldiers and manage day-to-day operations. Someone with the common touch who can walk into prisons and low places. Someone with good judgment who's good at hiring the right people. That's QB's downfall. I love the guy, and I admire his down-on-the-farm patriotism, but his judgment is bad. There's no excuse for how the little girls were treated up at the Nazi camp. That was on his watch." Quincey shook his head sadly. As if he wasn't in on it.

Quincey looked at me. A question in his icy blue eyes. "On the other hand, QB has exceeded expectations on the business side. At his suggestion, we built a private fight club in a warehouse up in the Valley, where we put on boxing matches every second Monday. QB is often featured and he never disappoints. By invitation only, it's LA's best kept entertainment secret. We have a fight coming up tomorrow, and it just so happens that QB needs an opponent. You see, Mr. Crane…" Quincey paused and stared at me. "QB was scheduled to fight Javier Fincus on Monday before a sold-out, full house at a thousand dollars a pop. This cannot fall through. Therefore, I'm asking you, or should I say, I'm telling you, you are going to fill in for Javier. QB's itching to fight you anyway." Quincey allowed himself a short chuckle. "Pure undiluted hatred, Mr. Crane, can make for one helluva fight. So that's the deal. *Mano a mano*. It'll be a start, Crane, it'll be a start."

Well. This was a giggle. If true. A reprieve, even if only temporary, was better than sitting here in this off-the-wall jail. And I was pretty sure I could take Tragg in the ring. At least I could make it interesting. But I didn't buy it. I knew this was a dance with death and no more, so I decided to go for the jugular. "I'm all over it, Tom. As soon as you tell me how you fucked up in 'Raq. How many men died on your watch, Tom? Ten? Twenty? One hundred? You need help, Tom. Sometimes, even you have to forgive the unforgivable. Even if it means forgiving yourself. So that you don't take us all down with you."

It's hard to describe the emotions that broke across Quincey's face. The light draining from his eyes. His face cracking open from forehead to chin. Nothing but pain and darkness within. Just as quickly it reformed. Lines where it had been smooth. Deeper lines where there already had been lines. Thought he was going to come at me, but he didn't. Spoke instead. Low intense heat. "That's what you don't understand, asshole. That's why I need Frank. Among other things, he was my fucking psychiatrist."

"I understand," I said. "I'm sorry he's dead. I wish he was alive so you could talk to him." For an instant, I really was sorry. But too late. I'd triggered a moment of clarity. Quincey decided to strike back.

"Look, Crane, I said my piece, what I want, and what I believe. But then you had to go and get nasty. So now, I'm going to tell you what the principals want, or rather, what they demand. I imagine you've probably figured it out anyway in that sniveling coyote brain of yours. You've pissed off too many people too many times, which is why you're here at this moment in time. All that's left is how to dispose of your body with the least risk of your criminal friends whining to their equally criminal friends in LAPD. Not that anyone would listen to them...Myself, I had hope for you despite your stubbornness and refusal to appreciate our largesse. I saw in you a man of some principle—confused, misguided, but perhaps salvageable. Now, however, you have become an inconvenience that must be disposed of."

He paused. Looked down at the gun in front of him. Continued. "You see, even though I personally want to keep you alive, my superior officers think otherwise. I don't like the aggravation of slugging you down to Tijuana and having *los Estatales* put a bullet in your brain. Too many people involved, too many potential problems. And anyway, you deserve better, Crane, you really do." He paused. "Particularly when QB has developed such feelings for you." His thin lips seized in a ghoulish smile.

"I guess you can't call it a bromance. It's more like a special version of brotherly love available only to those of us who know combat firsthand. I call it an aggromance. You just substitute aggression for eros." He was a smart son-of-a-bitch, but damned if I was going to tell him that. "I sense you share a special regard for Brother Tragg. It will make for an interesting evening of entertainment. And naturally, we hope Mr. Moore and Mr. Bott can be persuaded to join us."

He picked up his pistol and holstered it. Stood up, protecting his head against the low ceiling. I wanted to sweep his legs out from under him, but with my limited mobility, it would not be a good play. Things had taken a peculiar turn. But interesting. Better than being chained up in this creepy jail.

Quincey told me his soldiers would arrive around seven p.m. to transport me up to the fight club. I would be alone there until tomorrow evening with a light bag, a heavy bag, and a well-stocked refrigerator. My trainer would show up a few hours before the fight to help me devise a good strategy. Quincey told me Tragg had a sledgehammer right and a decent left hook. That I should box him, not try to brawl, or else he'd mop up the ring using me as detergent.

"Good luck, Crane. You're going to need it."

"Thank you, Tom. I'm sure I will."

CHAPTER FORTY-NINE

When we reached the fight club parking lot, the soldiers removed my hood and dragged me out of the van. Dizzy at first. Not sure where we were. Maybe somewhere up around Pacoima. Early October shadows inked the pavement, matching the black and gray of a wind-rattled sky. The head bogie, who looked like he might be Emery's younger brother, got up in my face. "Okay, baby, let's get moving."

Marched me across the parking lot…toward a large, washed-out gray stone building. At one point, Emery's kinsman clapped a meaty paw on my right shoulder and squeezed…hard. For a wild moment I thought they were going to kill me, and I tried to wrench free. The Benelli M4 pointed at my crotch convinced me otherwise. "Eyes forward, sumbitch. Don't get stupid."

They were big on security. Steel bars across the warehouse door and a deadbolt. While the other soldiers dealt with the locks, Emery's kinsman kept inching closer till he was right in my face. "Hey, asshole. I gotta message for ya." He slapped me lightly on the side of my face. "I believe you can do this, baby. You got those lucky eyes. The big man's gonna go down hard…Now go on. Get movin'." The door swung open and he half-herded, half-shoved me inside. The door closed.

I tried to suss the place, my vision hazy. It was maybe half-again the size of a basketball court. Girders and exhaust pipes criss-crossed the ceiling. LED high bay lights hung from the girders. There was no way out. Exhaust pipes too narrow to crawl through, even if I could reach them. The surprising part was the large, roofless structure nested inside the outer shell, a building within a building, which, I figured, was where the fight would be held.

A narrow walkway ran along the perimeter of the inner structure, and I recced it before going inside. No surprises. The loading dock doors were sealed tight as a drum. If my fate was to get in the ring with Tragg, so be it. Rather a bizarre start to my funeral rites, but I could think of worse.

The door to the inner building led into a small auditorium. Bleachers on three sides, wet bar on the fourth. Boxing ring in the middle. The smell of Two Kings Aftershave lingering in the air.

Beyond the auditorium, a carpeted hallway divided the living area on the right from the workout space on the left. The rooms were cubicles with modular dividers for walls. There were two back bedrooms with bunk beds, a bathroom, a den with bookshelves, a kitchen, and a living room that butted up against the back of the auditorium. The workout area reminded me of a high school P.E. department in miniature. Locker room, weight room, scaled-down basketball court.

Strange to be a condemned man wandering around this peculiar domicile-cum-gymnasium. Still, better than the river prison. I decided to focus on one thing only—gathering up strength for what lay ahead.

I wandered into the kitchen. Steaks were defrosting on a cutting board next to a grill pan. Tomatoes and fresh fruit in wooden bowls on the counter. A loaf of French bread still in the wrapper. Brown rice and broccoli in the fridge. Five crisp twenties lying on the counter. I pocketed the money. Grilled a steak and warmed up the brown rice and broccoli. Added the French bread with sweet butter. Ate slowly, thoughtfully, the strength flowing back into me. Then I made coffee.

Cup in hand, I scoped the gym. The wall behind the bar was

papered with boxing photos. QB Tragg. Everywhere. Tragg in a white satin robe with lime green piping holding his gloves above his head. Tragg, bare-chested and massive, standing over a fallen foe. Tragg, expressionless, in a Marquess of Queensberry pose.

Wanted to rip the pictures off the walls. Not a good idea. Calmed down and studied them. Tragg looked powerful but ponderous. To my dismay, the ring looked small. To stay upright, I was gonna have to get on the bicycle, but I was also gonna have to attack. Something stirred in the dim reaches...

The den was interesting. One small bookshelf dedicated to boxing, a second featuring crime fiction beginning with Hammett and Chandler. I selected a coffee table book called *Meet the Champions*. Sat down in a leather easy chair and flipped through the pages. The book started with Tyson and worked backwards. Great shots of Ali rope-a-doping in Africa, throwing unconventional right-hand leads that slowly turned George Foreman's face into mush. After a while, the images blurred. I closed the book and dragged myself to the back bedroom.

Hard to get to sleep...in the goddamned bunk bed. Thinking about death. What it feels like. If it feels like anything at all. Pissed off because if I died, I'd never get to say goodbye to Maleah. That hurt. She was a little girl, less than two years old, when Cassady and I brought her back from Guangzhou in Southern China. I'd been a good dad. Arm-in-arm on the couch watching horror films and comedies. Weekend walks and bike rides. Then the separation. Cassady and Maleah moved to Kensington. Maleah and I talked on the phone several times a week. She stayed with me every other weekend, and we had plenty of heart-to-heart conversations. She knew she could confide in me. We never discussed the Constantine matter or how it had led to our family splintering. Oddly, once she'd adjusted, Maleah said the separation was good for everyone. She now had two entire sets of friends and got to live in two different houses. And she didn't have to listen to Cassady and me arguing. I had to hand it to her. The girl had a stiff upper lip, which both pleased and frightened me. She was strong, had a lot of her mother in her and—I like to think—just enough of her old man. Finally, I slept.

CHAPTER FIFTY

Opened my eyes shortly before dawn. Didn't know how or why I was there. Reality returned in pieces...I was scheduled to fight a sadistic enforcer who was going to try and kill me. Seemed almost comical by light of day. Smart thing would've been to snap to, get cleaned up, drink some coffee, scramble some eggs, don fighter's togs, and get into the ring to develop a fight strategy. Instead, I lay there letting my mind wander...

Forty years ago, when I was an agile twelve-year-old lashed together with whipcord and baling wire, I'd retired from the ring. My quitting gave my father Adam an excuse to wallow in Jim Beam. Adam, who had fought Golden Gloves in Minneapolis before meeting my mother Geraldine and moving up to the Mesabi Range, began training me when I turned seven. By then, my mother had long since flown the coop. It was Adam, my younger brother Rafer, and me.

Adam preached Dempsey. Considered him pound for pound the greatest fighter ever. At least among the old-timers. Adam owned grainy newsreel footage of Jack's classic brawls with Jess Willard and Luis Angel Firpo. On muggy summer evenings, Adam and Rafer and I would sit in the living room watching Dempsey, a blur of speed, guts, and power, attack and destroy his gigantic foes. Ruffling my hair with a callused hand, Adam would explain what Dempsey was doing and why he was doing it, maniacally insisting all I had to do was listen to him and emulate the Manassas Mauler, and I, too, could be a champion.

After we'd digested the grainy footage, we'd descend to the basement to practice what Dempsey preached. Adam had been an inspired trainer—tough, stern, but quick to praise when I did something right. By the time I was ten, I was boxing in local Silver Gloves tournaments and winning most of the time. When I was twelve, we traveled to Minneapolis for a big tournament. First time I faced serious competition. Adam had warned me this would not be cake, and as soon as I got in the ring with my first opponent, a twelve-year-old kid from the inner city, I knew he was right. Six fights that weekend, each more brutal than the one before it. I won the first four. The fifth was a draw, and I lost the championship match to a black kid who knocked me out in the second round with a tight left hook to my liver that couldn't have traveled more than ten inches.

Adam took the loss in stride. On the long drive back to the Mesabi Range—made even longer by his habit of stopping at gin mills every forty miles or so—he did everything he could to build me up, explaining calmly what I'd done right and where I'd screwed up and how every fighter, even Dempsey, had lost now and then on the way up.

I didn't mind losing the fight. I knew Adam was right. Even Muhammad Ali lost a few times. Losing was not why I quit. I quit because I hit adolescence and started thinking about girls and rock and roll and what I wanted to do with my life. Realized I had choices, and there was no law other than Adam's stating I had to be a boxer.

My quitting crushed my father. Five years of living vicariously through little Nicky, now down the drain. Nothing left but a failed marriage, a mind-numbing job as town letter carrier, and a taste for whiskey. For a while he focused on training Rafer, but although my kid brother had heart, he lacked my speed, power, and killer instinct. After the boy endured a few one-sided losses, Adam threw in the towel.

Adam never forgave me and I never forgave him for refusing

to forgive me. From then on, he careened steadily downhill—even tried to kill me while in the throes of delirium tremens. Once in California, I never mentioned my early boxing career to Bobby or Tony. Admitted I was proficient in the art of street fighting, an entirely different game—vicious, unconscionable, but easier to master than the boxer's intricate science...There in the bedroom, I found myself wishing I could have worked it out with Adam. But no time to get maudlin. I had a fight to prepare for. I stood up and wandered into the bathroom

Checked myself in the mirror. Three or four days of gray-brown stubble. Recently shaved head. Bloodshot eyes, mouth frozen in a hard line. Bad motherfucker. Could've been Quincey's bastard working-class brother. Spat into the sink, stripped down, and got into the shower. Afterwards, I cobbled together a big breakfast of ham and eggs, toast with strawberry jam, and oatmeal with walnuts and brown sugar. Delicious. Last meal of the condemned? Or was it? Maybe Bobby and I could pull something off...Coffee in hand, I returned to the den, where I carefully perused the boxing books. I was looking for *Championship Fighting*, Dempsey's classic boxing manual. It had been Adam's bible. No luck. The fight club's boxing collection was more flash than substance. Very little on *how* to box. I wondered if Tragg had a real trainer or if he was simply a guy who liked to slug it out and enjoyed posturing like a paper champion. I hoped it was the latter.

CHAPTER FIFTY-ONE

My trainer was a piece of work—a white gym rat with hair growing out of his ears and nostrils and a livid scar across his left cheek. Tragg must've dragged him out of one of the downtown gyms. He showed up around 8 p.m., flanked by a phalanx of armed guards wearing brown bomber jackets. Said his name was Cy and called me Bucko. He unlocked the supply room and told me to "have at it." Then he waited in the hallway, humming "When a Man Loves a Woman," while I selected trunks, shoes, and a cobalt blue robe with emerald trim. Then he pointed to the locker room. "Take your time, Bucko. Lemme know when you're ready and I'll tape you up."

Put my clothes and shoes in one of the lockers. My handcuff key was still double-backed to the inside waistband of my jeans, my GPS device still in place. When I was ready, I called Cy, who motioned me to the trainer's station. He wrapped and taped up my hands and outfitted me with a pair of regulation black goatskin Cleto Reyes boxing gloves. Then we hit the ring and went to work.

First, he asked me what I knew, so I told him. He asked me to prove it so I did, first in slow motion, then at three-quarter speed. It came back quickly. Before long, I was moving freely, throwing left-right combos like I'd never left the ring. Cy whistled between his teeth, spat a load of phlegm into a plastic cup he set down in the corner of the ring, and told me to come at him. We sparred for a while at full speed, pulling our punches and avoiding each other's heads. Then I showed him some of the tricks Adam had taught me, including the Jack Dempsey falling step and power jab. This brought another whistle of appreciation. Finally, he waved me off, picked up his cup, and told me to follow him. He wanted privacy, so we headed for the back bedroom. One of the guards patted us down, found nothing alarming, and left the room. After Cy unwrapped my hands, he gave me a long look.

"So what gives, Bucko? What're ya doin' here?"

"Let's just say I'm not here by choice."

"I figured that. There's somethin' funny 'bout this. Usually the fighters come on their own. No guards or anything. Nuttin' like that. So what did ya do to piss the big boys off?"

"You don't wanna know."

He looked at me warily, sucking the inside of his upper dentures. Finally, he nodded his head. "I guess I don't. It ain't my business. So let's talk about how you're gonna kick Juiceboy's ass. Here are the rules. The first three rounds are for show. Nobody gets knocked down, but it's a big plus if somebody gets bloodied up. Rounds four and five are for the money. That's when the crowd goes crazy, and the betting goes through the roof. The big boys have a team of bookies right there in the crowd taking bets. I've been tryin' to figger out how to separate 'em from their money, but so far I haven't come up with anything good."

"How much do you get paid for doing this?"

"Me?" His expression turned cagey. "Pretty good. Pretty damned good, Bucko."

"Glad to hear it."

Then he analyzed Tragg in the ring. Said the big guy was slow but was nevertheless a pretty solid boxer. "So here's what ya do. During rounds one through three, don't show him what ya really got. Save it for round four. That's when you catch him napping. As soon as the bell rings for round four, you take control. You hit him with the falling step and the power jab and all that Dempsey shit. I guarantee you Juiceboy has never seen it before. You play this right and you might surprise us all. Wouldn't that be something? But if you fuck up, he'll kill ya."

My mind kept fading in and out. Not good. "What's he got?"

"The basics. Straight right, left hook, right cross. Good power and decent technique. He can hurt you with any of his punches."

"What about his jab?"

Cy shook his head. "That's the good news. It's purely for show. He throws it flat-footed. A child could shake it off. If you attack in round four and get him backin' off, he'll start jabbin' to buy time. First chance you get, you slip one of them pussy jabs and right cross him like a motherfucker. Like you showed me a few minutes ago in the ring. He'll clinch to buy time. You pull him into your body, then shove him away with both hands and nail him with an overhand sneaker hook. Just like Jack would've done. But you gotta land it square. He'll be fallin' away and you don't wanna waste it." He looked at me, a curious glint in his rheumy old eyes. "Where did you learn that Dempsey street-fightin' shit? I haven't seen anybody do that since my balls dropped."

I laughed. He was funny. "I learned it from my old man."

"Figures. It had to be an old-timer."

"What happens if we go five rounds and nobody gets knocked out?"

Cy smirked. "I've never seen that happen here. But if it does, it's extra innings, Bucko, extra fuckin' innings. But that's not gonna happen."

After that I slept for an hour, which wasn't long enough. Cy woke me up at ten thirty. I rubbed my eyes and sighed while he tapped impatiently on the face of his Rolex knockoff. I laced up my shoes and held out my hands to be wrapped. Cy shook his head. "The fighters get wrapped and taped up in the ring. To make sure everything's copacetic...It's a big crowd, Bucko. Wall-to-wall fat cats and their very expensive ladies. And in some cases, their boyfriends. Then you've got your divorcees and their boytoys. You add it all up and you know what it spells?"

I shook my head.

"Money, money, money, baby. That's what it spells." He checked his watch. "We go on in five minutes. What's your ring name?"

I shrugged. "I don't have one."

"For fuck's sake! Ya need one. What's your last name?"

"Crane."

"Crane? Like the bird or one of them machines that lifts shit?" I nodded. "All rightee, then. We'll introduce you as Kid Crane. Not that original, but it has a good ring." I nodded. I had other worries. "What's your height and weight?"

"6'1", 188. I fluctuate." Then I realized I was the same height and weight as Dempsey when he stepped into the ring with Jess Willard on July 4, 1919 in Toledo, Ohio. Could be a good omen. Maybe. We sat there in silence. Cy kept looking at his watch while running his tongue across the inside of his dentures. Finally, he stood up. "Okay, Bucko. Time to rock and roll."

I stood up and we filed toward the door. Then Cy stopped me.

"Wait. I forgot somethin'. You already know this fight don't end till either you or Juiceboy gets knocked out. But there's one other rule, and it's important. In these fights, there's no such thing as a TKO, and there's no neutral corner rule either. If you knock Juiceboy down, hit him again as soon as he gets up. If he knocks you down, roll away while the ref is counting. Otherwise, he'll duke ya while you're still shakin' the cobwebs out."

"I understand."

From the back bedroom to the ring was about ninety feet, but it felt like my own personal Via Dolorosa. And I was no JC. Head bowed, I trailed behind Cy. He wasn't having it. Spun around and got in my face. "Fuck that weak shit, Bucko. This is a prize fight. You gotta put on a show, get the crowd in your corner. So snap to, motherfuck." Then he looped his arm around me and gave my right forearm a reassuring squeeze. "Listen, Kid Crane, you're a fighter. We both know that. While you were asleep, I went out and put some money on ya. So I need ya to stop snivelin' and act like a man." Then he released me and marched solemnly down the hallway and into the gym.

CHAPTER FIFTY-TWO

The auditorium was electric. Cy held the rear door open. I could feel the energy. Then he leaned in and whispered, "Let's do it, Bucko. Let's kick Juiceboy's ass."
Walked in with my hands crossed high above my head. No Tragg. Not yet. Every eye was upon me. I mounted the stairs and slid between the ropes. Began bouncing up and down on the balls of my feet, like a college hoopster getting jacked before tipoff. Revolved in a slow circle, staring at the crowd. Five hundred dollar sweat suits, Rodeo Avenue jeans, bling and pearls galore. Big breasts, some real, some fake. Small breasts jacked up to make 'em look big. Boy toys stripped to the waist, eyeing each other while hanging on the arms of their sugar daddies. No sign of Bobby, which didn't surprise me. Had the feeling he was near. Motherfucker just fades into the mix. I recognized Quincey, who was holding a drink near the bar. He was talking to an older man with a crop of snowy white hair. Desmond Cole? Perhaps...
The house lights dimmed and the sound system crackled. Kicked in. The William Tell Overture. The lights came back on, and QB Tragg, a corpulent clown in a white satin robe, mounted the steps and plunged into the ring. He'd had his nose repaired since I'd last seen him, and I have to admit, it was an improvement.
The ref appeared wearing the obligatory black trousers, blue

oxford shirt, and black bow tie. He motioned me to my corner. I sat down on my stool, and Cy began wrapping and taping my hands. Then Cy pulled on my Cletos and secured the Velcro wrist wraps. The ref moved to Tragg's corner, where his trainer repeated the same process. Meanwhile, Cy popped in my mouth guard and slathered Vaseline on my cheeks, nose, eyebrow ridges, and forehead.

Quincey's friend, the gent with the white hair, appeared center ring. "Ladies and gentlemen, we want to thank you all for coming out. We have a great fight on tap tonight, and we think you're gonna love it. In the far corner, we have Kid Crane. The Kid is 6'1" and weighs in at 188 pounds. His reputation is that of a street brawler, but from what I hear, he's damned good in the ring. And he's going to need to be 'cause the Kid's opponent, in the near corner, is our undefeated house champion, Mr. Oliver "QB" Tragg. QB stands 6'2" and tips the scales at 235 pounds. Those of you who have seen him in action already know what a dangerous beast he is. And from what I hear, there's bad blood between him and Kid Crane, so this should be interesting.

"Our referee is Jim Mannix and our timekeeper is Jerry Randall. This is a five-round, no-decision, semi-pro fight. The men will fight till one of them is knocked down for the ten-count. If no one is knocked out in five rounds, the fight will continue. Other than that, we follow strict World Boxing Organization rules, with one exception. This fight is not governed by the neutral corner rule. That means after a knockdown, the man still standing is under no obligation to move to a neutral corner. This makes for a more exciting fight, which, we believe, is what all of you are here for. So, without further ado, let's get to it."

The ref called us over and went through the rules a second time. I pretended to listen, but mostly I stared at Tragg. His pupils were huge, and I realized he was coked up or on meth. He was gonna come out of his corner like a fuckin' berserker.

The ref motioned us to our corners. The bell rang, the crowd cheered, and Tragg charged. His jab was useless, like Cy had said, but he threw so many of them in such rapid succession I was winded from batting them away before I even got my bearings. Knew I had to hurt him and fast. Spun away, bounced off the ropes, and got on my bicycle. He chased me around the ring, firing his wuss jab like a lady's boot pistol spraying blanks, mixing in an occasional right that I slipped with ease. At first, I made no attempt to counterpunch. He landed a right to my spleen. Stung. I went into a low bob and weave, moving fast, no longer winded, my adrenaline kicking in. The crowd in full freakout mode. Weaving, I spun back against the ropes, rope-a-doped, slipped a telegraphed right, and bounced to open space, which closed quickly as Berserker Boy lumbered after me. He was slowing down already, and I knew what to do. Adam had pounded it into my child's brain. Parried a few more wuss jabs, then fired my first real jab with the classic Dempsey falling step and full-tilt explosion, catching Tragg square on his meaty right cheek. Then I shocked his liver with a tight left hook that couldn't have traveled more than eight inches. His mouthpiece popped out, and as he tried to counterpunch, I crossed him hard to the jaw. Berserker Boy crashed to the mat.

Stood over him, ready with another combination. The crowd, sensing their fun slipping away far too soon, booed loudly. The ref looked at his watch. Waited at least five seconds. Finally began the count in slow motion…three…four…five…six…seven…Tragg on his hands and knees. I didn't give a fuck about the crowd or the rules or anything else. I was gonna kill the motherfucker the moment he stood up, but the bell rang at eight and one-half. I walked stone-faced to my corner.

"MOTHERFUCKER! BUCKO!" Cy was beside himself—proud, thrilled, and amazed by how the first round had gone. As soon as I sat down, the adrenaline overload hit me. Thought I was gonna black out. Had to pop back up and bounce on the balls of my feet, trying to get my racing heart and mind in sync. Dimly aware Tragg's trainer was feeding him far more than smelling salts.

The bell rang. This time, Tragg was careful. No one, not even a berserker, truly wants his bell rung. I thought I could knock him out, but a sliver of caution reminded me I was still a prisoner. The fight had to go four rounds. No sense jumping through the trapdoor. Not with a rope around my neck. The crowd had been sky high, and now it plummeted back to earth.

Would've taken the round on points, but points were meaningless. Contented myself with firing a few decent jabs and pulling an occasional right cross to render it harmless. Tragg did manage to sting me with a couple of left hooks that might've knocked me down if he hadn't been pulling his punches just like I was pulling mine. The bell rang and I went back to my corner. My adrenaline was fading. Wondered if maybe it was time. Unlace my gloves. Bow my head. Let the whole damned mob beat me to death. Shook it off. Reached down deeper. The bell rang and I got to my feet.

Round Three was mostly a repeat of Round Two. We both landed punches that stung but did no real damage. The crowd got restless. Started talking shit. It wasn't pretty, but what the hell! Back in my corner after the bell, Cy was dead serious. "Listen, Bucko, he's a much better fighter than he's shown. He came out like a madman in Round One and you jolted him. Now he's figgerin' it out. You gotta take him this round. Don't let this go five. You're in no shape. He'll kill you if it goes five. Remember what I told ya. Cross him hard. When he clinches, you gotta go to work. And make your punches count. You gotta do this, Bucko. I got my rent riding on ya."

Sucking air. All I wanted was to close my eyes and drift. But the bell rang. It always does. This time, Tragg meant business. Came out strong, ready to do damage. I got on the bicycle and scrambled. Legs like lead, lungs screaming. Barely deflected two or three left hook, straight right combos. The crowd smelled blood. Then, like Ali in the jungle, Tragg began throwing straight lead rights, which I blocked every time except for the time I didn't. The punch caught me square on the jaw. He followed up with a badass left hook, straight right combo to my body. I went down hard.

Blacked out till the three-count when the screeching crowd or some lucky charm woke me up. At six, I rolled away from the giant towering above me, and at eight, I was on my feet rope-a-doping. Very little left in the tank. Tragg, equally winded, threw weak jabs and sloppy rights that I deflected or shook off. *Couldn't be real, but for a moment I swear I saw Adam, stone cold sober, gesturing with both hands, barking commands.* I slipped a jab and fired a stinging right cross. Tragg's head snapped back. He almost fell and looked confused. Instinctively, he leaned into a clinch. I dropped my head down over his left shoulder and grabbed his right elbow with my open left glove, pulling him closer. As he had throughout, the ref let us fight. I sucked in some air. Shoved Tragg violently away and exploded an overhand right sneaker hook. Square on his left temple.

Stopped. Thought he would drop. But he didn't. Instead, he swayed like a big animal teetering on a ledge. Grimaced. Arms out to steady himself. Still didn't fall. It was time. Consecutive shovel hooks to each side of his jaw. This time, the big freak toppled. This time, he didn't get up.

Stood there watching as the ref delayed the count for at least eight seconds. It made no difference. QB wasn't getting up. With my last remaining strength, I moved to my corner and collapsed onto my stool. Cy was amped—shouting something about money and Las Vegas. The crowd noise was earsplitting, and the ring began to whirl. Slowly, my head fell forward...

Quincey's voice, like an echo passing through dark water. "Great fight, Kid Crane."

A second voice, Quincey's friend, the putative Cole. "That was downright surgical, Thomas. Your boy here fought a helluva fight." The voices faded and I faded too. Much later, it seemed, I was walking down the corridor, with Cy propping me upright. In the locker room, he unwrapped my hands. Boxing togs off, street clothes on. Slowly, very slowly. The soldiers in their brown leather bomber jackets clustered around the door, talking about the fight. Took my time. Catching my breath and mulling it over. Where was the crack in their armor? If I couldn't find it, I had to create it. When I was good and ready, I turned and faced them. Decided to play them. No other choice. Proclaimed. "The bigger they come, motherfuckers. The bigger they come."

"Listen to the man." Emery's junior lookalike, dressed in brown like a delivery man, came forward. "Congratulations, Kid Crane. It's your lucky day. Me an' my crew are gonna be driving you back to your hotel." He grinned, but his eyes weren't smiling. Food scraps and missing teeth. "I'm Todd. That was a killer fight. Now hold out your hands." He snapped the cuffs on. Loosely. "Forward march, baby." We were just reaching the ring when Cy bobbed and weaved his way through the phalanx of guards.

"Good luck, Bucko." He saluted me while kissing a large bill. Then he saw the cuffs. "Holy fuck!" He stared, and I realized I'd forgotten to tip him. Then he was gone. I felt bad. He'd been my ally in my darkest hour.

The crowd was mostly gone now, but knots of stragglers loitered in the parking lot, drinking and laughing. Two or three of them cheered when I passed by, and I raised my cuffed hands in response. Gladiator on parade. It was cold and misty and the air felt good on my face. Could feel Quincey and his white-haired friend watching me from somewhere in the shadows. Where the fuck was Bobby? Stopped. Took a deep breath. Another. He was out there somewhere. I could count on that. Todd pointed, and I climbed into the maw of a dark blue Dodge cargo van.

CHAPTER FIFTY-THREE

I slumped back in my seat, feigning sleep. Todd on my right and a large shapeless creature who smelled of sweat, garlic, and tobacco on my left. The driver and another bogie rode up front. Ten minutes down the road, I jerked as if coming out of a sound sleep. I had one play. First lull, then attack. I sat up straight. Said I was hungry. "Let's go to In-N-Out, boys. I'll pay."

"You hear that?" said Todd. "Good idea. We've got a long drive."

"I'm not a boy," said the shapeless one on my left.

"Sorry, man."

"Fuggedaboutit."

"I'm serious about the food. I'm fuckin' starving. I entertained you motherfuckers. The least you can do is let me eat."

At first only Todd backed me, but the guys in front slowly came around. The shapeless one didn't vote. The In-N-Out was at First and Olive, near downtown Burbank. Set me back fifty bones. Todd watched carefully as I raised my cuffed hands to my shirt pocket and fished out the bills. We ate there in the parking lot, listening to hard rock on 95.5 FM. I joked with the soldiers between bites, telling them I used to be Mike Tyson's sparring partner, but that I got fired for knocking him down in the practice ring. Had them going for a while.

We finished our burgers and were almost done with our fries

when somebody knocked on the driver's window. The driver turned the radio down and hit the window control. "Hey, y'all. Ah'm lookin' for an all-night pharmacy. Gotta get a prescription filled. Can y'all help me?"

Bobby's voice. Heavy on the molasses. "Try lookin' up your asshole," said the driver. He buzzed the window back up.

Nothing soothes the savage beast like thick milkshakes and double cheeseburgers. By the time we pulled back onto I-5, the tryptophan was working. The shapeless fool started snoring, and Todd reached down and loosened his belt a notch. Knew I didn't have much time, but steeled myself not to rush.

"That was dope, Kid Crane. The way you took that asshole out. I thought you'd come through." Todd patted his pocket, meaning *cash*, not *gun*.

"That's the game I play." I spoke quietly and distinctly. The radio was playing, and I hoped only Todd could hear. "But I don't like the game you're playing. I know you're gonna hand me off to some TJ chop house. You're better than that, baby. Way better. You gotta get me out of here. Ten large, baby. Cash. You can split it four ways or however you want. One phone call and the money's on its way."

I didn't think he'd bite. But you always want to see how a fella will react. Todd was silent. I waited for a five-count and said, "Ten stacks, baby. Hell, play it right and you can keep it all yourself."

Silence. Then he spoke. "How'd you learn to box like that?"

"My old man was a good coach."

"Wish I'd had a dad like that."

"No, you don't. How 'bout it, Todd?"

Another long silence. Axl Rose was bawling "Welcome to the Jungle" on the radio. The shapeless one shifted toward me, and I had to push him away.

"I'm thinking."

While Todd was thinking, I took a deep breath and thought to myself, 'Fuck it, man. You had your chance.' I slumped back in the seat, crossing my hands in front of me. We came to a construction area, and traffic slowed to a near crawl. The driver swore loudly, and everyone, even the shapeless one, craned their necks to see what the problem was. Slowly and deliberately, as if it were as natural as eating or breathing (Bobby and I have both practiced this plenty of times), I slipped two fingers into my waistband and retrieved the handcuff key. Traffic picked back up again. The introductory chords to "Against the Wind" sounded on the radio as I quietly unlocked the cuffs.

 I waited until we'd passed 10 East and were approaching the 4th Street exit a mile from my office. Based on his hand movements, I was pretty sure Todd kept his piece in a left-side shoulder holster. Could I catch him napping and spirit it away by chutzpah and misdirection? Maybe, but the risk was huge. Instead, I took a deep breath, rose up in my seat as if stretching, and delivered a lethal back elbow to his left cheek, shattering his cheekbone. The sound of the *crack* in that confined space was sickening. Todd moaned in agony, and I deftly reached under his jacket, located his gun, slipped it out of its holster, and pointed it at his head.

 "Sorry, old boy. Now don't make me shoot you."

 Up front, the fourth crew member killed the radio.

 "Don't make me shoot anyone." My voice was firm, matter-of-fact, with the calm edge of a man who is no stranger to violence. "You can all live or you can all die. Your choice. Pull off on 4th and go down the hill. Drop me off at Little Tokyo. Then take your boy here to the hospital."

 I felt movement to my left and swung the handcuffs into the shapeless one's face. He screamed. For emphasis, I rammed the barrel of Todd's S&W .40 into his throat.

 "One more false move and you both get it."

 There were no more false moves. Todd moaned softly all the way—down the hill, over the forlorn and stately Fourth Street bridge, and along the straightaway to Alameda, while the shapeless one hyperventilated. The driver followed orders and

pulled over across the street from Little Tokyo.
"Open the door," I said.
Todd groaned. Slid the door open.
"Get out."
He slowly complied and I jumped out after him.
"Get back in."

But as he started to move, Bobby's Altima screeched to a stop in back of the van. Todd stopped, half-in and half-out, startled by the squealing brakes. Bobby jumped out and walked over, Sig Sauer in his right hand. Grabbed Todd by the scruff of the neck with his left. Leaned into the van. "I found the drugstore, mothafuckas." Leaned back out. Handed me the pistol. I thought he was going to punch Todd, but he didn't. Shoved him back inside instead. "All right, y'all. Get out'a here. 'Fore I use this." He produced a stun grenade. I grabbed the outside door handle and slid it shut. The van didn't move for a three-count. Then it pulled slowly away from the curb.

CHAPTER FIFTY-FOUR

Wiped Todd's handgun down with my shirttail and deposited it in a storm drain. Bobby and I jumped in his Altima, and he drove us around the corner onto Third and across the street into my building's parking lot. We ducked inside via the side door and took the stairs to the third floor. Felt good to be back in my office, if only for a little while. "Glad you didn't hit that poor fool."

"I didn't need to. You'd already done a pretty good job."

"I hated to do it. He saved my ass by getting his crew to go to the In-N-Out. I was fuckin' starving. Wouldn't have had the strength to escape without food." It was true.

"You didn't need to go to all that effort. I would've rescued you."

"How?"

"Well, it wouldn't have been pretty, but me and the 2nd Marine guys would've figured out something. But I'm glad you took care of it. Those fuckers are too expensive. Just having them on standby tonight is gonna cost us two stacks. Imagine if we'd had to stage a full-bore highway rescue? Which was the way I was leaning."

Bobby. The nonpareil.

Inside my office, everything seemed normal. My brace of black leather armchairs faced each other like they always do. I opened my safe and selected a fresh P22 Walther and a rarely used 9mm Colt Commander. Bobby put the coffee on. The pleasures of home.

Sat down on the edge of my desk. Bobby took an armchair. The office phone rang and I let it go to voicemail. No message.

"The fight," said Bobby. "What was it? MMA?"

"Nope. Marquess of Queensberry."

"You knock him out?"

I grinned. "With a little help from Jack Dempsey."

"Hmm." He gave me a quizzical look. "I've always wondered how you learned to box."

"Pretty simple, really. My old man taught me. Drilled me every day for years when I was really young."

"How come you never told me?"

"Just never came up. Mostly, I try to forget that part of my life."

That's when I saw the letter lying on the carpet near the door. An ordinary business envelope. My name, Nick Crane, in blue ink on the front. Tore it open.

Nick, I heard about the fight. Good luck!
Call me at 310-255-5757.
Adara

Stared at the note. Took a deep breath and started to call her number. Stopped. Told Bobby I had two things to take care of first. Asked him to stay close. Thought he'd object, but he didn't. Later, he told me I looked like Dante emerging from the ice at the bottom of hell when he spotted me standing there next to Todd's van.

I keep an old green 2008 Toyota Corolla on standby in our parking lot. For times like this. Holstered my guns, grabbed my eagle paperweight, and added a drop point hunting knife. Bobby locked up. Tuesday morning, two thirty a.m. Town like a crypt. Fourth Street Bridge empty, a sliver of moon floating in the southeast sky, Bobby tailing me in his Altima. East on 60 to Monterey Park. North on Garfield. When we got to Jack's office, Bobby parked on the street. I drove around to the back.

My rented Elantra sat quietly in the shadows. I grabbed the paperweight and got out of the Corolla.

When I got closer, I saw the broken glass on the ground. Someone had punched through the driver's side window. The door was unlocked. I flung it open. No dedicated burner in the glove compartment. Not surprised. Got in my Corolla and rocketed, Bobby close behind me. As fast as I was driving, I still couldn't match my own pulse rate. Empty streets, near empty freeways. When I reached the Eastern Avenue payphone, I dialed with shaky fingers.

"Nick?"

"Yeah."

"I figured it was you. Nobody else calls me this late."

"Have you phoned me?"

"No. Should I have?"

"No! Thank God you didn't." I damn near wept with relief.

"I *was* gonna call you in the morning. With important news."

"Good. But Greg, do *not* call me on the number I gave you. Under no circumstances. Unless you're yearning for a painful death."

"Jesus, Nick. I won't call that number. Lighten up. What the hell happened?"

"The phone was stolen. I'll explain later. Just keep working like you have been."

"I'm all over it."

"I'll call you later on today. Make sure to pick up. Keep your phone with you."

"Okay, Dad. I always keep my phone with me. Now let me get back to work. I have a shitload of emails to read."

CHAPTER FIFTY-FIVE

I phoned Adara. She gave me an address and asked me to meet her there. I asked her if she was being surveilled. She said she didn't think so. Said everyone's attention had been on the boxing match, but that I should make sure I wasn't the one being surveilled. Thirty minutes later, she ushered me into an apartment a few blocks west of The Grove in Mid-City. Wearing black jeans and a loose-fitting Romanian peasant blouse, she held a glass of red wine in her left hand. She was barefoot and her nose ring was gone.

"Oh no, Nick! Your face!" She pulled me into the room and slammed the door. Took a sip of her wine and handed it to me. "Kill it. There's more."

I needed little urging. She poured us both more wine, and we sat down across from one another.

"Is anybody else here?"

She shook her head, the gold flecks prominent in her light brown eyes. "I turned the surveillance off, video and sound. This apartment belongs to Thomas. He uses it for meetings and, I imagine, to meet his girlfriends. He was really busy with the fight tonight, so I went out with Jennifer. I usually do that on fight nights. Thomas thinks I'm sleeping at her house. He had no idea Desmond Cole was going to help you escape after the fight."

Hmm...Desmond Cole was going to help me escape? It

seemed like quite a stretch... But this bit of false news could wait.

"Is there any chance Quincey will come here looking for me?"

"None whatsoever. This is the last place he'd expect to find you."

"Good. Desmond Cole is the white-haired fella, right?"

She nodded. "That's him. Didn't he introduce himself?" Before I could answer, she said, "Listen, before I forget, I've got money for you. I'm sure you've used up most of the retainer."

"Affirmative. Thank you. Hang on, I've got to call my partner." While I phoned Bobby, Adara counted out ten stacks of Franklins, which she placed on the coffee table. I told Bobby he should knock off and get some sleep. He needed little urging. Adara put the money back in a small leather pouch and handed it to me. Then we talked.

Because I thought there could still be backup surveillance, I was careful and kept my voice down. Adara followed suit. Hard to hear each other. She motioned me over, and I sat down next to her on the couch. I didn't tell her Cole had not rescued me. Not at first. Told her I'd knocked out Tragg in the fourth round, and it was one helluva fight. Paused. We looked at each other. Her lovely brown eyes. Not perfect. More gold flecks around her left iris than her right. Which added to her charm.

"I imagine you've been through hell," she said. "Like I can't even imagine."

I shrugged, deadpanned, "It's forced me to brush up on my survival techniques." Waited for her to continue.

"I'm so glad you're okay. And I'm glad you're here." She squeezed my hand. Released it. "I had a good feeling based on how Thomas has been acting. He gets furious when things don't go his way. He does this slow burn thing that drives me crazy. He's been this way for at least ten days now. Mostly, we stay out of each other's way. *Allahu Akbar.* I think he's panicking, and that's not like him."

She shifted gears. "How did it go with my father?"

"I think it went pretty well." I leaned closer and described what we had agreed upon—the synchronized dual escape, the long underground sojourn, the state-of-the-art fake IDs, and the need to survive with less money.

She smiled. Said she was ready and wasn't worried about the ducats. Mohammad had been siphoning cash from the joint bank accounts for a number of years now and giving it to his Bostonian Iraqi friends to safeguard.

She smelled like oranges and red wine. I wanted to kiss her and pick her brain about the principals. Did neither. With Quincey still active, it would be hard to execute their dual escape. He had to be sidelined. Rowe had said an indictment would be filed before Thanksgiving. Too long. Way too long.

My wine glass was empty and so was hers. She refilled them and sat down next to me. I said she was smart to have had her letter delivered to my office. "Yes," she said. "That was my backup plan." She looked puzzled. "But didn't Desmond tell you to call me? When he rescued you from those paramilitary guys? He said he was going to intercept you in the parking lot after the fight. I thought it would be best for you to meet me here first, so I could explain things before he got here."

I was stunned. "He's coming here? What the hell for?"

Her turn to be stunned. "Wait. Did you even meet Desmond?" She stared at me. I shook my head slowly. "Then how did you…? Oh, Nick, you must have escaped some other way. How in the world did you manage that?" She squeezed my hand again. Briefly.

"I don't know how I did it." Lightly. "Just lucky, I guess."

"Does Desmond even know you escaped?"

"I'm pretty sure he knows by now…But not to get sidetracked, why is this Cole fellow coming here?"

"I'm getting there, Nick. Bear with me. I'm kind of in shock…How did you get away?"

"Oh, that." I shook my head and smiled. "I got lucky. In the parking lot after the fight, everybody was drinking and carrying on, and I kind of faded into the shadows where my friend was waiting. He whisked me away to my office, which is where I found your letter..."

She raised a sculpted eyebrow. "Really, Nick, that's a little far-fetched, don't you think? But it's all right if you want to be mysterious."

"It's kind of a need-to-know thing, Adara. My job is to protect you as much as possible. I'm sure you understand...So let's get back to Mr. Cole."

She pouted. Briefly. Spoke. "Okay. I get it. I'll just have to use my imagination...As for Desmond Cole, he'll be here at seven in the morning to talk things over. He'll bring coffee and pastry."

It was beyond strange. Quincey had wanted to give deadman-walking Crane a fighting chance in the ring with Tragg, and Cole, who I didn't know from Adam, had wanted to rescue me from Todd and his crew before they handed me off to a south-of-the-border death squad. Maybe. After the fight, Cole and Quincey had watched me being hustled into the van. They both must have gotten word that I'd escaped.

"Look," she said. "I think we're making progress. The principals are furious with Thomas and want him arrested immediately before he does any more harm. Desmond will explain where you come in when he gets here."

Where I come in? Jesus. That had been the problem all along.

My head was swimming. I asked the obvious question. "Do you trust Cole?"

Adara hesitated. Shook her head slowly. "The answer is no. Not entirely. I don't trust any of the principals, but I do trust Desmond on this. What you may not understand is that Desmond and the other principals have great respect for Thomas. They're disgusted with him, but they still want to save him from himself. The decision has been made to arrest him immediately before he does any more damage. Desmond will fill you in when he gets here. But the good news is this means you can rescue my father right after Thomas is taken into custody. I'll fly to Boston with you so that he and I can enter the safe house together. And we'll be in much less jeopardy with Thomas in prison. I believe this is our best chance."

I'll fly to Boston with you…I believe this is our best chance. Such a pretty thought, but so much could go wrong. The key was arresting Quincey. And I had another problem. Two glasses of red wine, and what I really wanted was to kiss her wine-stained lips. Deeply red. They parted when she spoke. It hit me in the chest like a warm hand from out of the impossible. She was a client. I groaned. Gave her a searching look.

She smiled. "Don't worry, Nick. We shouldn't have drunk so much wine." She stood up, took me by the hand, and pulled me to a standing position. "We need to get some sleep. Desmond will be here in a few hours. Your room is just down the hall."

She led me to the room. Queen-sized bed. She came in with me. I wanted her. Badly. She leaned in and kissed me on the lips. Tenderly. Blissful moment, but then she broke away, sighed, said goodnight, turned, and walked out of the room.

CHAPTER FIFTY-SIX

Desmond Cole's knock on the apartment door jolted me out of a restless sleep. I groaned and rolled over. Then one of my burners rang. Tony. Excited. He told me Bobby had phoned at the crack of dawn and explained that I had escaped from Thomas Quincey's crew. "Bobby said you were a fucking Houdini."

I smiled, despite my weariness. "Let's just say I'm good with locks."

Then Tony told me Raymundo Ochoa and his *compadres* were in town shopping for condos. If I could somehow rescue Gloria and Abrecia in the next few days, I could drop them off with Raymundo and his housekeeper at the Beverly Hilton, where they were staying. Raymundo would arrange to have them driven across the border within twenty-four hours. They would stay at his house in Culiacán until he got home from his real estate expedition. Then he would personally deliver the girls to Señora Iglesias. If she resisted, he would sweeten the pot until she gave in. But he didn't think it would be a problem. "She's a Mexican mother," said Tony. "I'm sure she hates Roberto, even in the grave, for cheating on her, but I don't think she'll turn her back on her kids' half-sisters."

I thought it over. A double or triple dealer he might be, but there was something about Raymundo—that fine specimen of corrupt retired Federale—that made me take heart. "Sounds good. Let's run with it. Have you located the girls' mother?"

"Elene's been fast-tracked to some border hellhole near San Pedro Island in Texas. She's applying for asylum. Her lawyer says she might be there for nine months or longer. He said he's going to fight for her." Tony paused. Cleared his throat. Spoke. "And I double-checked on the girls' legal status. They're Mexican citizens here illegally, which means they're deportable. I'm certain Roberto, first and foremost, would want the girls to be safe. And they'll never be safe here, Nick, not with things the way they are."

He was right. If by some miracle Elene got asylum and was on track for citizenship, then she might be able to have her girls returned to her here in the U.S. But those were big ifs. The important thing was to rescue the girls and get word to Elene as soon as we knew they were safe…

When I emerged from the bedroom, I found Cole and Adara sitting across from each other at a fifties-style, chrome-topped table in a little sunroom off the kitchen. That wasn't the problem. The problem was the small army of suits who scrutinized me balefully from their vantage point in the living room as I walked down the hallway to the kitchen. The one I made for their capo muttered something under his breath, his arms folded across his chest, his eyes watchful incisions under heavy brows.

"My personal bodyguards," said Desmond Cole. "It's more and more in vogue these days."

"Well, get them the fuck out of here." It was an order. I repeated it. *"Get them the fuck out of here."*

Up close, Cole was neither prepossessing nor repellant. With his regular features, thick, snowy white hair, and calm, wide-set blue eyes, he could have sprung from the pages of an AARP ad. Caucasian virtue *in extremis*. Wearing a sleekly cut white tuxedo.

"Nick Crane, sit down, sir." He gestured to a vacant chair next to Adara.

"Not till your cleaners hit the road."

Cole laughed. "As you wish, Mr. Crane." He stood up and called into the living room, "Dagmar, would you come here, please?" Dagmar, whose primary expressions seemed to be sullen and extra sullen, paid us the courtesy of unfolding his arms as he stepped into the kitchen.

"Everything's under control here. You and your men can take a break. I'll call you when I'm ready."

"What about his weapons?"

"Ah, that," said Cole. "I'm not averse to Second Amendment rights, and Mr. Crane surely won't be shooting anyone here at the breakfast table. You may go, Dagmar."

As Dagmar and his partners exited, I got my first taste of Cole's peculiar smile—friendly, accommodating, even joyous at times, but ever-shifting with the undertone of a man sharing a hidden joke to be grasped by only a select few. Adara poured me a cup of coffee. Then we got down to business. Or as much as you could get down to business with Desmond Cole…

"Thank you for agreeing to meet me here, Mr. Crane. As you know, I'm Desmond Cole. My friends call me Dee. You probably recognize me; I was the ring announcer at last night's fight. That was a fine exhibition, Mr. Crane. I can't remember the last time I've been so jazzed, and I was hardly the only one. I was a light-heavyweight myself when I was a young man. I could have been good, but I had my family's expectations to uphold, if you know what I mean?"

He paused. Time for magnanimous Crane. See where it took us. "I do know what you mean. I'm not sure I envy you, but I must say, you seem to wear it well. Your responsibilities, that is."

"Thank you. I appreciate that. I really do. But watching you knock QB's block off last night reminded me of what I could have been, what I probably should have been." Another bright and joyful smile, quickly replaced by a contemplative look.

I took a sip of coffee and put down my cup. Uncanny feeling

that everything had been preordained from the day Cole had casually dropped my name to Adara.

"So here we are. Feels like it's somehow inevitable." The ringmaster reading my mind. I didn't speak. Gnawed my lower lip.

"I think it's fair to say, Mr. Crane, that it's getting late in the game. The principals are getting impatient. The consensus is this has dragged on far too long. There's always that danger when working with friends. Which is what this is really all about, isn't it?"

Huh? Explain yourself, man. He did.

"We're still in mourning over the death of Frank Constantine—Thomas, in particular. It's a pain that does not go away. And now Rowe had to go and get himself killed. Again, because of you. Strange, isn't it? That means only Thomas and I are left…"

"Listen, Cole, I told Rowe to stay back, but he was a courageous motherfucker. I've got to hand it to him. If he had stayed back, Javier Fincus would have shot me in cold blood. Me *and* Bobby Moore. Rowe saved both our lives. So fuck off with your blame game. Frank Constantine had to be brought to justice. As for your friend Rowe, he chose to die a warrior's death. I salute him."

Long silence. Cole finally spoke, his blue eyes mournful. "I like your style, Mr. Crane. I really do. More importantly, I respect you, which is why I'm going to be frank and lay my cards on the table. The day you stole Frank's torture database is the day you signed away your freedom, if not your life. This has led to complications and disagreements on what to do with you. And you know how people waffle. It's human nature. When it was all four of us—Frank, Thomas, Rowe, and myself—we had considerable voting power as a bloc. We could often swing results in a positive direction. That's a fact you've obviously not considered while killing us off one after the other." He flashed a mournful smile. "But the long and short of it is, you are finished. Kaput. The question is, how do we want to handle your demise?"

This time, Cole didn't smile. Instead, he grimaced and his bright blue eyes seemed to cloud over. He rubbed them, controlling himself with difficulty. "Yes, Mr. Crane. Sometimes you have to laugh to keep from crying. Tears of a clown, you might say."

"I suppose we're all clowns in this game."

"The idea has been tossed around."

I nodded and tapped my fingers on the tabletop. "So just out of curiosity, who is responsible for the clusterfuck at the auto body shop?"

"Are you still thinking about that? You've got to put that behind you." Cole frowned and ran a hand through his hair. Elegant bastard. Then he stared past me as if the pale, yellow wall behind me contained the answer. Finally, he told me the principals were like the many facets of a diamond. Alliances would naturally form, but they would also shift, dissolve, and even shatter. But there were always four groups of four or five each. Groups were not required to vote as a bloc. "But you probably don't care about all that, Mr. Crane. What you care about is nuts-and-bolts stuff, like, *who the hell gave the order to ambush you?* All I can tell you is the decision was not made lightly. But you'd become too much of a distraction, especially for Thomas. You were given the chance to come in from the cold, but you made it clear you weren't interested.

"Therefore, Mr. Crane, the decision was made to have you...well, you know, damn it, man!" He paused, the picture of dejection. But not for long.

"But we digress, Mr. Crane. You're alive, at least for the moment, so why does it even matter?" He grinned impishly. "But remember. We did propose a solution. Mother's arms were open wide, but you declined her invitation. And I must say, the recent vote was close. Maybe there still is a way to persuade a few of the fence straddlers..."

He shifted gears. Effortlessly. "Frank Constantine was a dreamer, a brilliant man, but his childhood left him with indelible scars. Rowe and I, on the other hand, had stable upbringings and slid effortlessly into our niches. I can't believe Rowe is dead." Cole's eyes were distant. "We were all close. Rowe was the liberal and I was the pragmatist. Thomas was the man of action and Frank was the idealist. Rowe and I met at Phillips Exeter, and later on we met Frank and Thomas. They'd been childhood friends and shared a deep bond. Frank's death hit Thomas the hardest. And this, unfortunately, came on the heels of 9-11 and the invasion and reconstruction of Iraq." He paused. Moistened the inside of his lower lip with the tip of his tongue. Thinking. Continued.

They'd all served in Iraq. Frank was a psychiatrist, and Cole and Rowe were in logistics. Only Quincey saw active duty in the field, mostly in Al-Anbar province during the four-year battle to overcome the Insurgency. Cole explained that although Quincey could have risen through the ranks, he refused promotions and insisted on remaining a captain so he could be close to the troops. The key to defeating the Insurgency was bringing the Sunni sheikhs over to the Allied camp. They were ripe for change, sick of al Q'aeda and its absurd demands. All they needed was encouragement. Quincey had been magnificent. He drank tea with the sheikhs and dipped his fingers into the communal goat bowl. Held hands with Arab men in public in the approved tribal manner. Because of men like Quincey, by late 2007, most of the sheikhs, which in turn meant most of the Sunni tribes in Al-Anbar Province, had come over to the American side. Once he'd dipped into enough goat bowls and held enough hands to gain the trust of the people, Quincey had helped organize the local Sunni police and the Iraqi military at the grassroots level, and, with the sheikhs' blessing, he had spearheaded the reconstruction of schools and infrastructure.

Cole looked at us. "Perhaps you've heard the phrase 'winning the minds and hearts of the people?'" We nodded. "That's what Thomas did better than anyone. He was magnificent, and it gave him a sense of fulfillment…"

"But then he fucked up," I said softly. "And it ruined him. And now he wants everyone to pay."

"So you know," said Cole. "I guess that makes this easier."

"All I know is he lost five or six rifle teams. Around twenty troops. Through an intel error, which, I believe, could have been avoided."

Cole nodded. His eyes were sad. "Adara? Has Thomas ever told you exactly what happened?"

"He's only danced around it," she said quietly. "Thomas is a coward when it comes to the important things. All I know is he was infatuated with an Iraqi woman, who was somehow involved."

"Well, as I said to Mr. Crane, today is the day we lay our cards on the table. What I know is second-hand, coming from Frank, but I think it's basically accurate. Frank is the only one Thomas actually confided in. Are you sure you want to hear this?"

"Why not?" said Adara. "Thomas's debacle has brought me nothing but pain. More pain than you can imagine."

"What about you, Mr. Crane?"

I nodded.

CHAPTER FIFTY-SEVEN

"Her name was Akhtari, meaning wife of the Prophet. She was twenty-five years old and the daughter of tribespeople. I believe her parents were killed by Marine crossfire, but she lied and said they had died of natural causes. She showed up at Al-Alad Airbase at Camp Cupcake in the Hīt governorate in western Iraq in September of 2007, covered in black from head to toe. She said her parents were dead, and she was escaping from her brother, who beat her. She said her brother was in AQI, which was a problem. If we took her in, it would be a death sentence if she ever tried to go home again. Her death would be considered an honor killing. The Sunnis in Al-Anbar Province were nothing like the madmen in the Taliban, but they were still Muslims. Male honor was still paramount. When she begged and pleaded, the duty officer decided a nurse could examine her. Her story checked out. Her arms and legs were black and blue. That was enough. They made the decision to take her in."

Cole explained Akhtari was given a room and a job as a translator. She made the unbelievable sum of $1,000 a month. Once her bruises healed, she began wearing western clothes. Quincey met her a few months later in December. "She was gorgeous," said Cole. He turned to Adara. "Tall like you, Adara, elegant of face and figure. Thomas fell hard. Middle Eastern women are his weak spot. By then, his second divorce was final, and technically, he was a free man. Based on his status and reputation, Thomas had his own apartment. So did Rowe. It's amazing what a little money can do. Only Thomas and Rowe lived at Cupcake. Frank and I came and went, depending on where our duties took us. I came to Cupcake that February. I hadn't seen Thomas for six months. He was transformed, radiant like I'd never seen him. When I actually met her, though, I was disappointed. My sense was she cultivated a contrived sincerity. I can always spot that in a person. Maybe because I've been accused of having those same qualities." He smiled wanly, his eyes calm, knowing. "Of course, I said nothing to Thomas, just hoped it would run its course. I'd never known Thomas to remain interested in any one woman for long." Again, he turned to Adara. "Except for you."

Cole stopped. Pushed his chair back. Said what he was going to tell us was hard to tell. But he would try. He explained that along with winning the minds and hearts of the sheikhs and their tribes, it was also necessary to find and confiscate AQI's arms and IED caches, which were buried in literally thousands of places throughout the province. One night, after sex, Akhtari told Thomas that one of her older brothers, who was disgusted with AQI, had told her about a massive electronics cache concealed under the floor of a bombed-out primary school ten miles north of Hīt on the east bank of the Euphrates.

"She said her brother told her there were enough IEDs to rain hell on the Americans. She knew exactly where the school was because her cousins had gone there. Or so she said as she cozied up to Quincey in their comfortable bed and gave him directions to the schoolhouse."

Confiscating the IEDs could save an untold number of lives; speed was of the essence. Thomas had slipped out of bed before dawn. He got on the phone and dispatched six rifle teams and a truck convoy with orders to recover all of the radio controls and IEDS.

"Thomas thought it would be easy, damned near routine." Cole shook his head almost violently. "I don't know where he got that idea. Well, actually I do. He got it from Akhtari. And, of course, it was an absolute disaster. I think she must have phoned someone from the bedroom while Quincey was at his desk barking orders and dispatching the rifle teams. They were sitting ducks. No, they were worse than sitting ducks. They were cooked geese. The IEDs exploded at one-and-one-half-second intervals, like firecrackers, as they neared the ruined school. Eight Marines died more or less instantly. Thomas can give you their names, ages, and where they were from. One of them was a woman from somewhere in Kentucky. Five more men were shot and killed by snipers when they staggered or crawled from their Humvees. Thomas can also give you their personal information. Three survivors are now quadriplegics. One lives in Sarasota, one in Carson City, and one in Rice Lake, Wisconsin. Thomas visits them once a year and makes sure all their needs are provided for. Of the other eight, four were captured by AQI and made examples of. Their bodies were found in pieces in the desert a week or so later. Four men survived with only minor injuries. Of those four, one is in Soledad state prison, and one hanged himself last Christmas. The third is a child molester, and the fourth is an upstanding high school history teacher in Biloxi, Mississippi." Cole shook his head sadly.

"It was a nightmare. I wasn't at Cupcake when it happened. Thank God! It would have been too painful. I do know that although there was little overt blame, both the brass and the enlisted men were all too aware that Thomas had exercised bad, if not atrocious, judgment. For the rest of his tour, he kept his head down. He mustered out at the first opportunity, returned to the States, and left the Corps. He changed his name and began contracting with ICE a year later. He has never recovered psychologically, and I don't believe he ever will. The disaster in 'Raq is the real reason he is now such a fervent isolationist and nationalist. Not that 9-11 and the New York Public Library incident didn't contribute, but it was the 'Raq disaster that pushed him over the edge. This is not to say Thomas dislikes Arabs or Iraqis. It's far more complicated than that. He likes them a great deal, but he doesn't trust them."

"He certainly doesn't trust me," said Adara. Surprisingly, neither her eyes nor her voice suggested she was moved by the story.

"What about Akhtari?" I asked.

"She slipped away during the confusion and was never seen again. Presumably, she had someone waiting outside the camp."

Stunned. No other word for it. I tried to focus on the nuts and bolts. "What about the radio controls and communication equipment? Did the Marines make a second attempt, or did they just abandon it?"

"The former, with great care, but when they got there, the bird had flown. Nothing was left but some random ordnance."

A long silence I finally broke. "Okay, Cole. This explains a lot. I appreciate your candor. But tell me this. What exactly is Quincey trying to do here in the States? To the Muslim community?"

"You didn't hear this from me," said Cole, shaking his head. "Thomas now believes our road to salvation is to launch false flag operations here in the States designed to bring the country to such a permanent state of high alert that even the most sophisticated Islamic terrorist attacks would be intercepted and repelled. His grandiosity is astonishing. He has talked about launching a dozen terror attacks on the same day in twelve metropolitan areas, a kind of American *Kristallnacht*. At other times, he thinks it might be more effective to launch one attack per week for a three or four-month period. Imagine the apprehension by the fourth or fifth week. This is where you come in, Mr. Crane, at least in Thomas's mind. He wants to utilize your courage and organizational abilities. And I do think you'd be good at it. It would be a way for you to atone for the death of Frank Constantine." Cole lifted an eyebrow. "Although truthfully, it's probably too late for that now, even if you were interested, which I don't believe you are."

Jesus Christ. Cole was a slippery bastard.

"Thomas works with a task force that debriefs so-called high-risk individuals who are intercepted at the border. Sometimes they recommend federal charges, and other times they throw the luckless bastards back across the border. And, of course, there is the third option, to be used sparingly. This is where it gets ugly. The game is to identify promising candidates and turn them into programmed killers. But Thomas wrestles with this. In the morning, he thinks one thing; by evening, he thinks something else."

I nodded grimly. "What about him and Rowe pimping out the little girls? Turning them into sex toys?"

Cole shook his head. He wasn't going there.

I'd heard enough. "So tell me this, Mr. Cole. What exactly do you want from me? Adara told me the plan is to arrest Quincey immediately."

I sat back and waited.

"That is correct," said Cole wearily. No smile at all now. A sad, drawn face, but eyes as calm and quizzical as ever. "The plan is for you and your people to arrest Thomas and hand him off to LASD. He'll be charged with drug trafficking and will serve about twenty-four months in a federal facility. Otherwise, it would be LAPD and the FBI and God knows who else knocking down his door and dragging him away in disgrace. It would be a nightmare, and I don't want Thomas to experience that level of humiliation. He's suffered enough already."

What a hoot! No doubt Thomas had suffered, but what about everybody else, all his victims? Including yours truly. But I didn't say it. Instead, I pulled in my horns and said quietly, "What changes if I help pull this off?"

"As far as the principals are concerned, I'm not sure it changes anything. It may be too late for that. But let's pretend it's not. What are your terms?"

Just like with Mohammad on the Charles River Esplanade, I wanted to ruminate. Consider. Analyze. Construct a reasonable set of demands. But no time. Winging it as usual.

"I want three things. First, Adara and her father are to be set free immediately. I will finesse Mohammad's escape and arrange for him and Adara to be reunited in a private place. After that I will vanish for six months or so. When I come back, I will be left alone to run my company. And in the meantime, Mohammad gets his money back."

Cole guffawed. But only briefly. "Money, money. Why does it always get back to the dirty green? But all right. Mohammad gets his filthy lucre back—the money he earned off the bent backs of the Iraqi peasants. As far as total freedom for Mohammad and Adara, the answer is yes, at least for her." Cole turned to Adara. "Your life will be much better. I can promise you that. And your father's life will also be much better. But based on the contract he signed, he'll still need to be debriefed from time to time, but nothing intrusive. And I'll probably handle it myself. As for you, Mr. Crane, who can say? If it were only up to me, by all means, you could disappear for as long as you like and do anything you want when you return. But seriously, even if I were to lobby for you, which I definitely will if you help me out with Thomas's arrest, it will be an uphill battle to persuade the principals to back off. But it's worth a try. The first step is to have Thomas taken into custody in the most unobtrusive manner possible."

Well, the cards were on the table. Jokers wild. I was sick of Cole's bullshit equivocations, and, for a crazy moment, I considered shooting him in the head. Right there. At the kitchen table. But I didn't. I had to focus on my real goals. What Cole was offering was the devil's own bargain, but I didn't see what choice I had. If it all went well, and that was a big if, it would take Quincey completely out of the game, at least for now. Adara and Mohammad would be much better off. And if Mohammad came through with something in the mid-six figures range, I would be able to lie low with no immediate financial concerns. Then I remembered. "What about the eight girls and women who were being abused up at the Nazi camp? They must be given the right to seek asylum."

Cole nodded his head slowly. "They will have that right. Indeed, they will. But with expedited deportation being the order of the day, I don't think they have," his voice breaking, "much chance of succeeding. Of course, that might depend on who their lawyers are." He wiped his eyes. I was astonished. Was it real empathy or a great acting job? Either way, he recovered quickly. "But what I can do is this. I will talk to the appropriate people and make sure they're repatriated in the kindest, gentlest way possible."

Kindest, gentlest way. Where had I heard that before? "They deserve that as a bare minimum."

"Absolutely, Mr. Crane. I'll take care of it. It's the least I can do."

Then he said he was pretty sure any monkey business with the little girls was QB Tragg's play, and he believed it was just one or two isolated instances. I knew he was lying. If it was Tragg's play, why was Rowe minding them for Quincey? And why did none of these bastards even care? But I was boxed in. We had to take down Quincey, and we had to liberate Adara and Mohammad. And I had to rescue the girls in Ohio. I asked Adara what she thought.

Her gaze shifted from me to Cole and back. And then back to Cole.

"I want one other thing," she said firmly. "As soon as Thomas is in custody, my father and I—who have been unofficial wards of the State Department ever since we arrived here twenty years ago—will be given the right to apply for green cards. And our applications will be expedited."

Cole said he believed that could be arranged.

"All right then. I accept the terms. I can't speak for Mr. Crane, though."

I looked at them and they looked at me. Then I gave a single short nod.

CHAPTER FIFTY-EIGHT

Cole wanted to arrest Quincey on Wednesday, but I told him I needed one more day. A personal matter. He hemmed and hawed, but finally agreed.

He would schedule a twelve o'clock luncheon with Quincey on Thursday at his Bel Air estate. He would arrive before us in his Lambo. He assured us no one else would be there. Only Desmond and Tom. Old friends.

"It's like this, Mr. Crane. I want to make sure you understand. I need you to do me this small but important courtesy. LASD would love to dispatch a twenty-man team to tear Thomas's house apart, with half-a-dozen agencies along for the ride. But that's not what we want. We want his arrest to be as low-key as possible. That's why we want you to handle it. Calmly and discreetly."

"What about Quincey's soldiers?"

Cole waved off my concern. Said Quincey's soldiers were not allowed on his estate. Adara agreed that was generally true. Who wants hired guns hanging around when you don't need them? It was different out in the big world. There, they were a necessary evil. Cole said there would be no resistance whatsoever. He would personally disconnect the security system before we got there.

"Look," said Cole. "I hate like hell to do this to Thomas, but at least his last few minutes as a free man will be pleasant ones.

He and I will be enjoying moussaka on the patio. With his favorite endive salad and a bottle of Tempranillo."

I nodded. "We can do it. Without too much trouble, if, as you say, there is no resistance. If there is resistance, all bets are off."

Cole's turn to nod. He told me to sit tight. Called his security team and told them to bring the firepower. He didn't want us to carry our own guns. If things went south, and we had to shoot our way out, he wanted the bullets to be fired from untraceable guns. So much for his "no resistance" claim.

Ten minutes later, Dagmar and his goons lugged a good-sized chest into the living room and flipped open the latches. Manhunter's paradise. For myself, I selected a fifteen-round Glock 22 and an eleven-round Beretta 96, complete with suppressors, belt holsters, and cartridges. For Bobby, I grabbed a Sig Sauer 226P and a HK P30, with the requisite ammo and trappings. I checked each gun carefully. Cole was right. No serial numbers. I also chose four fifty-thousand-volt Tasers. Adara reached into her handbag and gave me five gate clickers. Then she retrieved a gym bag from her bedroom. To carry the weapons. It made a tidy little package.

Plan was I would meet with my crew and Adara at my office at eleven o'clock on Thursday morning. We would arrive at Quincey's estate at noon. Cole wanted us to be prompt because he had a wedding reception in Holmby Hills that afternoon. Which is why he had wanted to arrest Quincey on Wednesday. He asked us if we liked his white tux. Said he had just picked it up at a discount and was breaking it in. "Looks great on you," I said lightly.

"No, seriously, Mr. Crane. What do you think?"

"I think you wear it well."

"I do, don't I? There's something about good clothes that makes me feel like a million bucks."

Before I got in my car, Cole and I faced one another in the early morning light. First, he thanked me for escaping on my own so that he didn't have to engineer my rescue himself at great cost and aggravation.

"How would you have done it?"

"I had already called in my alpha team. They would have found a way."

Then he moved closer and put his right hand on my shoulder. Told me a warrant for the arrest of Thomas Quincey, aka Miles Amsterdam, was being fast-tracked based on Javier Fincus's proffer. They would notify Diego Smith. He suggested I arrange to have Diego and LASD meet us outside the gates of Thomas's estate. We would walk Quincey out to the street and hand him off to Diego.

"Simple as that," I said.

"Simple as that. LASD will keep Thomas in protective custody for a few days while we put the pieces in place. We have to make sure Thomas is not turned into a misunderstood hero who ends up getting a slap on the wrist. He needs to suffer to a reasonable degree; doing some time will wake him up. We'll do what we can to make sure we get the right AUSA when his case goes federal. I want him hit hard, but not too hard. This could make a huge difference in Thomas's life. It could bring him back to reality. And it could make a big difference in yours. I'll do everything I can."

Odd speech. I nodded grimly. Then we shook hands, one man measuring another. Then I got into my old Corolla and drove away.

CHAPTER FIFTY-NINE

With a trunkful of unmarked firearms, I started west on Santa Monica Boulevard. Angled up to Sunset. A late breakfast at Carney's, the railroad car diner across the street from the House of Blues. Then east on Sunset. Really just killing time while I made some phone calls. First Jack Snow. I tried to apologize but he cut me off. "I appreciate the sentiments, Nick, but no one on earth could have predicted those cocksuckers were going to bust in like that."

"Yeah, but what about your face?"

"It'll heal. I've been more scared taking a big hit on the gridiron back when I was a 130- pound wide-out." He laughed. "And my balls are intact. That's the good news. Ironically, the invasion was a good excuse to rearrange my books and weed out the duplicates." That's Jack. His world awash with silver linings. "It's a good lesson, Nick. Always lock your doors and keep a loaded gun close at hand. By the way, how did you escape from those maniacs?"

I told him that was a story for another time. We signed off.

Next, Caroline. She was at the ranch, her voice warm and friendly. A wave of relief. She told me her lawyers were rather mystified when she told them she was harboring eight refugees at her Grenada Hills stables, but when she told them they'd been rescued from a group of evil men and women, they came around.

"So they agreed to keep it on the down-low for a week?"

"They did. They better. I pay them a small fortune to keep their lawyerly mouths shut, except when it's time to open them. They told me that based on their workload, it would take them several days to research the legality of what I was doing." Then she said she was getting to know everybody except for Amy Li Kong's mother Soon Lin, who kept apart from the others and kept muttering about *the river*. I said I'd tell her why when we had more time. Then I sprang it on her, apologizing profusely for such short notice. Told her we had to fly to Ohio. Tonight. If she was shocked, she didn't show it. I asked her to text me the registration information for her private jet, a Citation XLS she stored at Bob Hope Regional Airport in Burbank. She laughed and said my tab was getting big enough to keep her in polo ponies for at least a year. I told her I was serious; we had to leave no later than five or six o'clock. She said okay and that she'd text me the information as soon as she got home.

After we hung up, I took a deep breath and called BK Knox. BK knows how to fly airplanes. I had talked to him right after my romantic interlude with Caroline. He'd told me he planned on hanging around for the next few weeks playing blackjack and lowball in the South County casinos. I had met him through Barry Camus, who told me BK was a good pilot and the soul of discretion. I had asked BK for his business card. For times like this. To keep the iron hot, I take him out to lunch once or twice a year.

Delighted when he picked up on the second ring. Not so happy when he told me he was having a wet lunch at the Cat 'n Kitty Lounge on South Normandie in South Los Angeles. "I'm sucking down some Tecates. Maybe you wanna join me?"

"I'd love to, BK, but I can't. Remember that job I mentioned?"

"Yeah, you need to go to Indiana or one of those fucked-up states."

"Actually, it's Ohio. We need to fly out of Bob Hope Regional no later than six p.m. tonight."

"What? Today? That's impossible."

"Why?"

"'Cause I'm off today. Kickin' it. Life is good."

"No, man, I really need you to do it. I'll pay extra if necessary."

"What the fuck! Barry warned me about you."

"You mean he told you I always keep my word and pay on time?"

"No, he said you're a pushy bastard who gets under people's skin."

"Sorry. I'm a little keyed up. You see, we're flying to Ohio to rescue two little girls from a sadistic foster home." Silence. I could hear him slurping on something.

He finally spoke. "It does sound interesting. And knowing what kind of company Barry keeps, what you're doing is probably highly illegal."

"Depends on how you look at it. We're the good guys here, and we'll be flying with a wealthy woman who's dedicating herself to saving these girls."

That worked. "Hmm? How much does she wanna pay for this?"

"She's not paying. I'm paying. What's your standard charge for a rush round trip flight to Gallipolis, Ohio."

"I don't have a standard charge for something like that." I could feel him nibbling at the bait. "Her plane, right?"

"Yessir. A Citation XLS." Silence.

"Ah, hell! Gimme five large, and I'll do it. And you pay all expenses, including refueling charges. When do we fly back?"

"Around noon tomorrow, I think. That's my goal." Damned good thing Adara had replenished my cash cache.

"What the fuck! I'm in."

"Good. I'll see you at five o'clock sharp at the airport. I'll text you the registration information for the Citation so you can get us cleared with the air traffic folks."

"Ten-four, baby. Old BK knows the good people up at Bob Hope. I'm all over it."

"Beautiful." We signed off.

Phoned Caroline. Told her we were on, and I'd meet her at her house at four p.m. Asked her to rent us a car in Gallipolis and to make hotel reservations for three separate suites for one night only. And to put it all on my tab. This time, she seemed to be listening closely. Sounded excited and a little nervous. We signed off. By now, I was nearly back to the Cradle Rest.

Then Tony. Told him that he and Bobby and I were going to arrest Thomas Quincey at his Bel Air estate at noon on Thursday. Based on the orders of a new mucky-muck. Said I'd give him the details later.

"Just like that," Tony said dryly. "After all this shit. That motherfucker's done a lot of damage. Maybe we should let him try to escape so I can shoot him in the back. That would cheer me up." Tony's not usually vindictive, but Quincey had arranged for the killing of Roberto. Or so Tony believed. And I was pretty sure he was right.

Then I walked him through my rescue plan. If all went well, Caroline and I would fly into Bob Hope Airport, with Roberto's daughters in tow, on Wednesday evening, no later than five or six p.m.

One more guy to call. Lyndon Naismith, Esq. Not sure he would cooperate, but either way, we were taking the girls. It was four p.m. Eastern Daylight Time when I phoned his office. The sweet-as-pecan-pie admin told me he was gone for the day. Not sure why, but I changed my mind and didn't leave a message. Thanked her and signed off.

Three hours to kill. Stopped in at the internet café on Green Street in Pasadena. Sent a few emails to Mohammad. Stuff about everyday life in Mesopotamia I was sure he already knew. Like the fact women were required to be up at dawn cooking the morning porridge. Then I fell asleep right at my computer. I was paying by the hour, and no one seemed to care.

When it was time, I drove to Caroline's house. Marveling as always at the sheltering foliage gracing her neighborhood. I was early. Someone in security directed me to one of her dens. Flicked on ESPN. Closed my eyes. Drifted. In nearly a deep sleep when she roused me.

We drove to Bob Hope Airport in my old Corolla.

CHAPTER SIXTY

BK was waiting for us at Caroline's hangar. On his arm, a pretty redhead in a blue jumpsuit named Priscilla. Couldn't tell if she was Asian or Latina or maybe Persian. She was hanging on BK's arm and talking on her phone. BK is 5'3" in cowboy boots. Which he wears 24/7. Big square body. Big square face. Cowboy shirt. Bolo tie. Rhinestone Elvis jacket. Military brush cut. Pronounced scar on his right cheek. His smile a grimace. His laugh a honk. Caroline tried hard not to stare.

BK said he needed to talk to me. We wandered into the hangar, where he gave the
Citation the once-over. "Very nice piece of machinery." He popped a couple of fruit-flavored tic-tacs into his mouth.

"Hope you're sober enough to fly."

"Hell!" Said with contempt. "Of course I can fly. I drink beer when I'm not working, but when I'm on the job, I'm as sober as Warren Buffett." More tic-tacs.

"Glad to hear it. Let's get moving."

"Just as soon as you hand over the cash." I sighed. Handed him a fat envelope. BK opened it and riffled through the bills. "Nothing I like better," he said, "than that crisp feel of brand-new Franklins."

We were in the air in forty-five minutes. I sat next to Caroline, our seats tilted back, sampling nuts, dark chocolate, and Prosecco. Priscilla joined us for a while. She smelled like cognac or brandy.

Uneventful trip. I was exhausted. After killing the Prosecco while chit-chatting with the women, I tilted my seat all the way back and tried to sleep. Tossed and turned a while, but finally went under. Woke up around ten when we landed at Samuel Gompers Airport outside of Tulsa to refuel. I knew jet fuel was expensive but had no idea how expensive. "Put it on my tab," I said to Caroline wearily.

"Not part of our deal," she said, smiling. I must've turned pale. She laughed and reached into her purse. AMEX Platinum did the trick. Sobered by the cost of this escapade, I told Caroline we'd repay her in full within two weeks. Tony was still sitting on most of Roberto's trafficking dollars, but I didn't want to touch that. As soon as Mohammad handed over the big money, I could pay off all obligations.

The next surprise came after we were once again cruising at altitude. I was nearing the end of *The Deep Blue Good-by*. It was amazing. Faced with terrible odds, Travis McGee had liquidated a small army of miscreants. Caroline was reading a trade magazine. I was hungry. Mentioned this, but she only laughed and pointed at the leftover nuts.

"What? No steak? No caviar?" Pretending to sound aggrieved.

"There's more nuts where these came from. In fact, I think I'm sitting next to one." She laughed, reached out, and stroked my cheek. "You poor dear. These planes don't have real kitchens, and we left so suddenly I didn't have time to call my caterer. For all your acquired savoir-faire, Nick, you're still a babe-in-the-woods."

I laughed. She had me pegged. "You're right. No culture in my house growing up. Unless you call boxing and football culture."

"Amazing," said Caroline. "The American Way...There was way too much culture in my house." We discussed the pros and cons of our upbringings and began talking about her schizophrenic son Peter, who, at age thirty, was about to get his degree in animal husbandry at UC Davis, where he and his pal Lou Hernandez shared an apartment.

Can't remember what we talked about next. Then came the third surprise. Caroline looked longingly at the empty Prosecco bottle. Nibbled her lower lip. Reached out and placed her fingertips in the middle of my forehead. Put her hands back in her lap. Spoke. Choosing her words carefully. "Nick, I loved what we did the other day. Right now, sitting here, I truly want to kiss you." She stopped. There was sadness in her smile. "But we can't do this on a regular basis. Make love, I mean."

I waited.

"It was good, Nick. And I like you a lot. But we're not right for each other. You know that." Her voice trailed off…

"Because we're worlds apart," I said finally. I reached for the nuts and a bottle of Perrier. The salt makes you thirsty…

We touched down at Gallia-Meigs Regional Airport at about one a.m. A profound gloom came over me as we straggled toward the taxi stand. I was little more than a shadow walking among shadows. Taking up the rear. Weary and sick to my stomach, I vomited quietly into a chain-link fence. Wiped off my mouth and trudged after them.

Caroline had booked us into a Quality Inn. The half-comatose deskman managed to
get us our key cards. On the way up to our rooms, I told BK to sit tight in the morning. I'd tell him when to Uber back to the airport.

CHAPTER SIXTY-ONE

Six hours of sound sleep. Up in time for the complimentary breakfast. Caroline, who was rustling through her suitcase, asked me to bring her back a cup of black coffee. BK and Priscilla were already in the lobby. Today she had opted for a baby blue velour jumpsuit. I grabbed some powdered scrambled eggs and toast. And a blueberry muffin. Sat down next to BK and told him I might need him to impersonate a lawyer named Lyndon Naismith on the phone in about an hour. Ran through the play.

"You motherfucker. That's gonna cost you another thousand."

"Only if we need to do it."

BK shrugged.

Then, per our plan, I sat down at a computer in the motel business lounge. Created a new Gmail address and sent an email to Mohammad. The byline read *Sumerian Gods*. I linked a photo of the big-eyed gods and hit send.

Went back upstairs. Caroline looked formidable, Amazonian, in a charcoal, pin-striped, tailored suit. She drank her coffee and we discussed strategy. Acted out a few scenes. Then we picked up our rental car, a silver Toyota Camry, and made a pit stop at a local Sears, where I bought a $200 off-the-rack suit, a red and blue striped power tie, and a pair of plain black dress shoes. Then we drove over to Thomas Brown Primary School.

Got out of the car and walked toward the visitors' entrance. Before we went inside, I ruffled Caroline's already mussed hair.

"Hmm," she said. "Sears man. Very sexy."

We followed the signs to the Principal's Office. I told the young admin I was with ICE and Caroline was with Social Security Services. "We need to talk to your Principal. We've just flown in from Tulsa."

She looked a little scared. "Okay, then, I'll call her. I'm a temp. This is only my second day."

"You're doing a good job," I said, smiling. I went over and sat down next to Caroline.

Certain parts of certain operations are like going on a blind date. You have no idea what to expect. The Principal, Ms. Juliana Sheffield, only made us wait five minutes. Good sign. Ten could have signaled hostility. While waiting, Caroline looked around for magazines. She should have known better. The new millennium. Not much to read, but plenty of inspiring slogans on the wall. And anti-bullying reminders: *Bullying Will Not Be Tolerated. Bullies Will Be Suspended.* Caroline's lips were moving soundlessly. Rehearsing her lines.

Ms. Sheffield came out, greeted us, and ushered us into her office. She looked about forty-five. Smooth brown hair cut shoulder length. A square jaw and slightly low forehead. Brown eyes. Matter-of-fact mouth. The type of woman Bobby Moore has been known to court. Pleasant voice, firm handshake. Her office was decorated with children's drawings, some cute, others just juvenile.

"So what can I do for you?"

"I'm Special Agent Bob Evans. I'm with ICE, Special Investigations Unit. My colleague here is Suzanne Morehouse. Ms. Morehouse is with Social Security, Homeland Health and Services."

Her eyes moved from me to Caroline and back. I leaned across her desk and showed her my license. She glanced at it and pushed it back at me. Did not ask for Caroline's. Which was a good thing. Time to execute. "We're here, Principal Sheffield, on an errand of mercy. You have two little Latina girls here, Abrecia Eliade and Gloria Diaz. As you may know, they're on an immigration hold and are being housed temporarily at a foster home outside of town here, pending deportation. We need to talk to them to see if they feel comfortable with a plan that their mother, who's being held in Texas, believes is in their best interest." I paused. Gave her space.

"Yes. I'm aware of the girls," she said slowly. She sat up straight, looking puzzled. "I don't know anything about their mother."

"Well, they have one," said Caroline brightly. "Abrecia and Gloria are very close to their mother." Her manner imperious but ever so subtle. "And she'll feel a whole lot better once she knows they're in a good home."

"Where would she be going, if I might ask?"

"Sorry, we can't disclose that. That's protected information due to their refugee status." Hangdog Crane interjecting. Head drooping forward. "I wish I could say more, but we've got to follow the rules."

"It was my impression these girls will likely be deported back to their native Mexico."

Not sure how she felt about that, so I played it both ways. "Well, that certainly could happen. Like I said, I wish I could tell you more. What I can tell you is while their mother's asylum case is being litigated, the girls will be welcomed into a warm, loving home, either here or in Mexico."

"They've been through a lot," said Caroline. "We discovered their mother filed green card applications for all three of them, and these applications have languished for over two years. They appear to have been pushed aside. We don't know why. We do know they would have their green cards by now if not for the…"

"Foul-up," I finished grimly. "So, if you could, Ms. Sheffield, please bring us the girls. And we'll need a room where we can talk to them." My father Adam could give orders that would make the short hairs stand at attention. I have the same talent, but try to keep it in check.

Ms. Sheffield caved. That was the easy part. But I wasn't sure about the girls. We met them in a conference room next to the teacher's lounge. Abrecia recognized me instantly and seemed pleased. Gloria looked bewildered and scared.

"Sit down, girls." Waited till they were ready. "This is my friend, Caroline. She's a federal agent too."

"What's that?" said Abrecia.

"We're people whose job is to help people."

"Right now, we want to help you," said Caroline, beaming the kind of concern only saints and the truly wealthy can manage. "You see, we have a good home your mama wants us to take you to. Did your mama ever tell you that you have brothers and sisters in Mexico?"

Abrecia's brown eyes widened. "Mama said brothers."

"That's right," said Caroline. "Brothers. I got mixed up."

"What are their names?" said Gloria in a low voice.

"I'm not sure," said Caroline. "Did your mama tell you their names?"

"I think," said Abrecia slowly, twirling a lock of her dark brown hair, "the big one is named Roberto and the little one is named Jorge."

"Roberto? That's Papi's name," said Gloria.

"Does Lyndon know about this?" asked Abrecia.

"Oh, yes. He's really happy about it."

"That's good." A moment later. "When are you going to take us?"

"We can take you now," said Caroline. "If you want us to. Would you like to come with us?" She looked so kind and patient. Years of practice caring for her schizophrenic son.

"I want to go," said Abrecia. "Do you want to go too, sister?" Gloria sat poker-faced. Finally, she managed to nod.

"Then tap your shoes three times," I murmured, "and we'll take you to a good home."

"I'll tell the Principal," said Caroline brightly. She rang the receptionist, who buzzed Ms. Sheffield.

This time, she arrived within a minute or two. I told her the girls had decided they wanted to come with us. Abrecia was firm in her assent. "Yes, Ms. Sheffield. We want to do what mama says. We want to go to our new home."

"I see," said Ms. Sheffield. "I need to talk to both of you privately." We left the girls sitting at the table and walked out into the hallway.

"I need to tell you something." Ms. Sheffield ran a hand across her smooth brown hair. "Moving little Gloria might be for the best. She gets bullied daily on the playground. If it's not outright—pushing, tripping, pulling her hair—it's subtle. Laughing behind her back, snickering, throwing spitballs in class. I've done what I can, God knows, but I haven't been able to stop it. So it's important Gloria's new caregiver knows that she needs to be treated with kindness and understanding."

"I'm really glad you told us that," said Caroline, "and we will pass the word along. Thank you, Principal Sheffield."

Ms. Sheffield needed to formally disenroll the girls before we could take them. She and her temp mashed together some paperwork that I signed with an incomprehensible flourish. I told her she would be receiving official notification by both email and snail mail. "Our department is rather stodgy. Could you give me your email address, please?"

She complied and Caroline wrote it down.

Abrecia was skipping with joy as we made our way to the parking lot.

CHAPTER SIXTY-TWO

Handling Ms. Sheffield had been easy. She had just enough respect for authority. I wondered if she knew ICE cannot legally force states and their institutions to turn over illegals. Truth is, I wasn't sure about public schools. Mostly, it's done voluntarily. Next came Rosie. I was anticipating trouble, but it had to be done. Driving out to the Munsons, I congratulated Caroline on her excellent performance. Told her the next step with Rosie would not be cake. Abrecia, who had been listening quietly, piped up, "Rosie's mean."

"Why, 'cause she makes you work so much?" Silence.

"What does she do?" asked Caroline.

"She's mean to Lala."

"Lala's one of the white girls, right?"

"Yes."

"What does she do to her?"

"I dunno."

"When does she do it?"

"Late at night."

Caroline gasped, and I swore under my breath. Recovered quickly. Told Abrecia not to worry. That we'd help Lala as soon as we could.

When we got to the Munson property, there were no cars in the driveway. I backed in so the front end of the Camry faced the road. Told the girls to get their stuff. While they trotted off to their trailer to collect their meager belongings, I wrote a note to Rosie stating a good home had been found for the girls and she would receive official notification in the mail. And that the county would also be notified. I even wished her good luck.

Gloria and Abrecia made several trips, and Caroline helped them load their stuff in the trunk. Meanwhile, I reread the note, folded it in thirds, and placed it in Rosie's mailbox. Caroline had just gotten the girls situated in the backseat when Rosie drove up in her F-150 and parked next to us, her rear end facing the road. I told Caroline to drive fifty yards down the road toward Gallipolis. Then pull over and wait for me. She needed little urging. I walked over to Rosie, who had jumped out of her pickup and was staring at the departing Camry.

I stopped about a yard away. "Hi, Ms. Munson," offering my hand, which she ignored. "We've found an excellent home for Abrecia and Gloria, so we are relieving you of your caretaking duties."

She stared at me, hands on her hips, her mouth working soundlessly. Finally, she spoke. "The hell you are. Who do you think you are?"

"You know who I am, Special Agent Terry Fry, at your service."

"You can't just take the girls."

"I already have."

"I'm calling 9-1-1." Took out her phone and brandished it like a weapon. Bluffing. Fleeting thought I'd like to weaponize Rosie's sturdy form and use her as a battering ram.

"If you call the police, I'm going to have to tell them about what you've been doing to Lala." She froze, her mouth half open. Maybe there was a soul in there somewhere, but I couldn't find it. The knife appeared out of nowhere. She lunged at me and I side-stepped. It wasn't pretty. First, I took the knife away; then she fought me with her bare hands. I let her hurt me for a while before I resorted to a left hook and right cross combination. Medium power. Hating myself. She went down.

Struggled to her hands and knees. Stared at me, her mouth trembling like a child about to cry.

I walked over and crouched down next to her. Reached out. Placed my hand on her shoulder. She resisted but only a little. "Okay Rosie. Here's what you are going to do—the one and only way you stay out of prison. This afternoon you go over to county social services and resign your post. Tell them to come pick up the remaining girls. Immediately. Then, get yourself some serious counseling. If you do as I say, I won't turn you in."

"H-how will we live?" She could hardly get the words out. "We depend on the county money." She looked up at me. In utter despair.

"I'm sorry, Rosie. You don't have a choice. Unless you want to go to prison. You'd be charged with criminal sex abuse of a prepubescent minor. So think it over. You'd be in with the other female sex offenders. I'm not sure you want that. You're looking at ten years if you don't cooperate. At least ten years. But I have a kind heart, Rosie, so I'm going to give you a chance. Lyndon will be checking up on you..."

I left her kneeling in the dirt, a large, rumpled creature beseeching the sky.

CHAPTER SIXTY-THREE

On the way into town, I called BK. Told him to register our return flight ASAP. He said it would take time 'cause he didn't know the locals. He would text me as soon as it came through. Asked if I wanted to pay a premium. I said yes. Grimly. The cost was mounting up. Financially and psychologically. And if this impersonating a federal agent bit went south, I'd be the one facing ten years. But you *never* plan on getting roped. It's the worst kind of luck.

Lyndon would check with the school, and Principal Sheffield would tell him two agents had taken the girls; one was with ICE, and the other was a formidable woman with wild red hair who dressed like a man and was articulate and straight to the point. If he dug deeper, he'd discover there were two male agents, Bob Evans and Terry Fry. And that the demanding woman was with some agency no one had ever heard of. On the other hand, Principal Sheffield had not opposed our "good home" mantra. She might tell Lyndon it was all for the best.

I sighed. Had to set Lyndon straight. The fact he was so close to the girls was eating at me. I parked and tucked the girls and Caroline into a back booth at a family-style restaurant a block down from Lyndon's office. While waiting for our food, I studied Google Maps on my phone. Stepped outside. Checked with BK, who said to sit tight; another thirty minutes and we'd be cleared. And to plan for a one o'clock take-off.

Then I got Lyndon on the phone. At first, he spluttered. I told him to calm down, that we could go bare fists or brass knuckles or knives or guns or even fucking maces and javelins, but I was taking the girls. Told him to meet me by the pond in the park next to the airport. Alone and on foot. And if he double-crossed me, I'd be very upset. Went back inside and asked Caroline to get my food to go.

I felt a trace conspicuous walking over to the pond, but I didn't want Caroline stranded without the car. A shame my brand-new suit was rumpled from my dust-up with Rosie. It was a humid day and I started to sweat. Took off the jacket and folded it over my arm.

Beat Lyndon to the pond by a minute or two. Enough time to take a few deep breaths and prepare for the onslaught. Which was rough. Mild-mannered Lyndon turned into a frothing pit-bull of a man. I listened patiently. No violence. He could punch me out. I didn't care. No violence because of the girls. And because I'd surely be arrested. None of this mattered to Lyndon. He could not control himself. Just kept screaming at me. After two or three minutes, I coughed and looked at my wrist.

"Okay, Lyndon. Sorry, but your time is up. I'm taking the girls. We've got a good home lined up for them while their mother goes through the asylum process." I smiled and tried to look sympathetic. "Go ahead and clock me if you want to, but Lyndon, baby, you're fighting the wrong guy. Abrecia told me Rosie is molesting Lala, one of the white girls. I pulled rank and told Rosie that if she didn't turn in her license immediately and return the other four girls to county social services, I would arrange for her to be charged federally. Criminal sex abuse of a prepubescent minor. Your job, Lyndon, is to do the right thing and make sure she complies. First step is she gives up all her girls and turns in her license. Then she enters counseling with a competent therapist who specializes in working with sex offenders. She'll probably have to enter a sex offenders' program. But I really don't want that poor, sick woman to go to prison. You're connected here in town. Keep it on the down-low, but make sure she does the right thing. And there's no time to waste."

He looked at me. Fury replaced by a kind of resigned misery. Rosie's fall hurt him badly, wounded his idealistic spirit. "C'mon, Lyndon, don't look at me like that. Don't shoot the messenger. Do you realize that fucking woman tried to stab me? With a rusty old hunting knife. Damn! Then, when I took the knife away, she tried to punch me out. That woman is tough as nails. It's a good thing the department insisted we learn martial arts. I had to resort to a little Krav Maga to subdue her." Lying Crane. I've never bothered to learn Krav Maga.

I gave this time to sink in. Spoke. "But listen, Lyndon, I think you would really like to say goodbye to the girls. And I know they want to say goodbye to you."

His pitbull persona beaten back down into his animal brain, in his cheap off-the-rack slacks and short-sleeved dress shirt, Lyndon looked better suited to small-town dentistry than this dirty game. He followed me grudgingly through the park and back to where the Camry was parked halfway between the restaurant and his office building. By now, Caroline and the girls had finished eating and were waiting in the car. Both girls had eased their way into the front seat. Gloria was actually sitting on Caroline's lap. When Abrecia saw Lyndon, she beamed. Gloria wriggled off Caroline's lap and within seconds, both girls had jumped up into Lyndon's arms. Caroline got out of the car and waited until Lyndon put the girls down. Then she offered him her hand. "SA Fry," nodding in my direction, "tells me you've done a wonderful job representing the girls. It's obvious they love you a whole lot." Lyndon nodded. Shook her hand solemnly. I told Lyndon I would send him the girls' address as soon as I knew it. Told him not to worry; they were in good hands. Offered him my hand, which he finally shook. Then the girls jumped up into his arms again. We waited.

Finally, he put them down. They trotted back to the Camry and got in the back seat.

We waved good-bye to poor, baffled Lyndon. Off to the airport. The girls' eyes got really big when we nudged them gently onto the plane. And stayed big while they bounced around like little jumping jacks until they finally passed out on Caroline and Priscilla's laps before bouncing awake again.

When we stopped in Tulsa to refuel, I took BK aside. I didn't want to take any chances. Ms. Sheffield or Lyndon could still decide to raise a stink. The state police could be called in. Which could be a prelude to disaster. Asked BK to radio ahead to get permission to land in San Bernardino. I would disembark with the girls, and then he could drop Caroline off at Bob Hope Airport in Burbank. I handed him five Franklins to seal the deal and called Tony. He said he was on it. Then I slept, catnaps only, most of the way to Berdoo. Every time I opened my eyes, there was Caroline playing with the girls. She was such a natural...

Tony and Bobby met us just off the runway after we landed in Berdoo. To my surprise, Caroline said she was coming with us. She wasn't willing to let go of the girls yet. I took her aside. Told her for reasons of operational security, it was better if she wasn't seen at the girls' destination.

"Oh? I can't be seen at the Beverly Hilton? What's wrong with you, Nick? You only use me when it's convenient? Is that what you're telling me?"

Stung, I gathered my thoughts. "I haven't used you, Caroline. You've helped me. You've been indispensable. And I had no other option. Without you, I could not have rescued these girls. You saved the day. I'd say you're a candidate for sainthood." Stopped, took a quick breath. "And you've got to admit, you've had a pretty good time."

She softened. To a degree. "I have had a pretty good time, but I'm going to see this through till the end. And it's no skin off your ass, Nick. So don't tell me what I can and cannot do."

I threw my hands up. Smiled. Know when I'm licked.

When I shook hands with BK, he tried to return the five Franklins. He said the original five stacks were enough. Nix. Bad form to take back money. Told him to spend it at the gaming tables. If he won, he could give me half the profit.

I rode up front with Tony in his SUV, while Bobby and Caroline entertained the kids in back. Tony and I didn't say much. Knew he was feeling a kernel of redemption—so was I. As in *gonna do one good deed before I die*. In one of Sun Tzu's less militant moments, he observed: *The supreme art of war is to subdue the enemy without fighting*. Which, with the exception of scuffling with Rosie, I had managed to do. It was a damn good thing, 'cause if I'd had to resort to brandishing a gun in Ohio, God only knows what might have happened...

Knew all of this was just a prelude to tomorrow's harder task. Arresting Quincey quietly at his Bel Air estate sounded simple enough. But I had used up plenty of luck already. How much was left in reserve? With the fates hard at work—spinning, measuring, and cutting...

When we got to the Beverly Hilton, Caroline and Tony took the girls inside. When she came back out, Caroline was smiling through her tears. Tony said everything looked good. He described the girls' squeals of delight when they found their room bedecked with toys and flowers. And then he thanked me. For a moment, there in the half-light in the front seat of his SUV, his brown eyes were warm again.

PART FIVE

CHAPTER SIXTY-FOUR

The following morning, while driving to my office to rendezvous with Adara and my crew, I bit the bullet and called Cassady.

"Hello. Who's this?"

"It's me."

"You sonofabitch!"

"Don't worry. We've made progress."

"You damned well better have. We flew in two days ago, and Maleah is already talking about dropping out of school."

"What the fuck? I told you to stay in England." Furious. At the same time, I felt a deep and abiding shame. Took a deep breath. "Tell Maleah dropping out of school is completely out of the question. As she very well knows. And tell her, with any luck, I'll be up in the City on Saturday to take her out to dinner."

"I don't want you going anywhere near our daughter. Not until you're completely in the clear. And if you do, I'll take out a restraining order."

Harsh, but understandable. "Okay. Tell Maleah you talked to me and everything's good." Hated eating crow, but one has no choice sometimes."

"Like hell it is." Then Cassady went for the jugular. "Nick, I want you to listen to me. I love you, but I can't stand any more of this. I've spoken to a divorce lawyer."

Long silence. Finally, I spoke. "Knock yourself out. If that's how you want to handle it. But we can work it out ourselves. Fifty-fifty. Tell the lawyer to go fuck himself."

"Good. Just so you understand."

"I do." I knew Cassady all too well. Too many lines had been crossed. She was drop-dead serious. I told her I'd be back in touch and signed off.

Next, I stopped at an internet café on Broadway. Created yet another Gmail account and sent the promised email to Mohammad. The byline read, "A God for Every Day of the Week." I attached a different picture of the big-eyed gods.

Got to my office at ten thirty; my crew was right behind me. Silence as I described our strategy. Basic plan was simple. Bobby and Tony and I walk onto Quincey's patio. He looks up from his moussaka, and Bobby slips a hood over his head. We stick a gun in his back and walk him out to the street. Load him up in Diego Smith's slammer van.

The men raised their eyebrows when I said Desmond Cole appeared to be Quincey's boss and a ranking member of the principals. "Problem is," I said, "I don't have an accurate sense of how the principals make decisions. Or who has veto power. I don't think it's Cole. But what I do know is Cole told me that if we manage to arrest Quincey, there's a slim chance I may get a reprieve."

"If you mean your death sentence may get commuted," said Bobby, "it's well worth a try."

I nodded grimly. "And it has to be a gentler, kinder arrest. No swat team bully-boy tactics. That's why Cole wants us to do it rather than LAPD or LASD. He thinks the cops would make a big stink and bust up the place."

"Well, at least they're good for something," said Bobby. Grim chuckles all around.

"Diego's all set," said Tony. "He and his people will meet us outside Quincey's estate. All we have to do is hand the bastard over. And I have the warrant in hand. I'm still trying to get LAPD to back me up, but I don't think it's going to happen. For some reason, they're saying it's strictly a county matter."

"Whatever," I said. "We'll take care of it with or without backup. Unless there are complications. Which, of course, there could be. My concern is this. Suppose Quincey wakes up and realizes Cole is setting him up? What happens then?"

"A clusterfuck," said Bobby shortly.

"Look," said Tony, "we all know anything could happen. Any fucking thing at all. We just have to be ready."

"Okay," I said. "Just so everybody understands…"

Then Adara described Quincey's house. It was a ten thousand square foot, two-story American Colonial country manor home with a finished basement on a five-acre lot. Outdoor parking for six cars. Four-car garage. Back patio ringed by sycamores. Olympic-sized pool and a seldom-used tennis court. And a guest house at the end of the long driveway, shielded from the main house by an overgrown orchard.

When it was time, I outfitted our crew with gate clickers and climbed into Adara's black Toyota Prius. We drove west. Bobby followed in his rented Altima, Tony in his F-150.

Bel Air lies in LA's Platinum Triangle, six square miles of ostentatious kitsch, clashing architecture, and boatloads of money. The California oaks and sycamores seem to grow out of massive hedges, screening the walls and security gates. God forbid you can see your neighbor's house.

Our plan was simple. When we got to the house, Adara would greet Quincey and Cole on the patio while I waited in the shadows. Then she would go inside to make sure Cole had remembered to turn off the burglar alarm. Tony and Bobby would join me. The three of us would wander back to the patio. Put the clamps on Quincey and hand him off to Diego Smith. Then in the evening, Adara and I would fly to Boston to rescue Mohammad. Simple as that. Maybe.

At five to twelve, we turned off Sunset and passed through the West Gate onto Bellagio Road. By now, I was seventy-five percent certain that arresting Quincey would not be simple. But after more than two weeks of constant tension and unrelenting violence, I was desperate to bring this ordeal to an end...

Once we were within spitting distance of the estate, I phoned Bobby and Tony. They were ready. Tony said LAPD had indeed proved to be useless, but that at the last minute, Raymundo and his crew had volunteered their services. "Fact of the matter is," said Tony, "Raymundo is itching to help arrest the mad dog who planned Roberto's murder."

"Good man," I said. "We just might need him."

At five after twelve, Adara and I drove in through the main gate and started up the long driveway that led to Quincey's oversized American Colonial home. On our left, a huge manicured lawn. The garage and outdoor parking were on the right. As we neared the garage, three men dressed as UPS drivers appeared in the road. Wrong. Dead wrong. "Oh, shit," said Adara. "The house is off-limits. What's going on?"

"Cut your wheels across the lawn." Adara needed little encouragement. She made a hard left and screeched across the lawn, clipping a masonry sundial. Three other men in blue suits were now chasing us. Cole's cleaning crew, Dagmar at the helm.

On the far side of the lawn, Adara angled the Prius so it pointed toward the gate. I hit Bobby on redial. Told him we had a war on our hands, and Quincey had apparently turned the tables on Desmond Cole. Said we had two choices. Retreat or attack.

"Attack," said Bobby. "That's why we're here."

I wasn't so sure. But no time to deliberate.

"Stop thinking," said Bobby. "We're going in."

"Okay," I said. "Go time."

I reached over and touched Adara's cheek. Fear in her eyes. And something else, too. Not surrender. Rather, resignation, which was almost worse. "Godspeed," I said. "Be careful. I'll call you when this is over."

I rolled out the passenger side and ducked behind a ficus hedge. Adara gunned the Prius diagonally across the lawn and out through the gate. Headed toward the Bel-Air Hotel, where she would wait for news.

Dagmar and his men had fallen back and were crouching, guns drawn, behind a privet hedge on the other side of the lawn. Their relationship to the UPS bogies? Friends? Allies? Teammates? It made no sense. Their immediate goal, though, was to shoot or capture me. But they were nervous. *Muy loco hombre.*

The main gate whirred and Bobby's Altima appeared. I called him and told him to wait at the head of the driveway until I touched base with Tony. "I'm behind a hedge on the lawn. Away from the driveway. FUBAR, baby. Quincey's got a whole army here. I've seen six already. I think Cole's cleaners have gone to the other side."

Called Tony. Briefed him quickly.

"I never thought it would be easy. Fuck 'em. We're going in."

The die was cast. "Okay. Stay on the perimeter until Bobby and I draw a crowd. Then move in and arrest every one of these fuckers. What are you carrying?"

"M4 Benelli and sidearms."

"OC?"

"You got it."

"Okay, then. It's dirty boogie time."

Bobby roared straight up the driveway. Soldiers shooting wildly, lunging for cover. He spun a U-ey in front of the guest house, came back down the driveway, and braked hard at the edge of the sycamore grove. He dove into the trees and found a vantage point with a clear view of both the patio and driveway. The UPS creeps retreated into the garage. Tony, Raymundo, and his crew of three, wearing Kevlar vests and armed with M4s and OC canisters, started up the driveway.

I sprinted down a narrow brick walkway on the far side of the house, past the servants' quarters, and onto the patio. Which was empty. Sudden pock-pock of pistol shots. Shotgun blasts and a scream. Sibilant OC bursts. Moaning, shrieks. Two more shots. Cursing. Silence.

Sig Sauer in hand, Bobby was crouching behind a raised planter bed. I joined him. The Benelli had done damage. Dagmar was cut in half. The five other goons were flailing around from the pepper spray. "Everybody get down. Move apart. Hands on the top of your head." Tony's voice, an ice pick on a grinding wheel. Four men got down on their knees. The fifth got a shot off, and Raymundo screamed. Couldn't tell where he was hit. Bobby emptied his clip into the shooter.

Beside himself, an enraged Tony jumped on the half-prostrate, dying soldier. Kicked him in the stomach and smashed his head with his shotgun buttstock.

"Tony, enough goddamnit! That's enough!" He looked at me, surveyed his handiwork. Shuddered. Then calm. "Bobby, help me cuff these guys. We'll lock 'em in the slammer van."

I shed my jean jacket and struggled into Dagmar's coat. It didn't fit, but would have to do the job. I looked at Bobby and Tony. "You know what comes next." They nodded. Strong men, brave and true. "Okay," I said, "let's see if the fat lady's gonna sing in tune."

CHAPTER SIXTY-FIVE

I entered the house through the patio door. Passed a Warhol of the young Mick Jagger. And one of John Lennon. Money, money, money. Good taste? Hmm. A Strauss waltz wafted through the floorboards. A modest library led to a screening room, where I found a circular staircase leading to the basement. Hesitated on the last step. And looked in.

A large finished room. A second staircase at the far end. Eight men—Quincey, Cole, and six soldiers. Cole, naked and covered in blood, was bent over a waist-high balance beam supported by uprights fastened to the floor and ceiling. Quincey, stripped to the waist, was wielding a four-foot rattan cane. He took a running start and laid into the helpless Cole. The cane whipped backwards and forwards. Thwack! Delivery. On the ass and thighs. No ordinary schoolboy caning, this. This was serious pain. A man could die this way. At the very least, Cole would carry the scars forever. I eased into the shadows and watched.

Ten more blows. It sickened me. Quincey finally stopped. Cole tried to stand up, could not. Slid to the floor and lay there gasping. Then he struggled to his knees. Pulled himself upright, using the balance beam for leverage. Fucker could take a beating. These were not ordinary men. They faced each other, Quincey lean and lithely muscled, Cole skinny, face contorted, loins in retreat, his thick white hair matted. Bleeding onto the floor.

Too far away for a Taser shot, and shooting Quincey in cold blood was not on the agenda. I inched forward. Bobby and Tony should arrive at any moment.

Ashen, dripping sweat and blood, Cole looked at Quincey, more with pity than anger. For all the world like a sorrowful father. Continuing a conversation that had begun before I arrived. "Goddamnit, Tom, I'm not betraying you. Why can't you understand that? I'm trying to save you from yourself, get you help before it's too late. Your plan to terrorize the American Muslim community is crazy. Sure, you might blow up a mosque. Hell yeah, blame it on Somali terrorists in Minneapolis. That might work at first, but it'll never work in the long run. You'll be exposed, and they will put you away for the rest of your life. Is that what you want, Tom? Don't you understand? You can't make up for the young men and women who died over there on your watch. They're dead, but you're still alive. That's all that matters. Pull yourself together, man. Please, Tom, I'm begging you."

Cole ran out of breath. He mopped at his face with his hand. Quincey stared at him. Then he spoke. No warm, soothing enema of a voice this time. Instead, a high-pitched rasp that made me shiver. The man was seriously deranged. "You, Rowe, all of you. You're all traitors. You've all betrayed me, everybody but Frank. None of you understand the kind of evil we face. It's not only Muslims. It's Iran, Russia, Syria, China, and the hordes of immigrants coming across our borders. We've got to put the clamps on, Dee. We've got to stop them. All of them. Why can't you see this? Wake up, Dee! Wake the fuck up!"

But Quincey gave Cole no chance to wake up. Instead, he ordered his men to lash Cole to one of the uprights. Facing Quincey this time. And it began all over again, the cane swooshing like a pterodactyl from the pit of hell. Chest. Stomach. Thighs. No direct blows to the face or loins. Not yet. Had the feeling they were coming.

Cole tried to talk between blows. Coughing and gasping. Fighting to get the words out. Something about how Quincey was being setup to take a hard fall by Marguerite Ferguson and her people. How they wanted to use him to do their dirty work. How it was all part of their master plan to round up Muslims and Mexicans. Put them in private prisons. Purify our land and blood...and make some serious money in the process. Finally, Cole shrieked, "I want to help you, goddamnit! Why won't you let me help you?"

Quincey stopped. Stared at Cole. Bowed his head. A moment of meditation. Then he stood up straight. Military posture. Walked up to Cole and slapped him hard with his right hand, a single shot, the whip dangling from his left. Cole staggered, held upright by his restraints. Quincey turned around, walked away, turned again, got a running start...

By now, I had eased closer. Tasers in both hands. Bobby was standing in the shadows near one staircase, Tony adjacent the other. Delivery time. The first dart caught Quincey right between his shoulder blades. He spun around, already spasming. The second caught him square in the chest. He collapsed, and Bobby came hurtling out of the shadows, a 230-pound Scud missile, taking out two of the goons. The third goon threw his hands up. Then Tony, wielding his Benelli. Two soldiers raised their hands, but the third threw down, hitting Tony point blank right in his Kevlar vest. Tony sprayed the shooter with three-inch shells.

Bobby had his three captives pinned down in the sights of his Sig Sauer. "Toss your weapons out on the floor! Now! One false move and I'll kill y'all." His drawl half syrup, half cold iron. I could smell their fear.

I helped Tony, shaken but still standing, handcuff his two surviving captives. He'd be sore for weeks, but his vest had saved him. He searched them while I covered him. Knives, brass knuckles, a brace of leather saps, and two Beretta Bobcats. Turned my attention to Bobby. In the nick of time. One of his prisoners had wormed a .22 caliber pistol from his ankle holster. I fired two rounds. The soldier screamed and dropped his weapon, bleeding from his right shoulder and left hip. Bobby shook his head, his face bone-white in the basement gloom.

I walked over to Cole. Released his restraints. Still bleeding, front and back, he staggered but stayed on his feet. Picked his boxers up off of the floor. Wiped some of the blood off his face and chest. Balled them up and threw them at the still-writhing Quincey. Then Cole got dressed. Slowly and deliberately. His black tuxedo was ruined. Once he was ready, he peered around the room. His gaze met mine, but with little hint of recognition. He walked over to Quincey, pulled him to a sitting position, and knocked him cold with a short right. Then he fell to his knees beside his fallen friend. Bowed his head and didn't move for a long time.

With Quincey still unconscious, Bobby and Tony and I went to work. We secured the five living soldiers and handcuffed them to the balance beam. Then Bobby handcuffed Quincey to one of the uprights. Diego Smith and his slammer van should be out front by now. But I wasn't sure if Quincey had backup waiting in the shadows. One way to find out. Gun in hand, and strangely weary as if I had been the one thrashed by Quincey's cane, I slowly climbed the circular staircase while Bobby and Tony hustled up the other set of stairs.

Came around a bend only to meet…holy fuck, QB Tragg, near the top. His grin ghastly, his S&W .40 trained at my forehead. I'll never know why he hesitated, but he did. Just for a split-second. Time enough for me to hit the deck and blast the sick fuck. Three shots—gut, heart, and throat. Then I climbed over the dying man and shoved him down the stairs. Force = Mass × Acceleration. Tragg was a big man. He picked up speed fast and smashed headfirst into the wall halfway down, which left him stretched across the staircase, blocking everyone's access. Selfish fucker, even in death.

Gunfire exploding outside. Tragg was only the advance. I stumbled out onto the driveway as Tony and Bobby barreled ahead. Two soldiers by the pool. Bobby knelt and blew one away while Tony and I chewed up the other. Quincey had, in fact, underestimated us. He had enough backup to overpower Raymundo's small crew, who had retreated behind my trusty ficus hedge, but not Diego and LASD, who trapped the remaining soldiers in front of the guest house. It was over pretty fast. The creeps threw up their hands, and Diego's team began securing them and escorting them to the slammer van. They were a motley crew. Hoodies and Army-Navy surplus khakis.

Diego strolled over, grinning. "Well, Crane, glad to see you're still standing. Not even a scratch. You are one lucky SOB."

"I'm glad you weren't ordered to stand down. We would have been screwed without you."

Diego shook his head. Reached for a cigarette. Remembered he didn't have any. Frowned. "They couldn't stop me. Maybe you haven't heard, but LASD is now part of a massive coast-to-coast operation to round up and deport illegals. It's called Operation Wetback, unofficially, of course. A little birdie told me there might be illegals here, and I figured it was my duty to investigate. The funny thing is, on the way over, I even had to divert a car of Fibbies looking for you. At least they said they were Fibbies. They were beating the bushes of pristine Bel Air. When they saw my slammer van, they waved me down and asked for directions to Quincey's house. Forgive me, Mother Mary, but I lied. It appears Quincey and his gang of thugs have friends in high places. But I think you already know that. The amazing thing is I show up here, and who do I see? My old friend Raymundo Ochoa, butt shot and bleeding. What are the odds of that?"

Huh? Diego knew Raymundo? I was beginning to think Raymundo knew every cop in Southern California.

"Is Raymundo okay?"

"The shot went through and through. He'll have a sore ass for quite a while, but he'll live. It's a good thing I brought a medic along. He stopped the bleeding and dressed Raymundo's wound before Quincey's last wave of creeps showed up."

"I'm glad he's all right. He and his crew were indispensable."

"He's a tough old street fighter. You're probably wondering how I know him. The truth is, I used to be in narcotics before I switched to homicide. Narcotics was too confusing, too many ways to go wrong."

Tony, tight-lipped from pain and exhaustion, joined us. "How's Raymundo?"

"Like I told Crane here, he should be fine."

"Good. I gotta go back inside to extract Quincey and all those fools we tied up in the basement. Mind if I borrow a few of your men?"

"Be my guest." Speaking fluent Spanish, Diego summoned a few of his men and explained the job. But before Tony could go back inside the house, Bobby walked over. "If you gents don't mind, I'm gonna go home and feed my goats. I haven't been home for what feels like forever." His leathery face broke into a huge, brown-toothed smile. "Then I'm gonna step out for a truly delicious *pescado* dinner. Maybe I can talk Leo from the auto body shop into joining me." He looked directly at me. "Unless he's still mad at you for outing his rat. Then I'm gonna…" He lowered his voice and spoke only to me, cupping his good hand and whispering in my ear. "Then I'm gonna go home and reread some of Frank Constantine's torture records. I believe I've been somewhat neglectful…" He grinned and clapped me on the shoulder.

"What the hell?" Playing dumb. But I already knew.

Bobby gave me a thoroughly triumphant look. "Let's just say I commandeered the important stuff before those assholes in the brown vans took the records back. It makes a nice alternative to TV." He grimaced, shook his head, and walked slowly toward his car.

***

Five minutes later, Quincey appeared, sandwiched between two husky deputy sheriffs. Saw me but didn't say a word. Bowed his head and kept walking. Then Cole, his black tux even blacker from dried blood. His mission accomplished, the principals would no doubt be pleased. Quincey would be incapacitated, at least for a while, and the rank-and-file Muslims of America would be spared a most painful persecution. Or would they? Weary beyond measure, his aspect skeletal, Cole's eyes were contrite, or should I say, seemingly contrite.

"So, tomorrow's the big day. Mohammad Ghaffari will be free at last." He smiled ruefully and looked me in the eye. "My own man betrayed me to Tragg, who informed Thomas."

"Well, they're both dead now, Dagmar and Tragg."

Cole nodded, but I had the feeling he didn't give two damns whether they were dead or alive. "Well, Crane, thanks for your help. Thank you for saving my ass. I was pretty well convinced it was curtains. I missed my wedding, but I can still catch some of the reception. It should be fun. A bunch of Polish Catholics dancing the Polonaise."

I looked at him. His tux was plenty rumpled, and the blood spots were seeping through. We shook hands. Then Cole turned and walked over to his Lambo. Before getting in, he stopped, turned, whistled piercingly, and went into a deep bob-and-weave, throwing jabs and left hook, right cross combinations. In slow motion. Who the fuck was this guy? Was there another double-cross around the corner? Another hall of blinding mirrors? Well, like Tony said, I'm a *muy loco hombre*.

CHAPTER SIXTY-SIX

A few hours later, I was halfway to the Long Beach airport when Agresti returned my call. I told him Mohammad's rescue was scheduled for eleven a.m. on Friday morning. Asked him if he was interested in joining the party. Said I could meet him at his office at nine. He hesitated for a moment, let out his breath, and asked, "You mean tomorrow morning, right?"

"Right."

Felt him deliberating on the other end of the line. "Nick, I know this sounds crazy, but I'm hearing spooks. I'm hearing national security wingnuts. It's got me worried."

"You and me both, brother." I didn't rush him, and he finally came around.

"Okay, Nick. I'm on board."

"Good. And one other thing. I need a safe house outside Boston for Mohammad and his daughter. Some kind of bootleg rental, spare no expense, cash in advance."

"I can handle that."

"Good." I signed off.

When I got to Long Beach International Airport, Adara was talking on her phone. She looked at me, waved one hand, and kept talking. I moved to a quiet spot and phoned Greg. He didn't pick up. I cursed and told him to call me ASAP. My burner rang sixty seconds later.

"Sorry. I was indisposed. What's up?"

"You're up. And I hope it's good."

"It's good all right. You were right. Tami Wheat, aka Marguerite Ferguson, is the key to all of this. Everything seems to revolve around her. After I found her email address, the spyware did the rest. Then once I got into her email, I started putting the pieces together. She connects to the NSC. She's some kind of independent contractor, wired up with the far-right elements in ICE, DEA, FBI, and God knows who else. These people...man, they have no fucking scruples. You can just tell. There's lots of talk in code and chatter about arresting a man named Thomas. If I'm not mistaken, we know this asshole. I thought he was *with them*. He *is* with them, isn't he? This whole thing is giving me a headache. The chatter says he was bringing Syrian terrorists across the border. It's fucked up, Boss. It's very fucked up."

"Yep." I thought back, remembering what Cole had said about Quincey's third option: *Identify promising candidates and turn them into programmed killers. Unleash them on the general population to fan the flames of terror. But Thomas wrestles with this. In the morning, he thinks one thing; by evening, he thinks something else.*

Rowe had placed the onus of the detentions squarely on ICE. But what if Marguerite Ferguson, who I had started to think might outrank even Cole, blamed Quincey for the porous border? As an ICE contractor tasked with protecting our border, he could end up being hoisted by his own petard. Which was more or less what Cole had said in Quincey's basement.

Greg told me Quincey was in regular contact with Marguerite and a man named Desmond Cole, but was not included in their group threads, which could get large. "It's freakin' amazing," he said. "There might be eight or ten people on these threads. And it's all kind of formal. They seem to be debating policy. So let me know where you want me to go from here. Right at the moment, I'm a little bit stumped."

I laughed. "I don't blame you, Greg. It's confusing as hell."

Goddamn. The threads were the record of the principals and/or their associates debating their policy decisions. Pukeworthy. But valuable. "Okay, Greg, I want you to do two things. First, record the names and email addresses of everyone in the long threads. Write the information down and save it in an encrypted folder. When you're done with that, I want you to focus on the most recent emails. Look for anything from Cole to Marguerite, and anything from Marguerite to Cole. Pay special attention when it's only the two of them. Try to figure out what their game is. If anything jumps out at you, call me right away. At this number. You've done a great job, Greg. I truly appreciate it. But don't let up now, 'cause the fat's in the fire."

The question was this—did Cole really want to protect me, or was his endless stream of equivocation all part of their vendetta against me? And why should he want to protect me? Because I was useful. And because we had arrested Quincey. And saved Cole in the process. There had been no indication Quincey was going to stop the caning.

"I'm on it," said Greg. We signed off.

Cole and Marguerite? What was their relationship? Had the feeling Marguerite might have been the fifth figure in their voting bloc. Before its members started dying. Cole, while strapped to Quincey's balance beam, had told him Marguerite was setting him up to take a hard fall. Yet Cole had not even mentioned her to me during our long, peculiar conversation at Quincey's mid-city apartment. Which was a tell in its own right.

CHAPTER SIXTY-SEVEN

Our plane left at four p.m. Once we were in the air, riding business class, I felt inexplicably shy. When the flight attendant came around, we ordered drinks and grilled chicken sandwiches with brie and arugula and cranberry mustard. After we'd eaten, we chatted quietly. Not about anything much. I didn't want to describe the mayhem in Bel Air, and Adara didn't ask. She smelled of lemon and orange, but with a hint of something else, something all too human—joy or expectation tethered by fear and pain—complex emotions that seemed to take on a material presence.

Finally, as our plane arrowed through complete darkness, Adara leaned close and said, "Thank you, Nick. I can't thank you enough. It's hard to believe Thomas is in custody. I have to pinch myself. I've been waiting for this day since practically the moment we moved to California. And I'm pretty sure my father and I will be much better off answering to Dee Cole instead of Thomas."

"You will be better off. We've got to hope rescuing your father goes smoothly. Unfortunately, there are no guarantees."

"I've got a good feeling about it," said Adara. She leaned even closer and pressed her cheek against mine. So soft and warm. Smooth like Caroline Best's breasts. I breathed her in. Let her fill me. Like a starving man in the desert drinking pure, sweet water. We stayed this way for a long time. Finally, Adara spoke.

"There's another good side to this. Since I won't be under Thomas's thumb anymore, I'm going to look into joining a repertory theater. I may contact Connie Reardon, my old drama professor at Hawthorne College. She was always after me to go farther in drama."

"I hope you do," I murmured softly. After that, we didn't talk much. At times, Adara moved closer; at other times, she moved away.

She had booked us two rooms at Breed's Hill Hotel on Charles Street north of the Commons, a few blocks from Agresti's office. When we got to Logan International, we picked up our rental car and drove to the hotel. I kept both eyes open, but saw nothing alarming. We staggered upstairs to our rooms just before two a.m. Said goodnight in the hallway. No ado, not even a kiss, as if Adara had decided the rest of her night would not include me.

My room was small but elegant, painted a deep burgundy. Desk lamps resembling candles. Queen-sized bed with stained-oak, colonial-style headboard. I took off my shoes and socks and propped myself up against the headboard, thinking. My mind kept returning to Quincey's basement. Could not get over the stoic way Cole had endured his horrific beating. These aristocrats seemed imbued with a hidden strength, which made them all the more terrifying.

When I began yawning, I took off my pants and shirt and lay down to sleep. Was just dropping off when I heard a knock on the door.

"Is that you, Adara?"

It was. She wore a blue bathrobe with white piping over a simple cotton negligee. "I can't get to sleep. Too much excitement, I guess. Maybe you'd like to talk for a while?"

I needed little urging. Put my pants and shirt back on. Then we sat there, yoga style, facing each other on top of the bed.

We spoke quietly, letting the mood arrange itself. Nothing about the recent traumatic events. Instead, pieces of our lives—lives so impossibly different yet in some ways similar. I talked about my mother who left when I was only three, and she spoke of hers—a kind, elegant woman struck down in her prime by a deranged servant.

After a while, during a break in our conversation, she said she was going to take a shower. "Don't fall asleep on me, Nick. Unless you really must."

She used my bathroom and I waited for her, dreaming. Her elegance, her rose petal lips, and her gold-flecked, earth-brown eyes. The work of an artist...And then, there she was in front of me. Backlit by lamplight, the whole mystery. From ankle to calf to blossoming thigh. From hair to face to throat to breasts to gently sloping belly. And there in the middle—a purely modern girl...

We started out slowly. Both a little shy. I kissed her lips softly. She sighed and moved closer. Draped herself about me, her arms slim and strong. I caught her lower lip between my teeth. Bit down gently, then harder. She gasped. I released her lip and her tongue darted into my mouth. Like lightning. It inflamed me. But I didn't hurry. There was no rush. One thing led to another, and before long I found myself, headfirst, in the wonderland between her thighs. By now, her sighs had turned to moans. When it was time, she came shrieking and muffled the sound with the bedsheet. This got her giggling. Then I got inside her. "Oh, Nick, honey!" She threw her head back and it was sweet abandon—her tawny throat so inviting, her breasts shimmying against my chest, and the supreme pleasure below...

After we'd recovered from the first time, she sat up in bed, her breasts damp, her nipples distended. She smiled. Joy with an edge of sadness that made it all the more joyful. Or...

The second time was different. Like plunging down a tunnel deep into the earth. A darker realm. Unchained sounds. Earthy smells. I crushed her breasts against my wounded chest and forgot everything except the woman who was loving me. Afterwards, she covered my face with kisses. Then we slept.

CHAPTER SIXTY-EIGHT

Woke up at seven-thirty, Adara by my side. I lay there with my eyes closed and breathed deeply—musk and perfume and the earthy smell of sex. I cradled her from behind; she rolled over and faced me. This time, we were calm and gentle. With a hint of sadness because we knew...Afterwards, we barely had time for a quick shower before heading downstairs for breakfast.

I asked for a table with a view of the street. Cold dark morning. Ominous sky. But beautiful in its own way. Famished. Both of us. I ordered the smoked salmon omelet and frittata. Adara chose Belgian waffles and their fancy egg sandwich. Then she ordered a second round of vanilla pancakes with fresh strawberries and maple syrup, which we shared. After the food was gone, we sat there looking at each other and smiling shyly.

But time. Had to get to Agresti's office. Tipped our waiter and the *maître d'hotel* and asked the concierge to get me a taxi...and walked Adara back up to her room. We locked the door behind us. She sat down on the edge of the bed, and I sat down beside her. The sweet and the bittersweet. We didn't say much. Mostly, we just held each other. Except at one point she murmured, "Nick, we are so good together." Something caught in her throat. She released me, sat up straight, and took a deep breath.

I looked at her, and I felt something I hadn't felt for nearly forever—something found and something lost on a cold, dark

New England morning. I couldn't explain what I was feeling, but it made my heart ache. I reached out and stroked the hollow of her elegant cheek. And wished we could vanish into some Neverland. Told Adara I would meet Mohammad and I'd bring him back, and then, with the help of my colleague Agresti, we'd take her and her father to a safe house.

As an added precaution, I had the cabbie run some counter-surveillance before dropping me off in front of Agresti's building. The sky was gunmetal gray except to the immediate north across the Charles River, where a wine-dark stain stretched like an angry wound.

No sign of Agresti's admin Valerie. Agresti himself sat behind her desk. There were fresh lines on his forehead that hadn't been there two weeks ago. I told him Quincey's team was on its last legs. At least for now. QB Tragg had gone to boxer's heaven, and Quincey was in jail facing federal charges for cocaine trafficking. I told him spiriting Mohammad away from the Esplanade should not pose too much of a problem. Barring unforeseen circumstances. Then I shut up and waited. To at least a count of ten.

Finally, he spoke. "Everything's ready." He looked at me strangely.

"Hit me, Agresti. What's up?"

He told me he'd been followed several times over the past few weeks and had received threatening emails. Although alarming, that was hardly the worst part. The worst part was the fact his garage had been firebombed. Fortunately, he and his fiancée were both at work when it happened.

"How much damage?"

"My boat was destroyed and all my sailing equipment."

"Your boat?"

"Yeah, my boat. You got something against boats?"

"Of course not. I guess they were sending a message."

"Something like that."
"When did it happen?"
"A few days after Jet drove you to Hartford."
"When was the last email?"
Agresti pondered. "Three or four days ago."
"Have you been followed since then?"
He shook his head.
"Any more emails?"
Shook his head again. Could feel the wheels churning.

"Like I said, Quincey and his people are mostly locked up or dead. Or so it appears. There's a new guy named Desmond Cole running the play. He's the shiftiest of them all, but seems less addicted to violence than Quincey. Maybe. Strangely, at this point, I'm actually authorized by him to liberate Mohammad. For whatever that's worth. So I need to get on with it. I don't expect you to come with me. Not after they bombed your garage. And you're about to get married. You don't need this shit." A little reverse psychology. I knew Agresti could see right through my ploy, but I also knew it would be hard for a take-charge guy like him, the tough as nails son of an even tougher Italian longshoreman, to simply wish me good luck and go on with his day.

Agresti was pissed. 'Cause I'd put him in this cross. I didn't blame him. He was scared, too, which pissed him off even more. And the assholes had fucked with his boat. That shit don't fly with Agresti. I looked him squarely in the eye. "Why don't you give me the address and the keys to the safe house, and I'll take care of it? In case there is a problem. And there could be. I'm not going to lie to you."

Long moment of silence. Then Agresti spoke. "I appreciate that, Nick. But just 'cause I'm worried doesn't mean I'm out. And it just so happens I need a serious cash infusion. The truth is, I'm a lot more comfortable being your muscle than I'd be sitting here on my ass wondering what the hell was going on."

I thanked him. With utmost sincerity. I've worked alone a lot in my life. More comfortable that way than most guys. But there are jobs where you want backup. This was one of them.

Told Agresti I thought he should bring along a couple of his most discreet law enforcement buddies. This got him rattled all over again, but then he calmed down and got on the horn. Took a few calls. Then he connected and arranged for two Southie policemen to meet us at the drop-off spot on Soldiers Field Road at eleven o'clock.

He was worried and it was contagious. What if Mohammad didn't show? Or Cole pulled a double-cross? Or Cole and Marguerite were working in tandem? Although Agresti and his people would be wearing iron, I felt naked without a firearm.

The purple stain hanging over the Charles River deepened into black as we shadowed the river on Storrow. My paranoia hit me hard as we passed under the Massachusetts Avenue Bridge. I suppressed a groan and stared straight ahead into the gloom. Agresti knew. "You're feeling it too. Aren't you?"

"Yep."

"Just proves you're human, my friend."

We pulled into the drop-off zone a few minutes before eleven. Agresti's people pulled in behind us. We waited. No sign of Mohammad. Ten minutes later, I looked at Agresti. He nodded grimly. We got out of his Fiat, and his people got out of their cruiser. In uniform. We huddled. Introductions were somewhere between brief and non-existent. I told the three men we would walk east through the tunnel and past the sailing pavilion. If there was still no sign of Mohammad when we reached Boston University, we would look for him in the university library. As a last resort. We'd proceed at the slow pace of the moon. Give Mohammad time to slip away and find us. For I could not believe he would not meet us as planned.

We stepped onto the road. I led the way. Agresti and the cops fell in three abreast behind me. We advanced slowly. With great care. Through the hardwood grove, heading east.

When we were ten yards from the tunnel, Mohammad

emerged from its dark maw.

"Mohammad! It's me! Nick Crane!"

At first, he looked bewildered. He stared at me, then turned and peered back into the tunnel. Satisfied, he waved and started toward us. He was no more than six feet away, and I was already reaching out to shake his hand when an old woman on a mountain bike rode out of the tunnel. The cold cracked my skull. I literally bowled Mohammad over, shouting, "Down! Get down!" Too late. For me. Her first shot skimmed past my skull. Shot two grazed my left forearm. Shot three buried itself in my belly.

Shot four came from our side. The last thing I remember, as the pain ripped through my gut and I went into shock, was watching the old woman topple off her bike.

CHAPTER SIXTY-NINE

I remember waking up in the operating room. Briefly. Medics in lab coats milling about. They seemed satisfied. Nodding their heads and bumping their fists. The absence of pain. That would change. Heavily sedated for now. Back under. Stayed there for days. Spectral world of shapes and shadows. In the deep in the dark water with a bright blue stream of liquid mist above me. That was the good part. The bad part was the sea-green raptors fanning the water with their powerful wings. To escape, I dove deeper into the cold and black, where even they could not follow. There were moments when I sensed Agresti was in the room, keeping silent vigil. Then the dark visions faded, and I was able to sleep peacefully.

Came to some days later. A nurse was adjusting my IV. In a private room. Lime green walls and a large window looking out over the parking lot. The morphine piercing the blood-brain barrier, a warm, drowsy feeling. I closed my eyes. When I woke back up, Marguerite Ferguson was sitting in a chair across from me, smiling like always.

She didn't speak. Just held that smile. For at least a seven-count. I matched her smile with a steady frown. She was the first to break. "Crane, I'm glad to see you're still alive. Otherwise, I wouldn't be able to tell you what a natural-born asshole you are. Because of you, Dee Cole lost his best girl, who was innocently riding her bike and keeping an eye on Mohammad. Some bystander said she shot at you, which is ridiculous. I have to admit, though, your Boston PD backup was a clever touch. I'm impressed. And just so you know, we found your armory. Not that impressive, though the plastic explosives do give one pause. No mattah. The contents of your little treasure trove have been duly registered and stored—to be turned over to the U.S Attorney's Office when the time is right." Threw me a big smile, her hair perfect as the Werewolf of London. Something about these folks and their hair.

I waited. Spoke. Voice rusty from disuse. "Damn, Marguerite, it's good to know I can count on you. Fabricating evidence, as always. This is almost as good as your Nick Crane killed Roberto Diaz fantasy."

This time, she laughed. Almost musically. I was surprised. "Perhaps that was a bit of a stretch. Fortunately, that case is closed. Mr. Diaz was murdered by a notorious narco-trafficker named Javier Fincus and two of his hired thugs. Fincus is indicted federally for meth and coke distribution. For the time being, his murder case remains with LASD, though that may change."

I found the control and buzzed my bed halfway to upright. Treated Marguerite to my best sarcastic smile. I was feeling pretty decent. With the help of my faithful morphine drip. Fuck this woman with her trim body, pinched mouth, and perfect hair. But cleverly. I was about to compliment law enforcement for its good work in arresting Fincus and his crew, but she spoke first. On to a topic she seemed to relish.

"In case you're wondering, Dee Cole and I had a little talk with Adara. At first, the little darling refused to confess to anything. She tried to hold her mud, as the saying goes. She thought she was a big brave girl now that her husband was in the can. All she would say was Dee Cole had authorized you to meet Mohammad on the Charles River Esplanade. To 'liberate him.' Which was a flat-out lie. And makes no sense because Mohammad wasn't even a prisoner in the first place. More like a guest of honor, you might say. But then we broke your little Adara. Hoo boy, did we ever break her! And when she started confessing, you couldn't turn the faucet off. She told us everything. How she hired you to travel to Boston to strategize with her pathetic little father. And how she led you to Thomas Quincey's house, knowing he would be helpless enjoying lunch with Dee. Oh, how she begged us to let her go! She even wept like a schoolgirl before agreeing to perform certain pleasurable acts upon my person. And then once she got started, she couldn't stop. That girl is a natural."

Hmm. Not exactly what I'd been hoping to hear. I took a deep breath. "Well, Ms. Marguerite, I appreciate your candor. And you're right, Adara did hire me to travel to this fair city to meet Mohammad. And you know why. To rescue him from your boy Quincey's control. That was my job. Period. And if I'm not mistaken, I've succeeded." Clamped my mouth shut. Let her make her play.

Right on cue, her smile dimmed. "Crane, you have been in la la land for ten days. A lot has happened. Thomas Quincey has admitted to conspiring to smuggle Mexican and Islamic terrorists across our southern borders. Intel had warned us about such terrorist infiltration, and boy howdy, were they ever right! And someone was pimping young girls on the side. Just awful. Though I don't think Thomas was responsible for that. In fact, several rather influential people are suggesting you might've had a hand in that nasty business."

Her smile gone, she was formidable. All the more reason to provoke her. "Dream on, Ms. Ferguson. The way I see it is like this. Mohammad and Adara are now free of Quincey and have their lives back. You should consider yourself a Good Samaritan. Purely by accident. Because you were the brave truth-seeker working with Quincey in the first place, which set the wheels in motion that ended in his arrest." I paused for air. Intermittent agony deep in my belly, where the bullet had abused my intestines. "But I'm pretty damned certain you were Quincey's co-conspirator in this nut job scheme to manufacture terror. Which is bound to catch up with you sooner or later." Paused. Closed my eyes and let the morphine carry me. Came out of it. She was smiling again.

"You have a big imagination, Crane. But go right ahead. Think whatever you like. You're still fucked every way but Sunday. It's all over the minute you walk out of this hospital. A team of crackerjack operatives will detain you and hand you off to me. Boy howdy, are we going to have a grand old time. You will be totally fucked…"

I rolled my eyes.

"I know," she said. "The truth hurts. It's not much to look forward to." She pantomimed holding something out at arm's length with her left hand and chopping it off with her right. "It really is great fun. I look forward to adding yours, or what was formerly yours, to my collection before I hand you off to the lads who will whisk you away to Scorpion Prison in Cairo. I'm told they are expecting you and are preparing to bring your sorry life to a slow and most painful conclusion."

Damn! The far right with a vengeance. Golden showers, ass rape, castration, and extraordinary rendition. Decided to try a different tack.

"So Marguerite, now that Quincey's walking the yard, I suppose you're going to have to take over." Left it open-ended. See what she would say.

"Take over what?" She was smiling again.

"You know. What I was referring to. The false flag operations. The acts of domestic terrorism. As a means of setting the stage for your final solution."

"My final solution? Are you crazy? The morphine is addling your brains, Crane."

"I don't disagree. I've got to get off this shit. But let me run it down. See if I'm on the right track."

"Be my guest, Crane. But please make it quick. I've got people to meet and can't stay here all day."

"I'd be surprised if you didn't have people to meet. An important woman like you. So I will make it quick. Your ultimate goal is simple. You want to build privately owned detention centers for Muslims and Latinos. All across our great land. On the taxpayer's dime. Financed partly by your friends in the Roach consortium. Partly through donations and investments. And, of course, whatever laundered Russian money you can scare up."

She deadpanned, but I could tell she was shaken. The truth hurts. While being caned by Quincey in the basement, Cole had let the cat out of the bag. I decided to finish this up. "Look, Marguerite, I'm tired. I took two bullets because of you, and one of them almost killed me. So do whatever you want. Indict me if you can. Have your goons take another crack at me on my way out of here. Maybe they can stop me. But I doubt it. And just so you know, I'm coming after you, honey, I'm coming after you." Paused. Didn't say another word. Neither did she. She stared at me for a long time. Smile completely gone. It wasn't just fury she was feeling, though there was some of that. It was more like recognition. Taking stock. Several times she started to speak. Every time she stopped. Finally, she stood up and walked out of the room.

CHAPTER SEVENTY

Adara came later that same afternoon. Pale, a bit unsteady, she had lost weight. She kept apologizing for, as she described it, "putting me in this hospital bed."

I looked at her. Most sincerely. "It's not your fault. This was hard for everyone—you, me, your father, and my friends. But we all did what we had to do, and it's worked out okay. I have no regrets. But here's what I want to know. I've been told Marguerite and Desmond Cole abducted you and held you for a day or two before releasing you. I want to know how you held up."

"What? How do you know about that?" She flushed slightly. "Has Dee Cole been here?"

"Not him. Marguerite herself. The dread Ms. Ferguson. She stopped by this morning, spewing threats and making an ass of herself. She claims she and Cole 'broke you.' I hope that's not true. She's a disgusting little woman."

Adara laughed mirthlessly. "The truth is, Nick, it wasn't that bad. Mostly, it was boring. It was obvious to me Desmond wouldn't let Marguerite do anything drastic. They abducted me on my way out of the hospital two days after you were shot. I was already upset because your doctors told me you had only a sixty-forty chance of surviving. Thank God you're out of the woods now. They took me to a cabin out in the Berkshires and cross-examined me. The whole thing was a farce, utterly pointless. They already knew I had hired you to rescue my father. They made a big deal out of trying to get me to admit that you and I had discussed using my father's money to smuggle terrorists across the Mexican border, which, of course, I denied. At one point, Marguerite acted like she wanted to have sex with me. I refused and she got nasty. At that point, Dee Cole stepped in and said me having sex with Marguerite was out of the question, but I should describe what you and I did in Boston. This naturally piqued the bitch's interest. So I went along with it, but I didn't tell them anything about what we actually did. Instead, I made stuff up. Silly stuff." Adara shook her head. "It was ridiculous."

"So, what did you tell her we did?"

Adara sighed. "Let's not go there now, okay? I'll tell you some other time. I'm afraid I did make you sound preposterous, which I apologize for."

"No need to apologize. It sounds like you handled it perfectly."

Adara smiled. "I did okay. I had them both laughing. By then it was late afternoon and everyone was tired. They knocked off and spent the evening watching *Braveheart*. The next day was pretty much a half-hearted repeat of day one. They wanted evidence you and I had conspired to sneak terrorists into the country. I gave them nothing, just stuck to the facts. They finally got sick of the charade, drove me back to Boston, and dropped me off at the Commons. I called my father, who was frantic. He was so glad to hear my voice. He sent Agresti to rescue me."

"Good old Agresti." I smiled. "I do have one request. Make sure your father pays Agresti. We both need the money, and I'm going to have to disappear for a while."

Adara nodded. "He already has. My father is a generous man."

We both fell silent. Maybe I gestured, or maybe it was her. Either way, she moved closer and eased into my arms. Ever so gently. Handle with care. Only nine days since the medics had dug a nine-millimeter slug out of my belly, along with a piece of my small intestine. I held her for a long time, her heart beating against my chest.

CHAPTER SEVENTY-ONE

After Adara left, I started missing her immediately. I kept thinking about the way she had looked at breakfast at the Breed's Hill Hotel, wolfing down vanilla pancakes with strawberries, her brown eyes shining after a night and morning of lovemaking. And all the other images. Her beauty. Her sadness. The way she held her wineglass. Her clothes. And most of all, her eyes the color of the earth before it rains. All this set against the terrible knowledge that the world, with its ways and means, would always stand between us.

Finally, I fell into a light sleep. Tossed and turned through the evening and into the night. Woke up around three a.m., my room dark and silent. Lay there for a long time. Thinking.

Then I disconnected my IV drip. Eased myself to a sitting position and swung my legs off the side of the bed. Stepped gingerly down onto the floor. And walked slowly across the room. Very weak. Extreme care. Back and forth five or six times until I was exhausted. My guts felt like someone was dragging them across an old-fashioned washboard. When I finally collapsed back onto the bed, I didn't bother to hook up my IV. Had to get off the dope. And quickly. Did not plan on hanging around this popcorn stand much longer...

Agresti showed up around eleven a.m. the next morning, sharp in a blue, double-breasted blazer. First a bit of chit-chat, then we got down to business. Mohammad had come through, just like Adara had said, to the tune of $600,000. Agresti had settled for one hundred large. I tried to talk him into taking a full quarter, but he refused. Handed me a debit card in my name with a balance of $480,000 with the pin number taped to it. Then he gave me $20,000 in cash. And a package containing four burner phones and four driver's licenses, one in my own name. And a bottle of broad-spectrum antibiotics. Not to mention a new wallet and a bag of clothes that he slid under my bed and told me to open when no one was around. Agresti had been a busy fellow.

My sincere thanks. He beamed...and said Bobby would pick me up outside of ER at three a.m., not tonight, but the following night, which was Thursday. Bobby would phone when he was ten minutes away. My job was to simply stroll out through ER and get in his car. He would be heavily armed and would provide me with the requisite firearms. In case anything came up. Which Agresti did not think was likely because I wasn't scheduled to be released for at least another five or six days.

Then came Cassady, her one and only visit. Brisk, light, and airy, like she didn't really care (even though I knew she did), the same way she had acted the night I met her upstairs at the Paradise Lounge in San Francisco thirty-two years ago. Same slim body. Same trim dancer's ass. Her hair tinted burgundy. Life in Kensington agreed with her. She actually sat down on the edge of the bed and stroked my cheek for a while. Said the doctors told her I was out of the woods, and she had told Maleah not to worry. Then she started laughing. Said she had called Bobby, who had confessed we were being paid a king's ransom for our troubles. Told me she was still going through with the divorce. But not until she got her cut.

I told her I understood. And that her share of the take would be a quarter of a million dollars. She whistled. Went back to stroking my cheek, poised and self-assured, glowing with health and prosperity.

"Easiest money I've ever earned." That pissed me off, but I didn't show it. After a while, she stood up, blew me an airy kiss, and walked out of the room.

I asked my nurse, a cheerful Filipina, to reduce my morphine to one-quarter of the dose they had been giving me. She said she would have to ask my doctor. Returned thirty minutes later and told me the reduction was fine. She adjusted the IV drip and said I was a brave fellow, but to let her know if the pain got too bad.

I spent most of the evening and half the night walking back and forth across the room. I was getting stronger. The pain was intense at times, but I toughed it out and just kept walking.

Maleah arrived the following morning. With her gospel-singing Kentucky roommate. I believe Cassady engineered it, but the girls came alone. I told Maleah I was very much alive and persuaded her and her friend, who spoke with a mountain accent, to tell me all about their classes at SF State. As Maleah spoke, her brown eyes flashed with delight as she expounded upon the idiosyncrasies of her professors. Made me think back to my own college days, same school, cold raw wind off the Pacific, earlier times, there with Cassady and Bobby. When it was time to go, Maleah asked her friend to step out into the hallway. Then she spoke her mind. Told me that although I was undoubtedly the most heroic person she had ever met, she couldn't bear the fact I was always in mortal danger. Those were her exact words. "Mortal danger."

I had no answers. Knew she was right. Not sure what came over me, but I told her it might be different if she was working for me. Even had the cock-eyed thought she and Greg Thurston would make a good couple. Blame it on the drugs. Or the lack thereof.

"I love you, Dad, but you've got to get it together." She kissed me on both cheeks. Stood up and walked to the door. Stopped, turned, and looked at me. Liquid welling up in her eyes. She smiled through her tears and walked out of the room.

CHAPTER SEVENTY-TWO

Then Cole came. A bit shame-faced, but equivocal as ever. "Sorry, old man, I tried to stop the hit, but I have no real control over Marguerite. But I want you to know it was NOT one of my people who shot you. And I'm glad you're alive. That's the important thing. I think you'll be interested to know that the Feds found half-a-dozen heavily armed Syrians training farther back in the canyon behind the Nazi encampment. I don't know how the hell Thomas conjured them up, but I'm starting to really dislike that son-of-a-bitch. One side is screaming Los Angeles is now a major terrorist target, and it's going to get ugly. The other side is trying to give Thomas a mere slap on the wrist so he can go back to work. The idea is he will turn the Syrians into paramilitary guys working with him to interdict real terrorists coming across the border. It's pure insanity. Meanwhile, his lawyers are trying to work out a sweet plea deal in which Thomas would plead guilty to what they call a phone count for the meth and cocaine. This could result in no more than a year in prison."

I shrugged. What a racket! No wonder Bobby and I call it the injustice system.

Cole shook his head. "Listen, old man, you've got to absorb the losses and steady the ship however you can. Sometimes, you may have to sacrifice a few scapegoats along the way."

Right, scapegoats like me. Decided to change the subject.

Asked him how Adara and Mohammad were doing.

Cole smiled and carefully skirted the fact they'd abducted Adara and given her the third degree. "Ah yes, our beloved Iraqi compatriots. I can tell you that they truly love their newfound freedom." His smile faded. "They're not the problem, however. You're the problem, Crane, if you really want to know the truth."

Somehow, that didn't surprise me. "I thought you said if I helped take Quincey into custody, it would swing the needle in my favor."

"I had hoped it would. But it's not working out that way. Naturally, the principals are impressed by your mettle, but they still think you're too much of a loose cannon. I've done everything I can."

Yeah, right! Like telling Marguerite when and where I was going to meet Mohammad. But I deadpanned, and we sat there looking at each other until Cole finally said, "If I were you, old boy, I would disappear. Lie low for a while and let things settle. And for God's sake, don't go anywhere near Los Angeles."

Hmm. The son-of-a-bitch was a mind reader. I nodded. "Sage advice, my friend. Exactly what I was thinking."

"I'm glad we agree on that. Well, I better be moseying on."

"Why? You've got another wedding to attend?"

Cole laughed. "Nothing like that. It's just that hospital rooms depress me." With that, he rose to his feet. We shook hands, a bit gingerly, and he walked out of the room, limping slightly, no doubt from the caning Quincey had administered with such enthusiasm there in the basement of his Bel Air home.

CHAPTER SEVENTY-THREE

Thursday morning, two a.m. I got dressed in the clothes and accoutrements Agresti had slid under my bed. Everything was filthy. Baggy trousers covered with paint. A flannel shirt that looked to have been dipped in crankcase oil. Minus the top three buttons. A ratty tee-shirt underneath. Surprisingly new tennis shoes, a perfect fit. And a beige headscarf stained with god knows what. Not to mention a dark gray, clip-on beard. I put on everything except the beard and headscarf. Spent the next thirty minutes walking back-and-forth across the room.

Then I took off the shoes (still wearing my hospital socks) and got under the covers. My gut was protesting, but nothing I couldn't handle. Very little morphine for the past twenty-four hours.

Bobby phoned at a quarter to three. Gave me instructions. I put on my shoes and beard and headscarf and walked out into the hallway. Quiet at this hour. Did not want to risk the elevator, so I took the stairs to the first floor instead and followed the signs to ER. Passed three or four employees who avoided my gaze. No one wants to confront a tall, bearded homeless dude who looks like he's been bathing in 30-weight motor oil.

But I wasn't worried about inside the hospital. Outside was the problem. In case Marguerite's people or Cole's people or anybody's people were waiting to slip the hood over my head the moment I stepped outside.

When I was sixty feet from the ER entrance, I slipped into an alcove. Called Bobby. Hospital cell phone reception is notoriously bad, and I could barely hear him. He said to wait until I heard shouts from outside. Then exit quickly. The getaway car, a brown and yellow Corolla, would be waiting.

Strange, but I did not make the connection. Too much stress, I guess. Or too little morphine. My guts were burning.

Then shouts. Cursing. Blows. A high-pitched scream. I shoved through the doors, walking fast. Two grown men were rolling around on the cement, punching and swearing. The man on the bottom uncorked another scream. Orderlies and ambulance drivers stood around watching. I came to the roundabout where the ambulances turn around. No Corolla. By now, hospital security was breaking up the fight. Actors in this peculiar drama.

I was fucked. Make a run for it? Where? Anywhere. Or nowhere. But with my injured gut, it might kill me. Then the Corolla appeared. First, it wasn't there. Then it was. The backdoor swung open and I crawled inside. There was Bobby, big as life in the backseat, grinning. Jet was behind the wheel. The same urban warrior who drove me to my riverfront meeting with Mohammad and then drove me to Hartford later that afternoon. "Goddamnit, Jack! Keep your head down until we're out of town." Jet barking orders from behind the wheel as we spun out of the ER parking lot on three-and-a-half wheels.

EPILOGUE

CHAPTER SEVENTY-FOUR

Jet took mostly backroads, heading north into Vermont. No sign of pursuit. No squawks or APBs. For the moment, I was a free man. Bobby had reserved a room for me at a Super 8 motel next to a truck stop ten miles north of Plattsburgh on the western shore of Lake Champlain. Where he had left his rental car and where I had a Hyundai Sonata, the blandest car in America, waiting for me.

We pulled into the motel parking lot at seven a.m. Bobby and I climbed out of the backseat. Not sure why—maybe it was the company—but my pain had lessened. Jet popped the trunk and Bobby extracted a suitcase. Jet and I shook hands. He hadn't changed. Same Bionic Man fingers. Bony face. Greasy hair. Dilated eyes. I handed him one stack.

"You're a good man, Jack," Jet said quietly. "This'll keep me and the old lady well for a week. Nothing I love more than buying wholesale."

"Glad I can help." Needs. All God's children have needs.

My motel room was basic. Very. Bobby and I went inside. I opened the suitcase. New cross-trainers, jeans, and denim shirts. And a lined, thigh-length denim jacket. And more IDs. You never know when they'll come in handy.

Bobby and I were both quiet. Not sure what to say. We had been through a lot and were still taking it in. Would be for a long time. When we did speak, our conversation kept returning to the years in San Francisco before Cassady and I moved to LA, before I started Nick Crane & Associates with Bobby's military disability money.

"Thirty years in LA," I said. "Thirty years and counting. That's a long time."

"Amazing we're still alive."

"We've been lucky. Let's keep it that way."

"Indeed," said Bobby.

Then Bobby told me Tony was depressed and had been calling in sick. "I never thought I'd find myself saying this, but I think he needs to get on an antidepressant."

"Aw, man, I hate to hear that. He blames himself for this whole mess. He's got to get over that."

And he would get over it. To a degree. But not until after our next battle with Marguerite and the principals. But that's another story. To be told on another occasion. Then I asked Bobby if he'd heard anything about Roberto's two little girls.

"Tony says they're fine. Living the good life on the ranchero. We ought to go down there and join them."

I smiled. "That's not a bad idea. What about the refugees up at Caroline's ranch?"

Bobby grinned. "This is where it gets interesting. According to Caroline's lawyers, she has every right to extend them hospitality for a reasonable period of time. The tricky part is arranging things so that they aren't held in some private hellhole while their asylum claims are being adjudicated after that reasonable period of time elapses."

Then we were silent, not envying their hard lot.

Bobby didn't want to leave, and I didn't want him to. We kept stalling. I gave him Greg Thurston's phone number and filled him in on my new plans for Nick Crane & Associates. For the time being, the staff would consist of Bobby, Audrey, and Greg. "You need to make sure the kid gets up to speed quickly. He doesn't know it yet, but he's gonna be our new rainmaker. Set him up with a handicap car. On the company dime. He's ready."

Then, to my surprise, Bobby produced a half-pint of Buchanan's Red Seal 21. We both drank from the bottle until it was gone. Then he clapped me on the back, and I kissed him on both leathery cheeks, Arab style. Then he was gone.

Spent the day sleeping. Pain still present, but bearable. Had started on the antibiotics. Taking no chances. My plan was to drive west later that evening. Take the northerly route across this great land. My destination: The Pacific Northwest.

Just before checking out that evening, I called Adara on one of the burners. She was surprised to hear from me but glad, which made me really happy. I told her I was going to disappear for a while, but I'd be in touch. She told me she had signed on with a local small theater to play Maggie in *Cat on a Hot Tin Roof*. Said it was a good opportunity to shake the rust off. Meanwhile, she had contacted Professor Reardon, who had agreed to put her in touch with several local theaters.

Then the good news. Cole was not making any unreasonable demands on either her or her father, and Marguerite had disappeared completely, at least for the time being. Mohammad's fortune was being replenished bit by bit, which made me laugh. It sounded like they were laundering the funds back into his accounts with requisite delicacy in the hope no one would notice they'd been rifled in the first place.

And then...

"Would you like me to call you from time to time?"

"Of course I would, Nick. And don't wait too long. A girl can get lonely, you know."

That was it. We signed off, and I packed up and checked out. Drove west into the maw of the great American darkness. Whistling and rubbing my guts at times to make the pain go away.

ACKNOWLEDGMENTS

I would like to thank all of my friends who supported me throughout the writing of *Rogues & Patriots*. Special thanks to BJW Nashe, my friend and early editor, who read and commented upon the manuscript countless times before I submitted it for publication, and to Peter Hoffman, who schooled me in the art of thriller writing and helped me discover the joy of writing in the first person. I also want to thank crime novelist Charles Salzberg for recommending my work to Down & Out Books and being unfailingly supportive since the day I met him on my crime blog back in 2014. Special thanks also to Eric Campbell and Lance Wright at Down & Out Books for very kindly agreeing to publish my work and to my editor Tom Hottle for helping to improve it. I also want to thank my cover designer Margo Nauert for her intriguing cover design and my boss John Brown for his unfailing good humor while teaching me the nuts-and bolts of private investigation. Finally, I would like to thank my late friend, Vietnam veteran Warren Larry Foster, for whom I feel the deepest affection.

PATRICK H. MOORE writes thrillers and crime novels. He is a Los Angeles-based private investigator and sentencing mitigation specialist. Since 2003, he has worked on over five hundred drug trafficking, sex crime, violent crime, and white-collar fraud cases.

Patrick studied English Literature and Creative Writing at San Francisco State University. While in college, he published numerous short stories and novel excerpts. More recently, in 2014, his first thriller, *Cicero's Dead*, was indie published by U.S. iNdIe Books. It was a finalist in the thriller category in the Beverly Hills Book Award Contest. In 2023, Down & Out Books published Patrick's PI political thriller, *27 Days*, which was a finalist in the Thriller category in the 2023 American Fiction Awards. *Rogues and Patriots* is the second book in a three-volume series in which LA PI Nick Crane fights the Principals, a violent cabal of right-wing extremists. Down & Out Books also published Patrick's recent novella *Setting the Record Straight*.

Patrick was one of the founders of *All Things Crime Blog*, which, in its heyday (2014 to 2017), was one of the most popular crime blogs in America.

On the following pages are a few
more great titles from the
Down & Out Books publishing family.

For a complete list of books and to
sign up for our newsletter,
go to DownAndOutBooks.com.

Pascagoula Run and Other Stories
Jeffery Hess

Down & Out Books
March 2024
978-1-64396-360-0

Amongst this assemblage are stories that have never been seen before, many of which have appeared in literary journals, magazines, or anthologies, and others that found their way into some of Hess's novels. Crime stories, all, and most on the Noir side of the spectrum.

The characters and their environs change, but the trouble never ends. They all bring it on themselves, but that doesn't stop any of them in moments like that. If you know, you know. Even if you don't, you'll be riveted by this stellar lineup of heroes and heroines and the damage they inflict.

Dark of the Day: Eclipse Stories
Kaye George, Editor

Down & Out Books
April 2024
978-1-64396-395-2

An anthology of stories to celebrate the April 2024 eclipse in North America. These stories are located in various places and are even of various genres and themes. What they have in common, besides featuring eclipses, are that they are all written by brilliant authors and will all entertain you. Read them before the eclipse, to get into the mood, or after, to nostalgically remember it.

Contributors include Cari Dubiel, Katherine Tomlinson, Carol L. Wright, Joseph S. Walker, John Rogers Clark IV, M. K. Waller, Toni Goodyear, Laura Oles, Bridges DelPonte, Eric Beckstrom, Kaye George, Paula Gail Benson, John M. Floyd, Debra H. Goldstein, Michael Bracken, and James A. Hearn.

The Killing Rain
Left Coast Crime Anthology 2024
Jim Thomsen, Editor

Down & Out Books
April 2024
978-1-64396-362-4

The Killing Rain is collection of short crime fiction, ranging from the cozy to the hardboiled, with each story depicting the Seattle area as a real or imagine place.

It's in conjunction with "Seattle Shakedown" — the slogan for the 2024 Left Coast Crime conference, slated for April 10-14 in nearby Bellevue.

Deception Specialist
A Jack O'Shea Novel
John Shepphird

Down & Out Books
April 2024
978-1-64396-363-1

Reformed-swindler-turned-private-eye Jack O'Shea was first introduced in a series of short stories published in *Alfred Hitchcock Mystery Magazine*. The debut won the Shamus Award. The second in the series was a finalist for the Anthony Award.

Seeking redemption from his criminal past, Jack investigates a murder at a shadowy Northern California mountain college—a "visa mill" with ties to Silicon Valley. As he uncovers the truth, Jack's life of crime catches up with him. Nothing is as it appears.

Made in United States
Cleveland, OH
23 January 2025

13455844R00217